The Evolution of Cajun & Creole Cuisine

By Chef John D. Folse, C.E.C.

CHEF JOHN FOLSE & COMPANY
Donaldsonville, Louisiana

Library of Congress Catalog Number 89-092468
ISBN 0-9625152-0-5

First Printing: January, 1990
Second Printing: March, 1991
Third Printing: May, 1991
Fourth Printing: March, 1992
Fifth Printing: December, 1992
Sixth Printing: June, 1993
Seventh Printing: April, 1994
Eighth Printing: October, 1995
Manufactured in the United States of America

Additional copies available from:

Chef John Folse & Company
2517 South Philippe Avenue
Gonzales, LA 70737
504-644-6000

Price: $19.95 plus $3.00 shipping and handling (total $22.95)

Also available:

Chef John Folse's *Plantation Celebrations*
Price: $24.95 plus $3.50 shipping and handling (total $28.45)

Chef John Folse's *Something Old, Something New...Louisiana Cooking
With a Change of Heart* (Heart-Friendly Cookbook)
Price: $21.95 plus $3.95 shipping and handling (total $25.90)

Louisiana residents add applicable state sales tax.

Table of Contents

Dedication

To: Laulie Bouchereau Folse, who has stood by me through the success as well as the failures in this business of cooking. She devotes her life to my dreams, content to remain in the background as a silent observer, never sharing the spotlight she so richly deserves. In addition, she proved to be a tireless editor, when I needed one so desperately. I couldn't have done it without her.

A Special Thanks

A very special thanks to the following persons, who without their help this book would never have been:

Pamela Castel, my Executive Assistant, who spent countless hours, days and weekends typing and proofing to get a good product to the publisher. Her dedication to the project was incredible.

Jose Garcia, the photographer, his talent behind the lens is unequalled in food photography. In addition, he is a true friend.

Reba Meliet, the artist, who created the scenes of Bayou country in such a splendid way on the following pages.

Walter Mayeux, the designer, who did the lay out of the covers and type.

Margie Larson, the liaison between all of the above. Her loyalty to my projects are only overshadowed by her ability to see them through.

Angus McIntosh, the Godfather of "Indigenous Cuisine". His words of wit and wisdom are found on many of these pages.

To the great staffs at Lafitte's Landing Restaurant and White Oak Plantation.....and you thought we'd never finish, Absolutely Nothing To It!!!!!

To the chefs of The American Culinary Federation. These men and women carve their existence out of the kitchens of America, as they "write the book" on the greatest evolution of cuisines in over a century.

Last but most important, to the thousands of Cajun and Creole chefs and cooks who came before me, laying the very foundation for our great cuisine. Without their talent and dedication, I would have had no base to build upon.

Chef John D. Folse, CEC, AAC

About the Author

Chef John Folse is the owner of two award-winning restaurants, a national catering and specialty event company and a manufacturing company in South Louisiana. His most famous, Lafitte's Landing Restaurant in Donaldsonville, has been recognized as one of the finest restaurants in and around New Orleans. White Oak Plantation, in Baton Rouge, houses his local catering division and Voila!, based in Louisiana, is his national catering and event management company. Louisiana Premier Products, in Gonzales, manufactures soups, sauces, entrees and meats for foodservice and retail establishments across the country and serves as the Corporate Headquarters. Chef Folse is the author of *The Evolution of Cajun & Creole Cuisine* published in 1990 and *Plantation Celebrations* published in 1994 and his latest work, *Something Old, Something New* published in 1995 and featuring heart-friendly Louisiana cuisine.

John is respected around the world as an authority on Cajun and Creole cuisine and culture. He hosts his own national television cooking show on PBS. He has taken his famous "Taste of Louisiana" from Hollywood to the Great Wall of China, opening promotional Louisiana restaurants in Hong Kong, Japan, Beijing, London, Paris, Rome, Bogota, and Taipei. In 1989, Chef Folse was invited to create the first ever Vatican State Dinner in Rome, and while there had a private audience with Pope John Paul II. In 1990, Chef Folse was named the "National Chef of the Year" by the American Culinary Federation, the highest honor bestowed upon an American chef. In that same year, his Lafitte's Landing was inducted into the "Fine Dining Hall of Fame", one of ten restaurants in America honored with this prestigious award. In 1987, Chef Folse was selected as "Louisiana Restaurateur of the year" by the Louisiana Restaurant Association and in November of 1988, the Louisiana Sales and Marketing Executives named him "Louisiana's Marketing Ambassador to the World." In 1988, Chef Folse made international headlines by opening his "Lafitte's Landing East" in Moscow during the presidential summit between Ronald Reagan and Mikhail Gorbachev. This opening represented the first time an American Restaurant had operated on Soviet soil. Immediately following this venture, John hosted ten Soviet chefs for the first Soviet American Culinary Exchange.

Chef Folse is the recipient of numerous culinary awards and recognitions, and has been honored by local, state and international governments for his continuing efforts to showcase America's regional cooking around the world. His most prestigious acknowledgments recently have been his selection as Commencement Speaker for Johnson & Wales University and the Culinary Institute of America, the largest culinary institutions in America. In 1994, he was elected National President of the American Culinary Federation, the oldest and largest professional chefs organization in the United States.

Jose L. Garcia, II

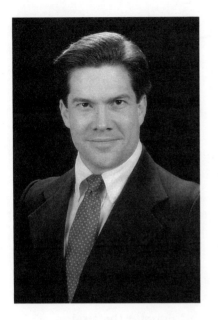

Photographer Jose L. Garcia, II collaborated with Chef John Folse in producing each of the color food photographs presented in this book.

Garcia, a native New Orleanian, graduated from Jesuit High School and Tulane University. A professional photographer since 1975, Garcia has operated his own freelance commercial studio based in New Orleans for the past seven years. Having pursued assignments ranging from political campaigns to fashion and product catalogs, Garcia began his association with Chef Folse after photographing the family residence where the Chef and his seven siblings were raised. The two soon discovered a common fascination with those things indigenous to Louisiana and the Cajun culture.

Occasionally accompanying Chef Folse to document his domestic travels, Garcia began capturing the chef's culinary art on film in 1982, emphasizing the roots of these Cajun creations by integrating elements of Louisiana culture, tradition or environment into as many of the compositions as possible.

These images are the latest crop to be harvested from this fruitful collaboration.

Bon Appetit!

Jose L. Garcia, II
3424 Bienville Street
New Orleans, LA 70119
(504) 482-8754

"So You Want to Cook Cajun and Creole..."

Prior to beginning our adventure into the cuisines of South Louisiana, it is imperative that I begin by outlining the basic principles, procedures, and terminologies that are unique to Cajun and Creole cookery. In the following pages, I'll be explaining stocks, sauces, rouxs and various other essentials in order for you to better understand how the rich heritages of the Cajuns and Creoles were adapted and developed in the New World to create the most exciting cuisine in America today. Certain Louisiana food customs, such as the boucherie, the cochon de lait, and the crawfish boil, will be covered for a better understanding of just how unique our cuisine and culture really is. After you read about the fascinating development of pralines, Cajun coffee, beignets, and hushpuppies, I know you will want to dig deeper and tackle the sections on gumbo and wild game.

It is important to realize that cultures and cuisines must constantly evolve. This evolution process is brought about when new ingredients and ideas are introduced into a region. Here in South Louisiana, the evolution process may be witnessed at every turn. The Cajuns today have more access to the outside world because of increased mobility, as interstates begin to cross the bayous and cities arise from our swamplands. An example of this process of change is the merging of cultures in New Orleans. Today it is difficult even for the locals to tell the Cajuns from the Creoles. However, we all agree that evolution is imperative, if our cultures and cuisines are to survive.

Though we will look into this evolution of Louisiana cuisines, I feel it is necessary to first understand from whence it came. Knowing the foundation of Cajun and Creole cooking will ensure a clear understanding of the direction we have chosen to take. As the young chefs of America travel into the bayous of South Louisiana and walk the French Market area of New Orleans, their creative juices cannot help but flow. The volumes of crawfish, crab, shrimp, oysters, wild game and other local ingredients lend themselves perfectly to the evolution process at the hands of these young masters. So for a moment, let's look into the past. This certainly will place a bright spotlight on the future of our magnificent cuisine, a cuisine constantly evolving for the better in South Louisiana.

The Cajun and Creole cultures are quite distinct and so are their cuisines. The Creoles were the European born aristocrats, wooed by the Spanish to establish New Orleans in the 1690's. Second born sons, who could not own land or titles in their native countries, were offered the opportunity to live and prosper in their family traditions here in the New World. They brought with them not only their wealth and education, but their chefs and cooks. With these chefs came the knowledge of the grand cuisines of Europe.

The influences of classical and regional French, Spanish, German and Italian cooking are readily apparent in Creole cuisine. The terminologies, precepts, sauces, and major dishes carried over, some with more evolution than others, and provided a solid base or foundation for Creole cooking.

Bouillabaisse is a soup that came from the Provence region of France in and around Marseilles. This dish is integral to the history of Creole food because of the part it played in the creation of gumbo.

The Spanish, who actually played host to this new adventure, gave Creole food its spice, many great cooks, and paella, which was the forefather of Louisiana's jambalaya. Paella is the internationally famous Spanish rice dish made with vegetables, meats and sausages. On the coastline, seafoods were often substituted for meats. Jambalaya has variations as well, according to the local ingredients available at different times of the year.

The Germans who arrived in Louisiana in 1690 were knowledgeable in all forms of charcuterie and helped establish the boucherie and fine sausage making in South Louisiana. They brought with them not only the pigs, but chicken and cattle as well. A good steady supply of milk and butter was seldom available in South Louisiana prior to the arrival of the Germans.

The Italians were also famous for their culinary talents. Since they were summoned to France by Catherine de Medicis, to teach their pastry and ice cream making skills to the Europeans, many Creole dishes reflect the Italian influence and their love of good cooking.

From the West Indies and the smoke pots of Haiti came exotic vegetables and cooking methods. Braising, a slow cooking technique, contributed to the development of our gumbos. Mirlitons, sauce piquantes and the use of tomato rounded out the emerging Creole cuisine.

Native Indians, the Choctaws, Chetimaches and Houmas, befriended the new settlers and introduced them to local produce, wildlife and cooking methods. New ingredients, such as corn, ground sassafras leaves or file powder, and bay leaves from the laurel tree, all contributed to the culinary melting pot.

I would be remise if I failed to mention the tremendous influence of "the black hand in the pot" in Creole cooking. The Africans brought with them the "gumbo" or okra plant from their native soil which not only gave name to our premier soup but introduced a new vegetable to South Louisiana. Even more importantly, they have maintained a significant role in development of Creole cuisine in the home as well as the professional kitchen.

Creole cuisine is indebted to many unique people and diverse cultures who were willing to contribute and share their cooking styles, ingredients and talent. Obviously then, Creole cuisine represents the history of sharing in South Louisiana. Early on in the history of New Orleans, the Creole wives became frustrated, not being able to duplicate their old world dishes with new world products. Governor Bienville helped to solve this problem by commissioning his housekeeper, Madame Langlois, to introduce them to local vegetables, meats and seafoods in what became the first cooking school in America. This school aided them in developing their cuisine in a new and strange land.

Creole cuisine, then, is that melange of artistry and talent, developed and made possible by the nations and cultures who settled in and around New Orleans. Those of us who know and love it, keep it alive by sharing it with the world.

The cuisine of the Cajuns is a mirror image of their unique history. It is a cooking style which reflects their ingenuity, creativity, adaptability and survival.

When the exiled French refugees began arriving in South Louisiana from Acadia in Nova Scotia, Canada, in 1755, they were already well versed in the art of survival. Their forefathers had made a home in the wilderness of southeast Canada in the land of "Acadie". Following their exile, these French Catholics found a new home compatible with their customs and religion in South Louisiana.

The story of "Le Grand Derangement" is memorialized in the epic poem EVANGELINE by Henry Wadsworth Longfellow. This love story tells of Gabriel and Evangeline, tragically torn apart when ten thousand Acadians were gathered and driven from their homeland. It took six days to burn the village of Grand Pre, and families were divided and put aboard twenty-four British vessels anchored in the Bay of Fundy.

The Acadians were forcibly dispersed, nearly half of them dying before a year had passed. Survivors landed in Massachusetts, Maryland, the Carolinas, Georgia (where some were sold into slavery), the French West Indies, Santo Domingo, Uruguay, Nicaragua, Honduras and the Falkland Islands. The main tragedy lied in the fact that the men were exiled first, to destinations unknown, with the women and children following later. As time passed, the struggle to reunite these families, in most cases, proved futile.

A large contingency of Acadians returned to the coastal seaports of France, their initial homeland, and eventually came to South Louisiana. Some were sent to England while others made their way back to "Acadie" to Sainte-Marie and settled on the French shore. Word rang out across Europe, Canada and South America that reunion with their husbands and fathers could be possible in the bayous of South Louisiana.

As wave after wave of the bedraggled refugees found their way to yet another land, the Acadians were reborn. They were free to speak their language, believe as they pleased, and make a life for themselves in the swamps and bayous of the French Triangle of South Louisiana. They were among friends, friends who enjoyed the same "joie de vivre" or joy of living.

Just as they had become such close friends with the Micmac Indians when they were isolated in the woodlands of Canada, so they befriended the native Indians here in South Louisiana. Friends were quickly made with the Spanish and Germans as well.

The original Acadian immigrants had come to Nova Scotia from France beginning in 1620. They were primarily from Brittany, Normandy, Picardy and Poitou. These fishermen and farmers had learned how to adjust, survive and make a life for themselves in Acadie. Once again, they were faced with the task of survival. Rugged as they were, the Acadians learned to adapt to their new surroundings. Armed with their black iron pots, the Cajuns, as they had come to be known, utilized what was indigenous to the area. No attempt was made to recreate the classical cuisine of Europe. None of the exotic spices and ingredients available to the Creoles were to be found by the Cajuns in Bayou country. They were happy to live off the land, a land abundant with fish, shellfish and wild game.

The Cajuns cooked with joy and love as their most precious ingredients, a joy brought about by reunion, in spite of the tragedy that befell them. To cook Cajun is to discover the love and experience the joy of the most unique American cuisine ever developed.

Cajun cuisine is characterized by the use of wild game, seafoods, wild vegetation and herbs. From their association with the Indians, the Cajuns learned techniques to best utilize the local products from the swamps, bayous, lakes, rivers and woods. Truly remarkable are the variations that have resulted from similar ingredients carefully combined in the black iron pots of the Cajuns.

Jambalaya, grillades, stews, fricassees, soups, gumbos, sauce piquantes and a host of stuffed vegetable dishes are all characteristic of these new Cajun "one pot meals."

From the Germans, the Cajuns were reintroduced to charcuterie and today make andouille, smoked sausage, boudin, chaudin, tasso and chaurice, unparalleled in the world of sausage making.

Cajun cuisine is a "table in the wilderness", a creative adaptation of indigenous Louisiana foods. It is a cuisine forged out of a land that opened its arms to a weary traveler, the Acadian.

So as you can see, South Louisiana has two rich histories and two unique cuisines: the Creole cuisine with its rich array of courses indicating its close tie to European aristocracy, and Cajun cuisine with its one pot meals, pungent with the flavor of seafood and game.

No wonder you want to cook Cajun and Creole!

CHEF JOHN D. FOLSE, CEC, AAC

"We may live without poetry, music and art;
We may live without conscience and live without heart;
We may live without friends, we may live without books;
But civilized man cannot live without cooks.
He may live without books, what is knowledge but grieving?
He may live without hope, what is hope but deceiving?
He may live without love, what is passion but pining?
But where is that man who can live without dining?"

Owen Meredith

Stocks in Cajun and Creole Cooking

As both Cajun and Creole cuisines are descended from their French classical and regional ancestors, I must place major emphasis on the importance of stocks in our cooking. What early Creole home would have been complete without the aroma of a constantly simmering stock pot filled with fish, shellfish or game bones.

Soups, sauces, marinades, sautes and braises all have as their essential base, a good, hearty and flavorful stock. Naturally, the bond between classical French stock principles and Creole cuisine is more recognizable than that of its Cajun cousin. In Cajun cuisine, to simmer ingredients that give flavor in a rich hearty liquid and then toss it out the back door would go against the grain of the hard-working Cajun. No, the Cajuns cooked anything they could hunt, trap or fish in a black iron pot, and the natural stock remained as the gravy. But the principles of Creole and classical stocks remained. Whole cuts of meat and plenty of seasoning vegetables went into the pot, but remained to become a part of the dish itself.

The evolution of crawfish bisque, from its classical origin, shows this development in Cajun cuisine. "Bisque d' ecrivisses" was a pureed crawfish soup in classical French cuisine. It was flavored with consomme and a mirepoix of seasoning vegetables, thickened with rice, strained and finished with cream. The dish was then garnished with stuffed crawfish heads. In Cajun cuisine, this dish finds its finest expression, but nothing is strained out! The vegetables remain and the dark Cajun roux gives the soup a character never touched in classical French cooking.

Courtbouillon is another example of the differences in French and Cajun cuisines. In classical cuisine, a courtbouillon consists of seasoning vegetables and spices, simmered in water producing a flavorful poaching liquid for fish and other seafood. In South Louisiana this becomes a dish in and of itself, as in Redfish Courtbouillon. The fish is cooked with vegetables and spices to create a sauce of inexpressible flavor with no loss or waste.

Many dishes in Cajun cuisine are this way. A sauce is created right in the pot without the fuss and waste of classical or even Creole cooking. Sauce Piquante quickly comes to mind. I've tasted Venison Sauce Piquante in my native St. James Parish that had the rich velvety character of an Espagnole Sauce, simmered all day by the chef of a French nobleman.

So remember, as we take that journey through Cajun and Creole cuisines, that the principles of stocks are essential.

Whether we make a hunter sauce from a game stock to grace a stuffed loin of venison or braise a rabbit as we create a "Lapin Sauce Piquante", in Cajun and Creole cooking the stock makes the difference. Here, old world principles have been adapted and local indigenous ingredients have been substituted to produce a cuisine that is truly American.

"Woe to the cook whose sauce has no sting."
Chaucer

Stock Techniques

Stocks have four major ingredients: bones, mirepoix (aromatic vegetables), bouquet garni (spices and herbs), and liquid (water, wine and/or stock).

1. *Bones*

Stocks can be made from any bones that you have in your kitchen. For a white stock, as in white veal stock, fish stock or chicken stock, simply wash the bones of blood and break or cut into manageable pieces, exposing any marrow. For dark stocks, such as brown veal stock, game stock or duck stock, brown bones well. A light coating of oil can aid in this process. Well browned bones add rich color and flavor to the stock. However, do not burn or char them, as this will make a bitter stock.

2. *Mirepoix*

Onions, shallots, scallions, leeks, celery, garlic, carrots, mushroom trimmings and tomatoes can all be used to infuse aromatic flavor into your stock, depending on what you have available in your kitchen. NEVER use bell pepper, cabbage, cauliflower or related vegetables as these make a stock bitter and/or overpower it. For brown stocks, the mirepoix can be added to the bones as they brown. For white stocks, they can be slightly sweated by sauteing before hand in butter. Size of cut depends on cooking time. For long stocks (beef, veal and game), larger pieces are fine. For quicker stocks (chicken, fish and shellfish), smaller sizes are required.

3. *Bouquet Garni*

Black peppercorns, parsley, whole thyme, bay leaf and cloves can be either tied up in a leek or in a cheese cloth and placed in the liquid. In the case of stocks that cook more than an hour or two, the bouquet garni should be added during the last hour and a half.

4.   *Liquid*

The whole purpose of stocks is to extract the color, flavor, nutrients and gelatin from the bones. Cold water is the mainstay in this process. It can be supplemented with either red or white wine as well. A double strength stock can be made by starting your stock with a previously made one that has been strained, cooled and skimmed of all fat. Cold liquid is used to draw the flavor out of the bones. In the preparation of a green vegetable like asparagus, hot water or steam is used and cooking time is shortened, to lock in flavor, color and nutrients. So therefore, in stocks, we use cold water and long cooking time in order to draw the flavor out. NEVER add salt to the water. When the stock simmers, the salt remains as the volume reduces and the stock will prove too salty. Stocks should be simmered slowly and skimmed of all impurities and fat which rise to the surface. This will produce a hearty, flavorful and clear stock.

Stocks & Sauces

The Roux

Stocks may be thickened by means of reductions, eggs, butter, vegetable purees, cream, foie gras, various starches and even blood. In classical French cuisine, the roux is the primary thickening agent. Equal parts of butter and flour are well blended over heat to create a roux. This process may produce rouxs of different colors and thickening capabilities depending on the cook's need. In Cajun and Creole cuisine, the roux has been raised to a new dimension never before experienced in other forms of cooking.

Butter, lard, peanut oil, bacon fat and even duck fat have been used in combination with flour to produce as many taste and color variations as there are cooks in South Louisiana. In classical cuisine, the brown roux is used for brown sauce, the blonde roux for veloutes and the white roux for bechamels. In Creole cuisine, a brown roux is made from butter or bacon fat and is used to thicken gumbos and stews requiring a lighter touch. The Cajuns, on the other hand, are the originators of the most unique rouxs in modern cookery.

The Cajun dark brown roux is best made with vegetable oil, although in the past, it was thought imperative that only animal fat be used. The flour and oil are cooked together until the roux reaches a caramel color. This roux has less thickening power, however, due to the fact that the darker the roux gets, the more the starch compound which thickens liquid breaks down. Thus, the thickening capabilities of the dark roux are diminished. The dark brown roux is the secret to traditional Cajun food because of the richness and depth it adds to the dish. Butter is used in classical and Creole rouxs, however, the Cajuns use only vegetable oil or lard to produce their lighter colored rouxs. Tan in appearance, these light rouxs are used primarily with vegetables and light meat dishes.

Nothing in Cajun country has a greater aroma than a light brown roux simmering with onions, celery, bell pepper and garlic. On many occasions, growing up in South Louisiana, my hunger was satisfied with a touch of this vegetable seasoned roux spread on a piece of French bread.

Certain gumbos are further thickened, in Bayou country, with either okra or file powder. Considering the variations in cooking time and fats or oils, the number of different roux possibilities are infinite. I will attempt to delineate six such rouxs, three used in classical cuisine, one used in Creole cooking and two that are strictly Cajun.

"What I love about cooking is that after a hard day, there is something comforting about the fact that if you melt butter and add flour and then hot stock, it will get thick! It's a sure thing in a world where nothing else is sure, it's a certainty, the stock will thicken!"

Nora Ephron

The Roux

THE BROWN BUTTER ROUX:

1/2 cup butter   **1/2 cup flour**

In a heavy bottom saute pan, melt butter over medium high heat. Using a wire whisk, add flour, stirring constantly until flour becomes light brown. You must continue whisking during the cooking process, as flour will tend to scorch as browning process proceeds. Should black specks appear in the roux, discard and begin again. This volume of roux will thicken three cups of stock to sauce consistency.

THE BLONDE BUTTER ROUX:

1/2 cup butter   **1/2 cup flour**

In a heavy bottom saute pan, melt butter over medium high heat. Proceed exactly as in the brown roux recipe, however, only cook to the pale gold state. This roux is popular in Creole cooking and will thicken three cups of stock to a sauce consistency.

THE WHITE BUTTER ROUX:

1/2 cup butter   **1/2 cup flour**

In a heavy bottom saute pan, melt butter over medium high heat. Proceed exactly as in the blonde roux recipe, however, only cook until the flour and butter are well blended and bubbly. Do not brown. This classical style roux is popular in Creole cooking and will thicken three cups of stock to a sauce consistency.

THE CREOLE ROUX:

The Creole roux can be made with lightly salted butter, bacon drippings or lard. As with everything regarding food in Louisiana, whenever someone attempts to reduce this wealth of food lore to written material, an argument breaks out. Let's just say that Creole rouxs vary in color the same as classical and Cajun ones. The Creoles, however, did have in their larder, butter for the roux, whereas any butter a Cajun may have had would have been saved for a biscuit or cornbread and never put in the black iron pot for a roux.

If a comparison statement can be made, it would be that generally speaking, Creole roux is darker in color than the classical French brown roux it descended from but not as dark as the Cajun dark roux.

THE LIGHT BROWN CAJUN ROUX:

1 cup oil   **1 cup flour**

In a black iron pot or skillet, heat the oil over medium high heat to approximately 300 degrees F. Using a wire whisk, slowly add the flour, stirring constantly until the roux is peanut butter in color, approximately two minutes. This roux is normally used to thicken vegetable dishes such as corn maque choux (shrimp, corn and tomato stew) or butter beans with ham. If using this roux to thicken an etouffee, it will thicken approximately two quarts of liquid. If used to thicken seafood gumbo, it will thicken approximately two and a half quarts of stock.

THE DARK BROWN CAJUN ROUX:

1 cup oil   **1 cup flour**

Proceed as you would in the light brown Cajun roux recipe but continue cooking until the roux is the color of a light caramel. This roux should almost be twice as dark as the light brown roux but not as dark as chocolate. You should remember that the darker the roux gets, the less thickening power it holds and the roux tends to become bitter. This roux is used most often in sauce piquantes, crawfish bisques and game gumbos. However, it is perfectly normal to use the dark brown roux in any dish in Cajun cooking.

This roux gives food such a rich character that I sometimes make shrimp and corn bisque with it, as well as a river road seafood gumbo that will knock your socks off. Slow cooking is essential to achieve that dark, rich color.

Some time ago, I was discussing the origin of the dark roux with my good friend, Angus McIntosh, a fine chef and aspiring Cajun. I've always contended that because the Cajuns cooked in black iron pots over open fires using lard as a base, the dark roux was discovered by accident when the fire got too hot and the flour over-browned. With their lean pantries in mind, the Cajuns kept the roux instead of discarding it. They enjoyed the flavor and kept doing it that way. Angus felt that it developed during the Cajuns' less affluent years as a means of enriching a soup or stew with flavor when the larder was not as full but the number of chairs at the table were many.

Either way, if properly done, the dark Cajun roux enriches food with color and flavor that is so fantastic it could only be Cajun.

Table of Sauce and Soup Consistencies Using The Roux of Cajun and Creole Cooking

THE BUTTER BASE ROUXS (The Classical and Creole Rouxs)

1 cup butter   **1 cup flour**

This recipe will thicken the following:

6 cups stock to a thick white sauce consistency.

8 cups stock to a concentrated soup consistency.

10 cups stock to a thick soup consistency.

12 cups stock to a perfect Louisiana gumbo consistency.

14 cups stock to a light gumbo consistency.

THE OIL BASE ROUXS (The Cajun Rouxs)

1 cup vegetable oil   **1 cup flour**

Cooked at 300 degrees F. for three to five minutes, this recipe will thicken the following:

6 cups stock to a thick brown sauce consistency.

8 cups stock to a thick gumbo consistency.

10 cups stock to a perfect Louisiana gumbo consistency.

12 cups stock to a light gumbo consistency.

It should be noted that the butter or oil base rouxs may be made well in advance, cooled, separated into half cup portions and placed in the refrigerator or freezer. The roux will keep well for months and always be available to you should an emergency arise.

Beef, Veal or Game Stock

6 Hours   2 Quarts

3 pounds marrow bones
3 pounds shin of beef
3 large onions, unpeeled and
    quartered
3 carrots, peeled and sliced
3 celery stalks, peeled and sliced
3 heads garlic, sliced in half to
    expose pods

2 bay leaves
4 sprigs parsley
15 black peppercorns
1 tsp whole thyme
1-1/2 gallons water
3 cups dry red wine

Preheat oven to 400 degrees F. Have your butcher select and save three pounds of beef or veal marrow bones and three pounds of an inexpensive shin meat or stew meat of beef. Place bones and shin meat in roasting pan and bake until golden brown, approximately thirty minutes. Place browned bones, meat and all remaining ingredients in a three gallon stock pot. Bring to a rolling boil, reduce to simmer and cook for six hours adding water if necessary to retain volume. During this cooking process, skim off all impurities that rise to the surface of the pot. Remove pot from heat and strain stock through fine cheese cloth or strainer. Allow stock to rest for fifteen minutes and skim off all oil that rises to the top. Return stock to a low boil and reduce to two quarts.

GAME STOCK:

To create the basic game stock, proceed exactly as you would for the beef or veal stock. The difference, however, is that you must substitute three pounds of duck, rabbit, venison or other wild game bones into the stock pot in place of the veal or beef bones. Other than the shellfish stock, game stock is used more often in Cajun and Creole cuisine than any other sauce base.

Changes

_____

_____

_____

_____

Fish Stock

1 Hour   2 Quarts

2 pounds fish bones, heads
    included
2 diced onions
2 diced carrots
2 diced celery stalks
6 cloves diced garlic
4 sprigs parsley

2 bay leaves
1 tsp dry thyme
6 black peppercorns
1 lemon, sliced
1 gallon cold water
3 cups dry white wine

Ask your seafood supplier to reserve two pounds of white fish bones and heads or two pounds of whole inexpensive white fish for this stock. Combine all ingredients in a two gallon stock pot. Bring to a rolling boil, reduce to simmer and cook for forty-five minutes. During the cooking process, skim off all impurities that rise to the surface. Add water if necessary to retain volume. Strain through fine cheese cloth or strainer. Return stock to low boil and reduce to two quarts.

Rm 81

Changes

_____
_____
_____
_____

Chicken Stock

1 Hour   2 Quarts

2 pounds chicken bones
2 pounds chicken necks, wings
   and gizzards
2 onions, finely chopped
2 carrots, peeled and thinly
   sliced
6 cloves diced garlic

2 celery stalks, finely chopped
2 bay leaves
2 sprigs parsley
1 tsp dry thyme
12 whole black peppercorns
1 gallon cold water
2 cups dry white wine

Have your butcher select two pounds of chicken bones and two pounds of chicken necks, wings and gizzards for this stock. Place all ingredients in a two gallon stock pot. Bring to a rolling boil, reduce to simmer and cook for one hour. During the cooking process, skim off all impurities that rise to the surface. Strain through fine cheese cloth or strainer and allow stock to rest for thirty minutes. Skim off all oil that rises to the surface of the stock. Return stock to a low boil and reduce to two quarts.

Changes

_____

_____

_____

_____

Shellfish Stock

1 Hour   2 Quarts

Comment:

The shellfish stock is the most utilized stock in Cajun and Creole cooking simply because it is the base for most of our soups and gumbos.

1 pound crab shells	6 cloves garlic, diced
1 pound shrimp shells, with heads	4 sprigs parsley
	2 bay leaves
1 pound crawfish shells, with heads	1 tsp dried thyme
	6 black peppercorns
2 onions, diced	1 sliced lemon
2 carrots, diced	1 gallon cold water
2 celery stalks, diced	2 cups dry white wine

Have your seafood supplier select one pound each of crab, shrimp and crawfish shells, including the heads if possible. Do not rinse the shells prior to beginning the stock. In the rinsing process, all fats are removed and herein lies the secret to a good shellfish stock. Combine all ingredients in a two gallon stock pot. Bring to a rolling boil, reduce to simmer and cook for one hour. During the cooking process, skim off all impurities that rise to the surface. Add water if necessary to retain appropriate volume. Strain stock through fine cheese cloth or strainer. Return stock to a low boil and reduce to two quarts.

Changes

_____

_____

_____

_____

Demi-Glace

1 Hour   1 Quart

Comment:

Demi-glace is an essential sauce in classical cuisine. I have incorporated this sauce into most of the dishes created at Lafitte's Landing Restaurant.

2 quarts beef, veal or game   **1/2 cup white roux (see recipe)**
** stock (see recipe)**   **1 ounce tomato sauce**

Equally divide the stock into two heavy bottom sauce pans and bring to a low boil. Using a wire whisk, add one half cup white roux into one of the sauce pans, stirring constantly as mixture thickens. Into the thickened mixture, blend tomato sauce. What you have just created is known in classical cooking as an espagnole sauce. If this sauce is not full-flavored, you may wish to add a mirepoix or bouquet garni. (see stock technique) Continue simmering while skimming all impurities that rise to the surface. As the espagnole sauce reduces, replace the volume with the stock from the second pot until all has been incorporated. Strain through cheese cloth or fine strainer. You may wish to add an ounce of sherry or brandy to add flavor.

Changes

_____

_____

_____

_____

Meat Glaze

1 Hour   1 Cup

1 quart beef or veal stock

Meat glaze or "glace de viande" is produced by reducing a rich, clear beef or veal stock to such a point that it napes or coats the back of a spoon. This is done by simmering the stock over medium to medium high heat in a heavy bottom sauce pan. As the stock reduces, you may transfer it from time to time to a smaller pot, straining it each time through cheese cloth. This syrupy mixture becomes firm and rubbery in texture upon refrigeration and coats meat giving it sheen and additional flavor. It also is used to enhance soups and sauces, and can be added to a Gastrique to give rich body to fine butter sauces. Glazes may also be made from chicken, duck, fish and game stocks and are known in classical cooking as glace de volaille (chicken), glace de canard (duck), glace de poisson (fish) and glace de gibier (game). Meat glazes may be kept refrigerated for weeks at a time.

Changes

_____

_____

_____

_____

Veloute

45 Minutes   2 Quarts

2 quarts chicken or fish stock   **1/2 cup white roux (see recipe)**
    (see recipe)   **salt and white pepper to taste**

In a heavy bottom sauce pan, bring stock to a low boil. Reduce to simmer and using a wire whisk, blend roux into the hot stock. Continue to whip until mixture is smooth and slightly thickened. Season to taste using salt and white pepper. Reduce heat to low and cook veloute approximately thirty minutes, skimming all impurities that rise to the surface. The veloute is the base for all great cream soups and flavored white sauces. It is the most practical of all mother sauces and is created with relative ease. In classical cuisine, the veloute is defined as an ordinary white stock. However, in Creole cooking, the roux is added to the white stock prior to calling it a veloute.

Changes

_____

_____

_____

_____

Hollandaise Sauce

15 Minutes   1 Cup

8 ounces unsalted butter
3 tbsps red wine vinegar
1/2 cup dry white wine
1 tsp lemon juice

dash of Louisiana Gold
Pepper Sauce
3 egg yolks
salt and white pepper to taste

In a small sauce pan, melt butter over medium high heat. Once melted, remove from heat and cool slightly. In a separate saute pan, add vinegar, wine, lemon juice and Louisiana Gold. Place over medium heat and reduce to approximately one half volume. Remove from heat and keep warm. In a stainless steel bowl, whip egg yolks with vinegar mixture. Place over double boiler and whip constantly using a wire whisk until egg mixture is double in volume, smooth and creamy. Do not allow mixture to overheat as eggs will scramble. Remove from heat and add melted butter in a slow steady stream, whisking constantly. If the sauce is too thick, add a few drops of warm water while whisking. Season to taste using salt and pepper and additional lemon juice if necessary. This sauce is best when served immediately. If allowed to cool, the butter will harden.

Changes

_____
_____
_____
_____

Bearnaise Sauce

15 Minutes   1 Cup

8 ounces butter
3 tbsps tarragon vinegar
1/2 cup white wine
1 tsp lemon juice
dash of Louisiana Gold
    Pepper Sauce

1 tbsp chopped tarragon
1 tsp chopped green onions
1 tsp finely chopped parsley
3 egg yolks
salt and cayenne pepper to taste

In a small saute pan, melt butter over medium high heat. Once melted, set aside and cool slightly. In a separate saute pan, add vinegar, white wine, lemon juice, Louisiana Gold, tarragon, green onions and parsley. Bring to a slight boil, whisking constantly, and reduce liquid by one half volume. In a stainless steel bowl, whisk egg yolks with vinegar mixture and stir until well blended. Place bowl over a sauce pan of boiling water and whisk constantly until egg mixture has doubled in volume and is smooth and creamy. Be careful not to overheat as eggs will scramble. Remove bowl from sauce pan and add melted butter in a slow steady stream, whipping constantly until all is incorporated. If the sauce should become too thick, add a few drops of warm water. Season to taste using salt and pepper and add additional lemon juice if necessary. This sauce is best when served immediately. If allowed to cool, the butter will harden.

Changes

_____

_____

_____

_____

Bechamel Sauce

30 Minutes   1 Quart

1 quart milk
1 small onion, diced
3 whole cloves
pinch of thyme
6 whole peppercorns

2 small bay leaves
1/2 cup white roux (see recipe)
salt and white pepper to taste
pinch of nutmeg

In a heavy bottom sauce pan, heat milk over medium high heat. Add onion, cloves, thyme, peppercorns and bay leaves and continue to scald milk with seasonings for approximately twenty minutes. Do not boil. Strain scalded milk through fine cheese cloth into another sauce pan. Bring back to a low boil and add roux, whisking constantly with a wire whip until all is incorporated. Continue to whisk until mixture achieves a nice white sauce consistency. Be careful that sauce does not scorch. When thickened, remove from heat and season to taste using salt, pepper and nutmeg. This sauce is the primary ingredient for all creamed vegetable casseroles and au gratin dishes. For more flavor in the bechamel, you may wish to add a small amount of chicken or fish stock as in the veloutes.

Changes

_____

_____

_____

_____

Nantua Sauce

1 Hour   2 Quarts

Comment:

Technically speaking, this sauce is in the bechamel family and is made by adding cream and crawfish butter to a basic white sauce. We have developed a sauce here in South Louisiana that is more closely akin to a veloute.

2 pounds crawfish shells, heads included	15 whole peppercorns
	1 gallon cold water
2 cups chopped onions	2 cups dry white wine
1 cup chopped celery	1/2 cup tomato sauce
1 cup chopped carrots	1/2 cup white roux (see recipe)
6 cloves diced garlic	1 pint heavy whipping cream
2 bay leaves	1/2 ounce brandy
1 tsp dried thyme	salt and white pepper to taste

In a two gallon stock pot over medium high heat, combine crawfish shells and heads, onion, celery, carrots, garlic, bay leaves, thyme, peppercorns, water, and wine. Bring to a low boil, reduce heat to simmer and cook thirty minutes. During the cooking process, skim off all impurities that rise to the surface. When cooked, strain stock through fine cheese cloth or strainer. Discard all stock ingredients and return hot stock to the pot. Bring to a low boil and reduce to approximately two quarts. Add tomato sauce and white roux, whisking constantly until roux is well blended and the sauce is slightly thickened. Reduce heat to simmer and cook fifteen minutes. Add heavy whipping cream and brandy and season to taste using salt and pepper. Strain sauce for a second time through fine cheese cloth or strainer, adjust seasonings and allow to cool.

Changes

_____

_____

_____

_____

Beurre Blanc

15 Minutes   1 Cup

Comment:

This sauce comes to us from the regional cuisine of Brittany. The city of Nantes, on the Loire, is famed for serving this sauce with Pike and Loire shad. Today in Louisiana, beurre blanc lends itself to many exciting variations.

1/2 cup dry white wine
2 tbsps white vinegar
1 tsp lemon juice
1 tsp finely diced shallots
1 clove diced garlic

1 tbsp sliced green onions
8 ounces chipped, unsalted butter
salt and white pepper to taste
1 tsp finely chopped parsley

In a heavy bottom saute pan over medium high heat, combine wine, vinegar, lemon juice, shallots, garlic and green onions. Stir constantly until liquid is reduced to approximately two tablespoons. At this point, the mixture is commonly known as a gastique. Reduce heat to low and add chipped butter, a few pieces at a time, swirling pan constantly. Do not stir with a metal spoon or whip, as hot spots may develop and butter will separate. Continue to add chipped butter, swirling pan constantly, until all has been incorporated. Remove from heat and season to taste using salt and white pepper. Garnish with chopped parsley.

Changes

_____
_____
_____
_____

Beurre Cajun

15 Minutes   1 Cup

1/4 cup crawfish tails with fat
1/2 cup dry white wine
1 tbsp lemon juice
1 clove diced garlic
1 tbsp sliced green onions

1/4 cup finely sliced andouille
dash of Louisiana Gold
   Pepper Sauce
8 ounces chipped, unsalted butter
salt and cayenne pepper to taste

In a saute pan over medium high heat, combine crawfish tails, wine, lemon juice, garlic, green onions, andouille and Louisiana Gold Pepper Sauce. Saute approximately three to five minutes or until all liquids in pan are reduced by one half volume. Add chipped butter, a few pieces at a time, swirling pan constantly. Do not stir with a metal spoon or wire whisk as hot spots will develop in the pan and butter will separate. Continue to add butter, a few pieces at a time, swirling pan, until all is incorporated. Remove from heat and season to taste using salt and cayenne pepper. This sauce is excellent when served over pan sauteed or charbroiled fish.

Changes

_____

_____

_____

_____

Beurre Creole

15 Minutes   1 Cup

1/2 cup dry white wine
2 tbsps lemon juice
1/4 cup jumbo lump crabmeat
1/4 cup diced tomatoes
1 clove diced garlic
1 tbsp sliced green onions

1 tsp tomato sauce
8 ounces chipped, unsalted butter
dash of Louisiana Gold
  Pepper Sauce
salt and cayenne pepper to taste

In a saute pan over medium high heat, combine wine, lemon juice, lump crabmeat, tomatoes, garlic and green onions. Saute approximately three minutes or until juices are rendered into the pan. Add tomato sauce, blend well into mixture and continue to cook until all juices have been reduced to approximately two tablespoons. Slowly add chipped butter, a few pats at a time, while swirling pan constantly. Do not use a metal spoon or wire whisk as hot spots may develop and butter will separate. Continue adding butter while swirling pan until all has been incorporated. Season to taste using Louisiana Gold, salt and pepper. This sauce is excellent over broiled or sauteed fish or grilled shrimp.

Changes

_____

_____

_____

_____

Beurre Rouge

15 Minutes   1 Cup

1/2 cup dry red wine   8 ounces unsalted, chipped butter
1 tbsp red wine vinegar   dash of Louisiana Gold
1 clove diced garlic   Pepper Sauce
1 tbsp sliced green onions   salt and cayenne pepper to taste

In a saute pan over medium high heat, combine red wine vinegar, garlic and green onions. Bring to a low boil and reduce until approximately two tablespoons of liquid remain. Add chipped butter, a few pats at a time, swirling pan constantly. Do not use a metal cooking spoon or wire whisk as hot spots will develop and butter will separate. Continue to add butter, swirling pan constantly, until all has been incorporated. Season to taste using Louisiana Gold, salt and cayenne pepper. This sauce is excellent over grilled fish or light meats.

Changes

_____
_____
_____
_____

Beurre Poivre Vert I

15 Minutes   1 Cup

3 tbsps green peppercorn liquid
1/2 cup dry white wine
2 tbsps lemon juice
2 cloves diced garlic
1 tbsp sliced green onions

2 tbsps green peppercorns
8 ounces unsalted, chipped butter
dash of Louisiana Gold
**   Pepper Sauce**
salt to taste

In a saute pan over medium high heat, combine peppercorn liquid, wine, lemon juice, garlic and green onions. Bring to a low boil and add green peppercorns. Continue to saute until liquid is reduced to approximately two tablespoons. Slowly add chipped butter, a few pats at a time, swirling pan constantly. Do not use a metal spoon or wire whisk as hot spots will develop and butter will separate. Continue to add butter, swirling pan, until all has been incorporated. Remove from heat and season to taste using Louisiana Gold and salt. This sauce is excellent when served with fish or veal.

RM 89

Changes

37

Beurre Poivre Vert II

15 Minutes   1 Cup

1/2 cup dry red wine
2 tbsps red wine vinegar
2 tbsps green peppercorn liquid
2 cloves diced garlic
1 tbsp sliced green onions
2 tbsps green peppercorns

2 tbsps meat glaze (see recipe)
8 ounces unsalted, chipped butter
dash of Louisiana Gold
      Pepper Sauce
salt to taste

In a heavy bottom saute pan over medium high heat, combine wine, vinegar, peppercorn liquid, garlic and green onions. Bring to a low boil and add peppercorns and meat glaze. Continue to saute, stirring occasionally, until liquid has reduced to approximately three tablespoons. Slowly add chipped butter, a few pats at a time, swirling pan constantly. Do not use a metal spoon or wire whisk as hot spots will develop and butter will separate. Continue to add butter, swirling pan, until all has been incorporated. Remove from heat and season to taste using Louisiana Gold and salt. This sauce is excellent over grilled tuna or veal dishes.

Changes

_____

_____

_____

_____

Stocks & Sauces

Beurre Citron

15 Minutes   1 Cup

1/2 cup dry white wine
3 tbsps lemon juice
2 tbsps orange juice
1 tbsp lime juice
2 cloves diced garlic

1 tbsp sliced green onions
8 ounces unsalted, chipped butter
dash of Louisiana Gold
  Pepper Sauce
salt and cayenne pepper to taste

In a saute pan over medium high heat, combine wine, lemon juice, orange juice, lime juice, garlic and green onions. Bring to a low boil and saute until liquid is reduced to approximately three tablespoons. Add chipped butter, a few pats at a time, swirling pan constantly. Do not use a metal spoon or wire whisk as hot spots will develop and butter will separate. Continue to add butter, swirling pan, until all has been incorporated. Season to taste using Louisiana Gold, salt and cayenne pepper. This sauce is excellent over broiled or poached fish.

Changes

_____
_____
_____
_____

Crawfish Butter

15 Minutes   1-1/2 Cups

Comment:

Crawfish butter is ideal for adding that unique Cajun and Creole flavor to any classical butter sauce. Simply place one tablespoon of this compound butter into any beurre blanc based sauce and miracles happen.

1/4 cup butter
1/2 cup chopped onions
1/4 cup chopped celery
1/4 cup chopped carrots

2 cloves minced garlic
1/2 pound live, whole crawfish
1/4 cup brandy
1/2 pound chilled unsalted butter

In a heavy bottom saute pan, melt butter over medium high heat. Saute onions, celery, carrots and garlic three to five minutes or until vegetables are wilted. Add crawfish, cover and swirl pan, approximately two minutes or until crawfish are pink in color. Simmer for three minutes. Deglaze with brandy being careful as brandy will ignite. Place all ingredients in a food processor with a metal blade and blend on high until well chopped. Remove mixture and chill. Once well chilled, mix crawfish mixture with butter. Blend crawfish flavor well into the softened butter. Force mixture through a fine screen sieve to remove all foreign debris and shells. Place in ceramic or plastic container, cover and chill.

Changes

Bordelaise Sauce

15 Minutes   1 Cup

Comment:

Bordelaise in the city of New Orleans, has a completely different look and taste than the bordelaise of classical cuisine. Bordelaise means "the sauce from Bordeaux." In classical cooking, the sauce begins with a red wine reduction. Originally, however, the sauce was made with white bordeaux and the key ingredient added during reduction was bone marrow. Often times, the sauce was garnished with rounds of marrow. The Creoles of early New Orleans, making do with what was available, changed this sauce completely and this is their version.

3/4 cup butter
3 tbsps olive oil
1/4 cup diced garlic
1 tsp cracked black peppercorns
1/4 cup sliced green onions
1 ounce red bordeaux wine

1 tbsp chopped pimentos
1/4 cup chopped parsley
salt to taste
dash of Louisiana Gold
  Pepper Sauce

In a heavy bottom saute pan, melt butter and olive oil over medium high heat. Add garlic, black peppercorns and green onions. Saute approximately two to three minutes or until vegetables are wilted. Be careful not to over-brown the garlic, as this will give the sauce a bitter taste. Deglaze with red wine and add pimentos and parsley. Season to taste using salt and Louisiana Gold. Remove from heat.

Changes

Remoulade Sauce

15 Minutes   2 Cups

Comment:

The recipe for the remoulade sauce of the River Road is found in the appetizer section of this book. I have taken this opportunity to give you a second version, the Creole style, thought to be the original Louisiana version.

1 cup olive oil
1/4 cup red wine vinegar
3/4 cup Creole mustard
1/2 cup sliced green onions
1/4 cup chopped parsley
1/4 cup diced celery

1 tbsp diced garlic
1 tbsp paprika
salt to taste
Louisiana Gold Pepper Sauce
    to taste

In a large ceramic mixing bowl, combine olive oil, vinegar and Creole mustard. Using a wire whisk, blend well until all ingredients are well incorporated. Add green onions, parsley, celery and garlic. Continue mixing until all seasonings are well blended. Add paprika for color and season to taste using salt and Louisiana Gold. Place in the refrigerator, covered with clear wrap, and allow to sit overnight. You may wish to serve a generous portion of this sauce over shrimp, lump crabmeat or simply as a salad dressing.

Changes

Louisiana Tartar Sauce

15 Minutes   2 Cups

Comment:

Tartar sauce is normally served with all fried seafood dishes in South Louisiana. You may wish to try this sauce as a dip for catfish beignets or as a topping for a seafood terrine.

1-1/2 cups heavy duty
    mayonnaise
2 tbsps lemon juice
1/4 cup chopped pimento olives
1/4 cup chopped sweet pickles
1 tbsp sweet pickle juice

1/4 cup chopped parsley
1/4 cup chopped capers
1 tbsp sliced green onions
salt to taste
Louisiana Gold Pepper Sauce
    to taste

In a large ceramic bowl, combine mayonnaise and lemon juice. Using a wire whisk, blend until well incorporated. Add olives, pickles, pickle juice, parsley, capers and green onions. Fold all seasoning ingredients into the mayonnaise until mixture is evenly blended. Season to taste using salt and Louisiana Gold. If you prefer a more tart taste, add a little lemon juice or white vinegar. If a sweeter taste is preferred, add more sweet pickle juice or a touch of sugar. Cover with clear wrap and refrigerate overnight for flavors to develop.

Changes

_____

_____

_____

_____

Louisiana Seafood Cocktail Sauce

15 Minutes   2 Cups

Comment:

Cocktail sauce is one of the seafood sauces found primarily in the city of New Orleans. This sauce has many variations but most are tomato catsup based and spiced with a touch of horseradish.

1 cup tomato sauce
1/4 cup catsup
2 tbsps red wine vinegar
3 tbsps Worcestershire sauce
1 tbsp horseradish
1/4 cup chopped bell pepper

1/4 cup chopped celery
1 tbsp diced garlic
salt to taste
Louisiana Gold Pepper Sauce
    to taste

In a large ceramic bowl, combine tomato sauce, catsup, vinegar, Worcestershire and horseradish. Using a wire whip, blend until all ingredients are well incorporated. Add bell pepper, celery and garlic and season to taste using salt and Louisiana Gold. Continue to blend until all seasonings are evenly mixed throughout the sauce. Adjust seasonings to your taste should more sweetness or tartness be desired. Cover and refrigerate overnight for flavors to develop. This sauce is always served with boiled seafood.

Changes

44

Marchand de Vin

30 Minutes   2 Cups

Comment:

The wine merchant sauce is probably the most famous of the New Orleans sauces. Though the original version in classical cooking employed bone marrow, we have elected to remove this ingredient in the Creole version.

1/4 cup butter
1/4 cup finely minced ham
1/2 cup finely sliced green
   onions
1/4 cup finely minced garlic
2 tbsps finely minced onions

1/2 cup dry red wine
1 cup demi-glace (see recipe)
1 tsp salt
1/4 tsp cayenne pepper
pinch of cracked black pepper

In a heavy bottom saute pan, melt butter over medium high heat. Saute minced ham, green onions, garlic and onions three to five minutes or until vegetables are wilted. Deglaze with red wine and reduce to one half volume. Add demi-glace and return mixture to a simmer. Season to taste using salt, cayenne pepper and cracked black pepper. Continue to reduce until sauce is slightly thickened and all flavors are well incorporated. This sauce is best served over any sauteed or grilled meat or veal.

Changes

_____

_____

_____

_____

Louisiana Style Hunter Sauce

30 Minutes   2 Cups

Comment:

This is the most complex flavor derived from a demi-glace. The sauce is dependent on the concentration of wild game flavor in the stock. I recommend this sauce with all venison and roasted wild duck dishes.

1/4 cup butter
1/4 cup diced wild Louisiana
   mushrooms
1/4 cup sliced green onions
1 tbsp diced garlic
1/4 cup diced ripe tomatoes

1 ounce dry red wine
1 ounce brandy
1 cup game demi-glace
1 tbsp chopped parsley
salt and cracked black pepper
   to taste

As previously mentioned, this is the most complex of demi-glace flavorings. Similar to the Grand Veneur or Royal Hunt sauce, the Louisiana Hunter Sauce can turn any simple roasted game into a culinary masterpiece. Take the time to accomplish the game stock and this sauce will be quite simple.

In a heavy bottom saute pan, melt butter over medium high heat. Add mushrooms, green onions, garlic and tomatoes. Saute for approximately five minutes or until vegetables are wilted. Deglaze with red wine and brandy. Reduce heat to simmer and cook until volume is one half. Add game demi-glace and parsley and season to taste using salt and cracked black pepper. Simmer for approximately five minutes or until the sauce is slightly thickened and full-flavored.

HINT: Refer to the demi-glace recipe and make demi-glace from two quarts of rich game stock. This should yield one quart of rich full bodied game demi-glace.

Changes

_____

_____

_____

_____

Brown Meuniere Sauce

15 Minutes   1 Cup

Comment:

The brown meuniere sauce is the most popular sauce at Lafitte's Landing Restaurant. Its tart taste and rich flavor goes well with both meat and fish. However, many exciting variations may be made using meuniere as the mother sauce.

4 ounces demi-glace
2 ounces dry white wine
1 ounce lemon juice

1/2 pound cold, unsalted butter
salt and cayenne pepper to taste

In a sauce pan over medium high heat, combine demi-glace, wine and lemon juice. Using a wire whisk, stir until all ingredients are well blended. Bring to a low boil and reduce until the liquids are about one half in volume. Slowly whisk in cold butter, a few pats at a time, swirling pan constantly while butter is incorporating. Pan must be swirled constantly as hot spots will develop and the butter will break down. Continue to add butter, swirling constantly, until all is incorporated. Season to taste using salt and cayenne pepper and keep warm. Since this is a basic butter sauce, it cannot be reheated as butter will melt and separate. If allowed to chill, it will return to the solid state. ·

Changes

_____
_____
_____
_____

Creme Fraiche

12 Hours   1 Cup

Comment:

Creme Fraiche is similar to heavy buttermilk or sour cream. We use this unique cream to finish many of our demi-glace based sauces. Not only does it tend to smooth out the flavor but it gives the sauce a nice tangy bite.

8 ounces heavy whipping cream   **3 tsps buttermilk**

In a ceramic bowl, combine cream and buttermilk. Cover with clean cloth and let set at room temperature for eight to twelve hours. Most cooks will combine the cream with the buttermilk and place on a pantry shelf overnight. The finished creme fraiche should be placed in a covered container and stored in the refrigerator. You may also wish to use this sauce as you would heavy whipping cream or sour cream.

Changes

_____

_____

_____

_____

Appetizers

Reba Meliet © 1989

49

Appetizers

When people in South Louisiana meet, there are two things they love to do. One is talk and the other is eat. Whether a social event or family gathering, the table is always over-filled with sumptuous appetizers, showcasing Louisiana's bountiful seafood and wild game harvest.

Crawfish, oysters, crabmeat and shrimp make up the majority of hors d'oeuvres in Cajun and Creole cooking. With such specialties as Oysters Marie Laveaux, Oysters Rockefeller, Shrimp Remoulade, and Stuffed Mushrooms Dominique Youx, the appetizers often times prove to be more interesting than the main meals.

Today, with the evolution process in Cajun and Creole cooking, we find such dishes as Smoked Terrine of Catfish, Shrimp Malarcher and our infamous Cajun Fettuccine taking the place of these early masterpieces.

> *"A man is in general better pleased when he has had a good hors d'oeuvre placed upon his table than when the scholars speak of Rome."*
>
> Samuel Johnson

Lump Crabmeat Viala

30 Minutes   6 Servings

Comment:

The building housing Lafitte's Landing was formerly the Viala Plantation House. Built in 1797, the home figured prominently in the life of the pirate, Jean Lafitte. This crabmeat dish is named in honor of the old Viala Plantation.

1 pound jumbo lump crabmeat

SAUCE PREPARATION:

1-1/2 cups mayonnaise
1/4 cup chopped green onions
1 tbsp chopped parsley
1 tbsp chopped tarragon
1 tsp chopped dill
1 tsp diced garlic

2 tbsps lemon juice
dash of Louisiana Gold
     Pepper Sauce
dash of Worcestershire sauce
salt and cayenne pepper to taste
1/4 cup finely diced red bell pepper

Remove shells from lump crabmeat, being careful not to break lumps. Place crabmeat in a covered bowl and refrigerate. In a food processor with a metal blade, combine all ingredients except red bell pepper. Whip on high speed for approximately one minute, then adjust salt and pepper seasonings to taste. Continue to blend one minute longer. Place mixture in a serving bowl and blend in diced red bell pepper for color. Cover tightly with clear wrap and refrigerate overnight. It is important to remember that the flavor of tarragon and dill will only be experienced after sauce has been resting over eight hours. Remove from refrigerator, test for seasonings and adjust if necessary. Add lump crabmeat, blending carefully into sauce. Place on romaine lettuce leaves and serve with garlic flavored croutons.

Changes

Lump Crabmeat St. Martin

45 Minutes   6 Servings

Comment:

Remember for that next cocktail party, this dish makes an excellent hors d'oeuvre and should be served hot with garlic croutons or crackers.

1 pound jumbo lump crabmeat
1/4 pound butter
1/4 cup chopped onions
1/4 cup chopped celery
1/4 cup chopped green onions
1 tbsp diced garlic
2 tbsps flour
3-1/2 cups hot whipping cream

1 ounce dry white wine
1 tbsp lemon juice
dash of Louisiana Gold
    Pepper Sauce
1/4 cup grated Parmesan cheese
salt and cayenne pepper to taste
1/4 cup diced red bell pepper
1/4 cup chopped parsley

In a two quart heavy bottom sauce pan, melt butter over medium high heat. Add onions, celery, green onions and garlic. Saute three to five minutes or until vegetables are wilted. Be careful not to brown vegetables. Sprinkle in flour, blending well into mixture. Using a wire whip, whisk hot cream into sauce pan stirring constantly until thick cream sauce is achieved. Reduce heat to simmer and add white wine, lemon juice and hot sauce. Add Parmesan cheese, stirring constantly so mixture will not scorch. Season to taste using salt and pepper. Add red bell pepper for color. If mixture becomes too thick, add a small amount of whipping cream or hot water. Remove from heat and gently fold in lump crabmeat. Place in souffle ramakins, garnish with parsley and serve with garlic croutons.

Changes

52

Crabmeat Spinach Pate

45 Minutes   6 Servings

Comment:

Although not a traditional pate, this spinach dish, when allowed to cool in a pate mold, resembles the real thing. When served in a hot chafing dish with garlic croutons, this dish becomes a wonderful hors d'oeuvre.

1 pound jumbo lump crabmeat
1/4 pound butter
1/4 cup chopped onions
1/4 cup chopped celery
1/4 cup chopped green onions
2 tbsps diced garlic
1/4 cup diced red bell pepper

2 10-ounce packages frozen spinach (thawed)
2 cups bechamel sauce (see recipe)
1 cup heavy whipping cream
1/2 cup grated cheddar cheese
1 tbsp Pernod or Herbsaint
salt and cracked black pepper to taste

In a two quart heavy bottom sauce pan, melt butter over medium high heat. Saute onions, celery, green onions and garlic until vegetables are wilted. Add red bell pepper and thawed spinach to vegetables and, using a metal spoon, chop spinach well into mixture. Saute five minutes, add bechamel sauce, cream and cheddar cheese, and stir constantly until mixture is bubbly and cheese is melted. Incorporate Pernod into pate mixture and season to taste using salt and cracked black pepper. Cook five additional minutes adding small amounts of milk or cream, should sauce become too thick. Remove from heat, fold in lump crabmeat and adjust seasonings if necessary. Transfer mixture to small souffle cups. Serve with garlic croutons. Try serving in a hot chafing dish as a great hors d'oeuvre. Mixture may be allowed to cool and then served as a cold spinach spread.

Changes

_____

_____

_____

_____

French Fried Crab Claws

30 Minutes   6 Servings

Comment:

Home style frying units, such as Fry Daddy or Fry Baby, make deep frying simple for the home kitchen. Also be aware of the nice "lite" frying oils available on the market today. Using these will make deep frying a lot healthier.

FOR BATTER:

1 cup milk
1/2 cup water
2 eggs

3 tbsps Creole mustard
salt and cracked black pepper
   to taste

In a one quart mixing bowl, combine all of the above ingredients. Whisk with a wire whip to ensure mixture is well blended. Set aside.

FOR BREADING:

2 cups yellow corn flour **
2-1/4 tsps salt
1-1/2 tsps granulated garlic

1-1/2 tsps cracked black pepper
1-1/2 tsps cayenne pepper
1-1/2 tsps dry thyme

In a one quart mixing bowl, combine all of the above ingredients. Set aside.

(Continued)

Changes

Appetizers

(French Fried Crab Claws continued)

FOR FRYING:

1 pound cleaned crab claws   **1-1/2 quarts vegetable oil**

In a home style deep fryer, such as a Fry Daddy or Fry Baby, preheat oil according to manufacturer's directions, or to 375 degrees F. Place crab claws in batter mixture and allow to set ten to fifteen minutes. Drain all excess liquid from crab claws and bread well in yellow corn flour. Shake off all excess breading and deep fry a few dozen at a time until claws turn golden brown and float to top of frying unit. Remove and drain on paper towels and serve hot, with cocktail or tartar sauce. (see recipe)

** **NOTE:** Yellow corn flour may be found in most gourmet shops or food stores. It may be found packaged and pre-seasoned as a seafood breading mix such as Zatarain's Fish Fry. If unavailable in your area, plain flour or equal parts of flour and yellow corn meal may be substituted.

Changes

_____

_____

_____

_____

Terrine of Smoked Catfish

1 Hour   20 Servings

Comment:

This recipe has become one of our most popular hors d'oeuvre items, as we bring Louisiana cooking around the world. Companies such as Delta Pride Catfish in Indianola, Mississippi, are making farm raised catfish a household word.

FOR SMOKING:

4 5-8 ounce fillets   1 tsp dry basil
1/2 cup olive oil   1 tsp cracked black pepper
1/4 cup red wine vinegar   dash of Louisiana Gold
1 tsp dry thyme   Pepper Sauce

Preheat homestyle smoking unit according to manufacturer's instructions. Pre-soak any wood chips such as pecan or hickory in root beer for a unique flavor. Combine all the above ingredients, blend well and pour over catfish fillets. Allow to set at room temperature approximately thirty minutes. Smoke fillets for approximately thirty-five to forty minutes or until flaky. Remove and allow to cool.

(Continued)

Changes

_____

_____

_____

_____

(Terrine of Smoked Catfish continued)

FOR TERRINE:

4 5-8 ounce smoked fillets
1 cup heavy duty mayonnaise
1/2 cup sour cream
1 tbsp diced garlic
1/4 cup chopped parsley
1/4 cup diced red bell pepper
1/4 cup diced yellow bell pepper
2 tbsps cracked black pepper

1 tbsp lemon juice
1/2 ounce sherry wine
1 tbsp Worcestershire sauce
dash of Louisiana Gold
   Pepper Sauce
salt to taste
2 pkg unflavored gelatin dissolved
   in 1/4 cup cold water

Coarsely chop smoked catfish. In a two quart mixing bowl, add all remaining ingredients, blending well to incorporate seasonings into the mixture. Adjust salt and pepper if necessary, and pour mixture into a terrine mold. Place in refrigerator covered overnight. When serving, remove from mold and garnish with French bread or garlic croutons. To enhance the presentation of the smoked terrine, you may wish to color two cups of mayonnaise, one with red food coloring and one with green. Using a pastry bag with a star tip, pipe colored mayonnaise around the base of the terrine. You may also wish to garnish the top of the terrine with a small amount of the colored mayonnaise and a fresh tomato rose.

Changes

Catfish in Puff Pastry

1 Hour   25 Pieces

Comment:

This classical presentation of farm raised catfish will be the hit of any formal hors d'oeuvre event.

FOR SAUCE:

1/2 pound white crabmeat
1/4 pound butter
1/4 cup chopped onions
1/4 cup chopped celery
1/4 cup sliced green onions
2 tbsps diced garlic
2 tbsps flour

2-1/2 cups hot whipping cream
1/2 cup grated Parmesan cheese
1/4 cup chopped parsley
1/4 cup diced red bell pepper
1 ounce sherry wine
salt and cayenne pepper to taste

In a heavy bottom sauce pan, melt butter over medium high heat. Add onions, celery, green onions and garlic and saute approximately five minutes or until vegetables are wilted. Using a wire whisk, add flour into mixture, stirring constantly. Do not brown. Add heavy whipping cream and Parmesan cheese, continuing to whip as mixture thickens. Should sauce become too thick, add a little milk or hot water. Allow to cook approximately ten minutes until bubbly and smooth. Add parsley, red bell pepper and sherry wine. Season to taste using salt and pepper. Add white crabmeat and fold well into mixture. Remove from heat, set aside and allow to cool.

(Continued)

Changes

_____
_____
_____
_____

(*Catfish in Puff Pastry* continued)

FOR BAKING:

3 5-8 ounce fillets
1 cup water
1/4 cup melted butter
1 tsp lemon juice

1 bay leaf
1/2 tsp dry thyme
salt and cayenne pepper to taste
1 tsp paprika

Preheat oven to 350 degrees F. Place fillets in baking pan with one inch lip, and add water, butter and lemon juice. Season fish with bay leaf, thyme, salt and pepper. Sprinkle paprika over fish to enhance color. Bake approximately fifteen minutes or until flaky. Remove and cool. Oven should remain on 350 degrees.

TO ASSEMBLE:

1 10"x15"-sheet of frozen puff
   pastry

2 eggs, beaten

Cut catfish fillets into 1 inch cubes. Cut puff pastry into 2-1/2 inch squares. Place one teaspoon of sauce in center of puff pastry square and top with one cube of baked catfish. Fold pastry to form a triangle over the catfish cube, and seal edges by crimping with a fork. Brush with beaten egg for even browning. Place in oven and cook until golden brown, approximately ten to twelve minutes. Remove and serve immediately.

Changes

_____

_____

_____

_____

Cajun Catfish Beignets

45 Minutes   50 Beignets

Comment:

This is a new presentation of an old idea. Deep fried catfish served hors d'oeuvre style will give your party the flavor of the Old South.

FOR BATTER:

5 5-8 ounce fillets
1 cup milk
1/2 cup water
2 eggs

1/2 cup yellow prepared mustard
1 tsp granulated garlic
1 tbsp cracked black pepper
1 tsp salt

Cut catfish fillets into one and one half inch cubes. In a one quart mixing bowl, combine all remaining ingredients, whisking well to incorporate seasonings. Add catfish cubes and allow to set at room temperature for fifteen minutes.

FOR BREADING:

3 cups yellow corn flour **
2-1/2 tsps salt
2 tsps granulated garlic

1-1/2 tsps cracked black pepper
1/2 tsp cayenne pepper
1/2 tsp dry thyme

In a two quart mixing bowl, combine all breading ingredients. Mix well to ensure proper blending of spices. Set aside.

(Continued)

Changes

60

(Cajun Catfish Beignets continued)

FOR DEEP FRYING:

5 5-8 ounce fillets, cubed   **1-1/2 quarts vegetable oil**

In a home style deep fryer, such as a Fry Daddy or Fry Baby, preheat oil according to manufacturer's instructions or to 375 degrees F. Remove catfish cubes from batter mixture and place in yellow corn flour. Coat beignets well on all sides and shake off excess breading. Deep fry a few at a time until golden brown or until catfish floats to top of fryer. Remove to drain board or paper towels and place beignets in a hot chafing dish. Serve with cocktail or tartar sauce. (see recipe)

** **NOTE:** Yellow corn flour may be found in most gourmet shops or food stores. It may be sold as a packaged pre-seasoned seafood breading such as Zatarain's Fish Fry. If unavailable in your area, plain flour or equal parts of flour and yellow corn meal may be substituted.

Changes

_____

_____

_____

_____

Shrimp Malarcher

45 Minutes   6 Servings

Comment:

This dish was named in honor of the famous Malarcher sugar planters of River Road Louisiana. Their sugar plantation was located in Convent, Louisiana, West of New Orleans. Today, Occidental Chemical Company occupies the site.

3 dozen 21-25 count shrimp,
   peeled and deveined
1/4 pound butter
1 tbsp diced garlic
1/4 cup chopped green onions
1/4 cup sliced mushrooms
1/4 cup diced red bell pepper
1/4 cup diced yellow bell pepper
1/4 cup diced green bell pepper

2 tbsps flour
1 ounce dry white wine
2-1/2 cups hot shellfish or chicken
   stock (see recipe)
1 tsp lemon juice
1 tsp parsley
salt and cracked black pepper
   to taste

In a heavy bottom saute pan, melt butter over medium high heat. Saute garlic, green onions and mushrooms approximately two minutes or until mushrooms are slightly wilted. Add red, yellow and green bell pepper, stir into mixture and cook one additional minute. Add shrimp and stir fry into vegetables until shrimp begin to turn pink and curl, approximately two minutes. Sprinkle in flour and blend into dish until white roux is achieved. The flour will absorb most of the liquids in the pan and act as a thickening agent for the sauce. Deglaze with white wine and add hot stock, whisking well into seasoning mixture. Add lemon juice and parsley and season to taste using salt and cracked pepper. Cook until sauce is thickened and shrimp are perfectly cooked, but not overdone. Additional chicken stock may be added, should sauce become too thick. This dish may be served in an au gratin dish or heated chafing dish with garlic croutons.

Changes

_____

_____

_____

_____

Creole Shrimp Butter

45 Minutes   12-15 Servings

Comment:

Shrimp Butter is an excellent substitution for the traditional pates or terrines. Also, a small amount of shrimp butter added into a finished seafood sauce will work miracles.

1 pound 150-200 count shrimp,
   peeled and deveined
1/2 cup chopped onions
1/2 cup chopped celery
1/4 cup chopped green onions
1 tbsp diced garlic
3/4 pound cold butter
2 tbsps tomato puree

1 tsp sugar
1 tsp red wine vinegar
1 tsp lemon juice
1 tsp Worcestershire sauce
1 tsp Louisiana Gold Pepper Sauce
salt and cayenne pepper to taste
1/4 cup finely diced red bell pepper
1 tbsp finely chopped parsley

In a one gallon stock pot over medium high heat, boil shrimp in lightly salted water until shrimp are pink and curled, approximately three to five minutes. Remove from water and cool. Once shrimp are cool, place metal cutting blade in a food processor. Place shrimp, onions, celery, green onions and garlic in processor and chop on high speed for approximately thirty seconds. Add all remaining ingredients except red bell pepper and parsley. Continue to blend on high speed until all ingredients are well chopped and smooth butter is achieved. Add red bell pepper and parsley and blend three seconds for color. Pour into terrine mold and refrigerate overnight for flavors to develop. Serve with toast points or garlic croutons. You may wish to serve the terrine on a silver platter garnished with boiled shrimp and a confetti of colored vegetables.

Changes

South Louisiana Shrimp Remoulade

30 Minutes   6 Servings

Comment:

Remoulade sauce may be found in any restaurant in South Louisiana and in as many recipe versions. The remoulades of New Orleans are normally Creole mustard based and highly seasoned. This, however, is the River Road version.

FOR BOILING:

3 dozen 21-25 count shrimp,
   peeled and deveined
2 quarts cold water
1 diced onion
1/2 cup diced celery

3 bay leaves
1/4 cup lemon juice
1 sliced lemon
4 tbsps salt
2 tbsps cracked black pepper

In a four quart stock pot, over medium high heat, add water and all seasoning ingredients. Bring to a rolling boil, reduce to simmer and allow to cook fifteen minutes for flavors to develop. Bring mixture back to a rolling boil, add shrimp and stir approximately three to five minutes. At this point, shrimp should be pink and curled. Test for doneness, being careful not to overcook. Once water returns to a boil, shrimp should be perfectly done. Pour off boiling water and replace with cold tap water to stop the cooking process. Drain and place shrimp in a serving bowl. Cover with clear wrap and refrigerate. This may be done the night before.

(Continued)

Changes

(*South Louisiana Shrimp Remoulade* continued)

FOR SAUCE:

1-1/2 cups heavy duty
   mayonnaise
1/2 cup Creole mustard
1 tbsp Worcestershire sauce
1 tsp Louisiana Gold Pepper
   Sauce

1/2 cup finely diced green onions
1/4 cup finely diced celery
2 tbsps finely diced garlic
1/4 cup finely chopped parsley
1/2 tbsp lemon juice
salt and cracked black pepper
   to taste

In a two quart mixing bowl, combine all of the above ingredients, whisking well to incorporate the seasonings. Once blended, cover and place in refrigerator, preferably overnight. A minimum of four hours will be required for flavor to be developed. When ready, remove from refrigerator and adjust seasonings to taste. Place six shrimp on a leaf of romaine or other colored lettuce and spoon a generous serving of remoulade sauce on top of the shrimp. Do not sauce shrimp prior to service, as they will lose their firm texture.

Changes

_____

_____

_____

_____

Bayou Shrimp Beignets

1 Hour   25-30 Beignets

Comment:

Shrimp Beignets are somewhat similar to seafood fritters or shrimp patties. Try placing two to three beignets on toasted French bread with tartar sauce to make an interesting poboy sandwich.

1 pound 150-200 count shrimp, peeled and deveined
2 quarts vegetable oil for deep frying
1/4 pound butter
1/4 cup chopped onions
1/4 cup chopped celery
1/4 cup chopped green bell pepper

1 tbsp diced garlic
1/4 cup finely chopped green onions
1 tbsp flour
2 eggs
1/4 cup lemon juice
1 tbsp sherry
salt and cracked black pepper to taste
2 cups seasoned Italian bread crumbs

Preheat oil in home type deep fryer, such as Fry Daddy or Fry Baby, according to manufacturer's directions or to 375 degrees F. In a saute pan over medium high heat, melt butter. Saute onions, celery, bell pepper and garlic for approximately three minutes or until vegetables are wilted. Add green onions and saute one additional minute. Sprinkle in flour and blend well into vegetable mixture to form a white roux. (see roux technique) Do not allow to brown. Remove from heat and set aside. In a food processor with a metal blade, chop raw shrimp for approximately thirty seconds. Add eggs, lemon juice and sherry, and blend three additional seconds. Spoon shrimp mixture into saute pan with cooked vegetables and season to taste using salt and black pepper. Using a metal spoon, chop shrimp into vegetable mixture until all is well incorporated. Sprinkle in just enough bread crumbs to absorb any extra liquids. Roll beignet mixture into one and one half inch oblong patties and coat well with seasoned Italian bread crumbs. Deep fry a few at a time until golden brown and beignets are floating to the top of the oil. Remove to drain board or paper towels. May be served with cocktail or tartar sauce. (see recipe)

Changes

Honey Broiled Shrimp

30 Minutes   6 Servings

Comment:

Sugar cane syrup is widely used in South Louisiana as a marinade for wild game or as a unique flavoring in certain dishes. Though called Honey Broiled, the interesting flavor in this dish is made possible by the use of sugar cane syrup.

**3 dozen 21-25 count shrimp,
    peeled and deveined**
1/2 cup honey
1/2 cup Louisiana cane syrup
1/4 cup white wine
1/4 cup sherry

2 tbsps cracked black pepper
1 tbsp diced garlic
1 tsp dry tarragon
1/2 tsp dry basil
1/2 tsp dry thyme
1 tbsp chopped parsley

Preheat oven to 375 degrees. In a one quart mixing bowl, combine all ingredients except shrimp, and blend well using a wire whisk. Since the cane syrup and honey must be blended, take special care to whip properly and incorporate all seasonings. Place shrimp in a baking pan with one inch lip. Cover shrimp with syrup mixture, making sure that all shrimp are well coated. Use all of the honey broiled mixture. Place in oven and bake ten to fifteen minutes or until shrimp are pink and curled. Remove from oven, place six shrimp on each serving plate and coat generously with the cooking liquid. Serve with hot French bread.

Changes

_____

_____

_____

_____

Oysters Marie Laveaux

1 Hour   6 Servings

Comment:

Marie Laveaux was the voodoo queen of Bourbon Street. Legend has it that the pirate, Jean Lafitte, often met Marie at the Old Absinthe House late in the evening, and enjoyed oysters on the half shell and traded the secrets of Barataria Bay.

FOR OYSTERS:

3 dozen select oysters,
   reserving liquid
3 tbsps butter

1 tsp chopped garlic
1 tsp chopped parsley
1/2 ounce Pernod or Herbsaint

In a heavy bottom saute pan, melt butter over medium high heat. Add garlic and parsley, and saute approximately two minutes. Add oysters and cook until edges begin to curl. Do not overcook. Deglaze with Pernod and cook additional one minute. Remove oysters, reduce cooking liquid to one half volume, and reserve for sauce.

(Continued)

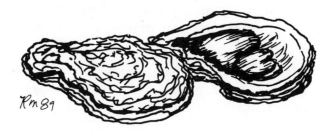

Rm 89

Changes

_____

_____

_____

_____

Appetizers

(*Oysters Marie Laveaux* continued)

FOR SAUCE:

1/4 pound butter	1 ounce dry white wine
1/2 cup diced onions	reserved cooking liquid from
1/4 cup diced celery	oysters
2 tbsps diced garlic	reserved oyster liquid
1/4 cup chopped green onions	pinch of nutmeg
1/2 cup white crabmeat or	1/4 cup diced red bell pepper
cooked chopped shrimp	1/4 cup diced yellow bell pepper
2-1/2 tbsps flour	salt and cracked black pepper
3 cups hot whipping cream	to taste

Preheat oven to 375 degrees F. In a one quart heavy bottom sauce pan, melt butter over medium high heat. Add onions, celery, garlic and green onions and saute approximately three minutes. Add crabmeat or shrimp and saute additional one minute, stirring constantly. Sprinkle in flour and using a wire whip, stir until a white roux is achieved. (see roux technique) This roux will act as a thickening agent for the sauce. Add heavy whipping cream and white wine, while continuing to blend with the wire whip. Bring to a low boil, stirring constantly as mixture thickens. Add cooking liquid from oysters as well as reserved oyster liquid. Reduce heat to simmer and cook approximately ten to fifteen minutes, adding hot water if necessary, should sauce become too thick. Add nutmeg and colored bell peppers and season to taste using salt and pepper. Place six oysters in each of six au gratin dishes. Top with generous serving of sauce and bake until bubbly. You may wish to sprinkle Parmesan cheese on top prior to baking. This dish should be served with garlic croutons or crackers.

Changes

_____

_____

_____

_____

Oysters Bayou Teche

1 Hour   6 Servings

Comment:

Of the oyster dishes famous in South Louisiana, none are known more widely than Rockefeller and Bienville. The Cajuns of Bayou Teche had their own specialty and I prefer it to either one of these now world famous oyster dishes.

2 dozen fresh shucked oysters,
    reserve liquid and shells
1/4 pound butter
1/4 cup diced onions
1/4 cup diced celery
1/4 cup diced red bell pepper
1 tbsp diced garlic
1/4 cup chopped green onions
1 cup claw crabmeat
3 tbsps flour

3 cups heavy whipping cream
1 ounce dry white wine
1/2 cup finely sliced mushrooms
1/2 cup grated Parmesan cheese
1 ounce sherry
1/2 cup chopped parsley
2 egg yolks, beaten
salt and cayenne pepper to taste
1 cup seasoned Italian bread crumbs

Preheat oven to 450 degrees F. In a two quart heavy bottom sauce pan, melt butter over medium high heat. Add onions, celery, bell pepper and garlic. Saute approximately three to five minutes or until vegetables are wilted. Add green onions and claw crabmeat, blending well into vegetable mixture. Sprinkle in flour and using a wire whip, stir until white roux is achieved. (see roux technique) Flour will act as a thickening agent for the sauce. Add heavy whipping cream and dry white wine. Using the wire whip, stir constantly until sauce begins to thicken. Add sliced mushrooms and Parmesan cheese, stirring well as cheese melts and mixture continues to thicken. Add sherry and chopped parsley. Combine oyster liquid with beaten eggs, blending well. Remove sauce pan from heat and quickly whisk in egg yolk mixture. Season to taste using salt and cayenne pepper. Allow to cool slightly or until sauce can be spooned without dripping. Place one oyster on each of twenty-four shells, top with equal servings of sauce and sprinkle generously with seasoned bread crumbs. Place on baking pan and cook on center oven rack until sauce is bubbly and bread crumbs are well browned. Serve immediately.

Changes

_____

Oyster and Andouille Pastries

1 Hour   6 Servings

Comment:

This is an excellent example of the evolution of Cajun and Creole cooking. The flavor of oysters and andouille, added to a classical butter sauce and served over French pastry, brings our cuisine into the 1990's.

2 dozen select oysters, reserve liquid
2 sheets 8-1/2" x 13" puff pastry
1 egg beaten
1/4 cup melted butter
1/2 cup diced andouille sausage
1 tsp diced garlic
1/4 cup sliced mushrooms

1/4 cup chopped green onions
1/4 cup diced tomatoes
1/4 cup diced red bell pepper
2 ounces champagne
1 cup heavy whipping cream
1/4 pound chipped cold butter
salt and cracked black pepper to taste

Preheat oven to 400 degrees F. Place two sheets of puff pastry, one atop the other, and cut into three inch squares. Lightly butter a large baking sheet and place squares of puff pastry evenly on the baking pan. Brush top of pastry with beaten egg, as this will enhance the color. Bake pastry until golden brown, approximately ten to fifteen minutes, remove and keep warm. In a heavy bottom sauce pan, melt butter over medium high heat. Saute andouille, garlic, mushrooms, green onions, tomatoes and bell pepper approximately three to five minutes, or until vegetables are wilted. Add oysters and oyster liquid and deglaze with champagne. Saute until edges of oysters begin to curl, about two minutes. Add heavy whipping cream, bring to a slight boil and reduce cream to one half volume. Once cream is thickened to sauce consistency, slowly add chipped butter, two to three chips at a time, swirling pan constantly until all butter is incorporated. It is important to swirl pan around burner and not to stir with a spoon, as butter may break down if hot spots occur. Continue until all butter has been added. Season to taste using salt and pepper. Place pastry square in center of six inch serving plate, remove top half of pastry and fill with equal parts of oysters and oyster butter sauce. Top with other half of pastry and serve.

Changes

Marinated Oysters

30 Minutes   6 Servings

Comment:

Marinated oysters, like smoked oysters, offer we Louisiana cooks a nice versatility when considering oysters as an appetizer dish. The longer the oysters set in the marinade, the better they will become.

3 dozen freshly shucked
   oysters, reserve liquid
2 cups olive oil
1 finely sliced sweet Vidalia
   onion
1/4 cup finely diced onions
1/4 cup finely diced celery
2 tbsps finely diced garlic
1/4 cup finely chopped green
   onions

1/4 cup finely diced red bell pepper
1/4 cup finely diced yellow
   bell pepper
4 bay leaves
1/4 cup red wine vinegar
1 tbsp lemon juice
1/2 cup sherry wine
2 tbsp cracked black pepper
1 tsp salt

In a heavy bottom sauce pan, heat olive oil over medium high heat. Add sliced onions, diced onions, celery, garlic, green onions, bell peppers and bay leaves. Saute approximately three to five minutes, or until vegetables are wilted. Add oysters and saute until edges are slightly curled. Do not overcook. Remove from heat and add oyster liquid and all remaining ingredients. Place oysters and all cooking liquid in a ceramic bowl. Allow to cool, cover tightly with clear wrap and refrigerate a minimum of twenty-four hours. Stir occasionally to keep all oysters in marinating liquid. Serve with croutons or on lettuces as a salad, using marinade as the dressing.

Changes

Oysters Rockefeller

1 Hour   6 Servings

Comment:

This, the most famous of all oyster dishes in Cajun country, was first developed at Antoine's Restaurant, by Jules Alciatore in 1899. Named Rockefeller because of its incredibly rich flavor, the original recipe included no spinach.

2 dozen shucked oysters,
    reserve liquid and shells
1/4 pound butter
1/4 cup diced onions
1/4 cup diced celery
1/2 cup chopped green onions
2 tbsps diced garlic
2 10-ounce packages cooked
    frozen spinach (thawed)
2 tbsps flour

1 cup heavy whipping cream
1/2 ounce Pernod or Herbsaint
1/2 cup tomato sauce
1 tsp sugar
2 tbsps Worcestershire sauce
1 tsp Louisiana Gold Pepper Sauce
salt and cracked black pepper
    to taste
4 cups rock salt

Preheat oven to 450 degrees F. In a two quart sauce pan, melt butter over medium high heat. Saute onions, celery, green onions and garlic, approximately three to five minutes or until seasonings are wilted. Add cooked spinach, and using a metal spoon, chop well into the vegetable mixture. Cook until spinach is hot and well incorporated into seasonings. Add flour and blend well into mixture, being sure to remove all lumps. Add whipping cream and oyster liquid, stirring constantly until sauce is thick and bubbly. Incorporate Pernod, tomato sauce, sugar, Worcestershire and Louisiana Gold. Continue stirring until all is well blended. Season to taste using salt and pepper. Place rock salt on the bottom of an 11x14" baking pan. This will ensure that the oysters will not tip over while baking. Place one oyster on each shell and top with generous serving of Rockefeller sauce. Place on baking pan and bake until hot and bubbly, approximately ten to fifteen minutes. Serve four oysters per person.

Changes

_____

_____

Cajun Fettuccine

45 Minutes   6 Servings

Comment:

This pasta dish was first introduced at Lafitte's Landing Restaurant in 1981. Pasta was coming of age in American cooking, and South Louisiana had the perfect ingredients for such a dish. Today, this dish is found throughout America.

3 cups cooked spinach fettuccine
1/4 pound butter
1 tbsp chopped garlic
1/4 cup chopped green onions
1/4 cup sliced mushrooms
1/2 cup diced tomatoes
1/2 cup diced andouille
1/2 cup 50 count shrimp, peeled
   and deveined
1/2 cup lump crabmeat

1/2 cup cooked crawfish tails
1 ounce dry white wine
1 tbsp lemon juice
1 cup heavy whipping cream
1/4 cup diced red bell pepper
1/4 pound chipped cold butter
1 tbsp chopped parsley
salt and cracked black pepper
   to taste

In a two quart heavy bottom sauce pan, melt butter over medium high heat. Add garlic, green onions, mushrooms, tomatoes and andouille. Saute three to five minutes or until all vegetables are wilted. Add shrimp, crabmeat and crawfish. Cook for an additional two minutes. Deglaze pan with white wine and lemon juice, and continue cooking until volume of liquid is reduced to one half. Add heavy whipping cream and, stirring constantly, reduce until cream is thick and of a sauce like consistency, approximately five minutes. Add diced red bell pepper and chipped butter, two to three pats at a time, swirling pan constantly over burner. Do not stir with a spoon, as butter will break down and separate if hot spots develop in the pan. Continue adding butter until all is incorporated. Remove from heat, add parsley and season to taste using salt and pepper. Gently fold in cooked fettuccine and serve. May be chilled and served as a cold pasta salad.

Changes

_____

_____

Smoked Breast of Mallard

2 Hours   6 Servings

Comment:

Today, chicken is used more and more on grills and smokers to produce variety in salads and appetizers. We are replacing the traditional breast of chicken with its bayou counterpart, breast of mallard.

6 boneless duck breasts
1/2 cup vegetable oil
1/4 cup Louisiana sugar cane syrup
1/4 cup dry red wine
2 tbsp Worcestershire sauce
1 tbsp Louisiana Gold Pepper Sauce

1/2 cup diced onions
1/2 cup diced carrots
1 tbsp finely diced garlic
2 tbsps cracked black pepper
1 tsp salt
1 tsp dry thyme
1 tsp dry tarragon

Preheat a homestyle smoker according to manufacturer's directions. You may wish to flavor pecan or hickory chips by soaking them in root beer for a unique flavor. In a one quart mixing bowl, combine all ingredients except duck breasts. Using a wire whip, whisk well to blend all seasonings. Add duck breasts to mixing bowl, cover with marinade and allow to set at room temperature for one hour. Smoke for approximately one to two and a half hours, testing for doneness after one hour. Remove from smoker, slice into quarter inch strips and serve with Creole mustard sweetened with a small amount of Louisiana cane syrup. The sliced breast may also be used on a salad or in a gumbo.

HINT: Domestic duck or Long Island duckling may be substituted in this recipe.

Changes

75

Mallard Duck Sausage

1 Hour   20 6 inch Sausage Links

Comment:

Though I am using mallard duck in this recipe, the sausage has been made at Lafitte's Landing using all types of wild game including rabbit, venison and alligator. It continues to be a novelty, whenever it is served.

2-1/2 pounds wild mallard
   duck, deboned
2-1/2 pounds pork
1/2 pound pork fat
1/2 pound bacon
1/4 pound butter
2 cups diced onions
1 cup diced celery
1/2 cup chopped green
   onions

2 tbsps diced garlic
1/2 cup port wine
1/4 cup cognac
1 tbsp dried thyme
1 tbsp cracked black pepper
1/2 cup chopped parsley
salt and cayenne pepper to taste
6 feet sausage casing

Grind duck, pork, pork fat and bacon using the fine cutting blade of a meat grinder. Once ground, place in a mixing bowl and remove all visible sinew or bone which may have passed through cutting blade. Set aside. In a heavy bottom saute pan, melt butter over medium high heat. Saute onions, celery, green onions, and garlic until wilted. Remove from flame and add port wine and cognac. Return to stove top, being careful as cognac will ignite on open flame. If using an electric range, ignite saute pan using a kitchen match. Cognac will burn approximately two minutes. Reduce liquid to one half volume.

(Continued)

Changes

_____

_____

_____

_____

(Mallard Duck Sausage continued)

Add thyme and cracked black pepper, blending well into mixture. Remove from heat and cool to room temperature. Add sauteed seasonings to ground meat mixture and blend well to incorporate all seasonings into sausage. Add parsley for color and season to taste using salt and cayenne pepper. To check for proper seasoning, form a small patty and saute in hot oil for a few minutes. Taste and adjust seasonings if necessary. You may stuff into casing, using the sausage attachment on your grinder or take the mixture to your local butcher for stuffing. This mixture will stuff approximately three feet of sausage. Once stuffed, poach links in simmering water for five to ten minutes, then place on baking sheet in 375 degree oven for ten to fifteen minutes. Slice sausage into one inch serving pieces and serve with Creole mustard as an hors d'oeuvre, or serve six inch link as an appetizer. You may wish to create one of the Cajun or Creole butter sauces to accompany this sausage. (see recipe)

HINT: Domestic or Long Island Duck may be substituted in this recipe.

Changes

_____

_____

_____

_____

Terrine of Wild Rabbit

2 Hours   3 Pound Terrine

Comment:

Normally in Cajun and Creole cooking, we prefer the daube glace or jellied pork to the cooked terrine. In this recipe, however, we have borrowed the classical presentation and substituted our wild Louisiana rabbit.

FOR MARINADE:

2 dressed rabbits,
    approximately 2-1/2 pounds
    each
1 pound beef marrow bones
    (see butcher)
1 pound cubed pork butt
1/2 pound bacon
1/2 pound pork fat

1/2 tsp salt
1 tbsp cracked black pepper
1 tsp dry thyme
pinch of dry sage
pinch of allspice
2 whole bay leaves
1/2 cup cognac

Using a sharp knife, trim loins from back of rabbit. Set aside and continue to debone all remaining meat from legs and back of rabbit. This should yield approximately one and a half pounds of meat. Using the bones of the rabbit and one pound of beef bones, proceed with game stock or Fonds de Gibier (see recipe). Reduce the stock to approximately one cup and chill this essence of rabbit for later use in the recipe. Place rabbit, pork, bacon and pork fat along with all seasonings and cognac in a ceramic mixing bowl. Using your hands, mix all ingredients well to coat meat with marinating mixture. Allow to remain at room temperature three to four hours or in refrigerator overnight.

(Continued)

Changes

_____

_____

_____

_____

(*Terrine of Wild Rabbit* continued)

FOR TERRINE:

1/4 pound butter
1/4 cup finely diced onions
1/4 cup finely diced celery
1/4 cup finely diced green onions
1 tbsp finely diced garlic
2 tbsps cracked black pepper
1/2 cup finely diced mushrooms

1 cup finely diced andouille
1 ounce brandy
2 ounces port wine
1 tsp dry thyme
salt to taste
2 whole eggs
1 pound sliced bacon

Preheat oven to 350 degrees. In a heavy bottom saute pan, melt butter over medium high heat. Saute onions, celery, green onions, garlic, black pepper and diced mushrooms approximately three to five minutes or until vegetables are wilted. Add diced andouille, saute additional one minute, then remove saute pan from fire. Add brandy and port wine and return to heat, being careful as liquor will ignite once reaching flame. Reduce liquids in pan to approximately one half volume. Add essence of rabbit which was produced from the rabbit bones. Add dry thyme and season to taste using salt. Remove from heat and set aside to cool. Remove marinated meat from refrigerator and, using a meat grinder, twice grind all meats and fat with the exception of the trimmed rabbit loins. Once ground, add all cooked seasonings and whole eggs. Mix well to incorporate all seasonings. Meat may be tested for proper flavor by pan frying a one inch patty in butter. Adjust if necessary. Completely line a two quart terrine mold using the sliced bacon. Allow enough of the bacon to overhang the terrine to be used when covering the top of the mold. Fill to one half of the mold by pressing meat mixture into all corners. Place rabbit loins down center of mold, and continue filling until terrine is completely full. Any remaining pieces of pork fat may be placed on top to add moisture. Cover terrine mold and bake in water bath for approximately one hour. When done, clear juices will run from the top of terrine. Remove from oven and cool. Once cold, terrine may be sliced and served as an appetizer.

Changes

Sauteed Chicken Livers Orleans

30 Minutes   6 Servings

Comment:

Chicken was so predominant on the farms in early Louisiana that many a unique chicken dish emerged from the Cajun kitchen. This recipe dates back to the early 1900's and today is still a favorite in the city of New Orleans.

2 dozen chicken livers
1/4 pound butter
1/4 cup diced onions
1/4 cup diced celery
1/4 cup sliced green onions
1 tbsp diced garlic
1 bay leaf
1 pinch file powder

1 pinch dry thyme
1 pinch of basil
2 ounces brandy
1 cup veal demi-glace (see recipe)
salt and cracked black pepper
    to taste
2 tbsps finely chopped parsley

In a heavy bottom saute pan, melt butter over medium high heat. Saute chicken livers until brown on all sides, approximately five minutes. Add onions, celery, green onions, garlic, bay leaf, file powder, thyme and basil. Continue to saute until vegetables are wilted, about three to five minutes. Deglaze pan with brandy and add veal demi-glace. Bring to a slight boil, reduce heat to simmer and cook an additional five minutes. Season to taste using salt and cracked black pepper. Remove from heat and add finely chopped parsley for color. Serve four pieces of liver covered with sauce in au gratin dish, or over toast points or pasta.

Changes

_____

_____

_____

_____

Stuffed Mushrooms Dominique Youx

45 Minutes   6 Servings

Comment:

Dominique Youx, a notorious general of Jean Lafitte, some say his half brother, went on in life to become one of New Orleans' leading politicians. He was quite a cook, and this recipe is dedicated to his memory.

24 jumbo fresh mushrooms
1/4 pound melted butter
1-1/2 cups chopped mushroom
    stems
1/2 cup finely diced green
    onions
1/4 cup finely chopped parsley
1 tbsp finely diced garlic
1/4 cup diced red bell pepper

3/4 cup white crabmeat
1 ounce sherry
1 tsp lemon juice
salt and cracked black pepper to taste
1/2 cup seasoned Italian bread crumbs
1/4 pound melted butter (for sauce)
4 ounces sherry wine (for sauce)
2 ounces dry white wine (for sauce)

Preheat oven to 450 degrees F. Wash mushrooms well, remove stems and finely chop stems for recipe. In a saute pan over medium high heat, melt butter. Add mushroom stems, green onions, parsley, garlic and red bell pepper. Saute approximately three to five minutes, or until vegetables are wilted. Add white crabmeat, sherry and lemon juice. Continue cooking an additional two to three minutes. Season mixture to taste using salt and pepper. Add Italian bread crumbs, a little at a time, until stuffing is of proper texture but not too dry. Using a teaspoon, fill each mushroom cap with generous serving of stuffing. Place six mushrooms in each of six au gratin dishes and top with melted butter, sherry and white wine. Bake in oven ten to fifteen minutes or until mushrooms are golden brown.

Changes

Eggplant Belle Rose

1 Hour   6 Servings

Comment:

Normally, eggplant is thought of simply as a vegetable here in Louisiana. However, once again, we are borrowing from the classical style to produce a new dish, certain to take its place as a tradition on the Louisiana table.

FOR BATTER:

1 medium size eggplant   1 egg
1/2 cup vegetable oil   1 cup flour
1/2 cup milk   salt and cayenne pepper to taste
1/4 cup water

In a saute pan, preheat oil to approximately 350 degrees F. In a mixing bowl, combine milk, water, and egg. Season to taste using salt and cayenne pepper. Whisk well using a wire whip. Cut six slices from center of eggplant, approximately 1/4 inch thick. Place in eggwash and set aside. Season one cup of flour to taste using salt and pepper. Remove eggplant from eggwash, dip in flour and pan fry until golden brown and tender to the touch, approximately three minutes on each side. Drain and keep warm.

(Continued)

Changes

_____

_____

_____

_____

(Eggplant Belle Rose continued)

FOR SAUCE:

1/4 cup melted butter
1/4 cup sliced green onions
1 tsp diced garlic
1/4 cup chopped mushrooms
1 pound crawfish tails or lump
    crabmeat
1/2 ounce white wine

1 tsp lemon juice
salt and cayenne pepper to taste
12 ounces brown meuniere sauce
    (see recipe)
6 ounces hollandaise sauce
    (see recipe)
2 tsps chopped parsley

In a saute pan, melt butter over medium high heat. Saute green onions, garlic and mushrooms approximately two to three minutes. Add crawfish tails or lump crabmeat, stir and cook one additional minute. Deglaze pan with white wine and lemon juice. Season to taste using salt and pepper. Continue cooking until crawfish or crabmeat is thoroughly hot. Place two ounces of meuniere sauce in center of serving plate and top with one eggplant medallion. Distribute an equal amount of crawfish or crabmeat on each eggplant and garnish with hollandaise sauce and chopped parsley.

Changes

_____

_____

_____

_____

Crabmeat Stuffed Summer Squash

45 Minutes   6 Servings

Comment:

Once again, we take a traditional vegetable of Bayou country and incorporate a different twist to create a dish that will certainly give the cook something to experiment with. Try using some of your local vegetables in this recipe.

3 medium size yellow summer squash
1/4 pound butter
1 cup diced zucchini
1/4 cup diced onions
1/4 cup diced celery

1 tbsp diced garlic
1/4 cup diced red bell pepper
1/2 pound lump crabmeat
1 tsp lemon juice
salt and cayenne pepper to taste
1 cup seasoned Italian bread crumbs

Preheat oven to 375 degrees F. Slice yellow squash lengthwise into two equal halves. Remove neck from squash and finely dice for recipe. Place squash halves in pot of boiling water and cook for eight to ten minutes, or until skin is tender. Remove from water and allow to cool. In a heavy bottom saute pan over medium high heat, melt butter. Add diced zucchini, diced yellow squash, onions, celery, garlic and bell pepper. Saute approximately three to five minutes or until vegetables are wilted. Add lump crabmeat and fold gently into mixture. Add lemon juice and cook one additional minute. Remove from heat and season to taste using salt and pepper. Add bread crumbs, a little at a time, until squash mixture is held together but not too dry. Using a metal spoon, scoop seed section from center of yellow squash and discard seeds. Divide stuffing equally between six halves, stuff and place on baking pan. Sprinkle with additional bread crumbs and bake ten to fifteen minutes until squash is golden brown.

Changes

_____

_____

_____

_____

Soups

Gumbos, Soups, and Bisques

There are as many recipes for gumbos and soups in South Louisiana as there are cooks, and EVERYONE in South Louisiana cooks! I'm not just talking about loosely held opinions, but the solid, time-honored family traditions that are kept secret, argued over and fought for. Everyone considers theirs to be the gumbo of gumbos, and every other cook's soup not worth eating.

This local phenomenon probably stems from the fact that gumbo is unique to Cajun and Creole cuisine and that it is the product of so many diverse cultures and cooking traditions. There is just as much controversy surrounding the origin of gumbo as there are opinions held as to what makes a gumbo truly great. One such difference of opinion is the notion that it descended from the French courtbouillon. I contend that "bouillabaisse" was indeed the forefather of gumbo. Now everyone knows how important "the French Connection" is in the history of gumbo, but to designate courtbouillon, that spiced and seasoned poaching liquid, teaming with aromatic vegetables, as the forefather of gumbo is to ignore an obvious fact: courtbouillon gave birth to an entirely different dish here in South Louisiana!

Recipes abound in French cuisine for courtbouillon. It is usually water based, with or without wine, and seasoned with aromatic herbs and vegetables. The purpose of the seasoned liquid is to give flavor to the fish and seafoods that are poached in it. The idea of removing the poached fish and throwing out the seasoned water with its herbs and vegetables would have been very rare in early Creole homes and unheard of by a hardworking Cajun who could subsist on such a broth.

No, Creole and Cajun cuisine abounds with dishes termed "courtbouillons", entrees that originally were smothered or poached seafood dishes, and much later came to be thickened with a roux. In these dishes, the flavorful liquid, the herbs, and the vegetables all stay in the pot and become part of the feast.

Soups

There are considerable reasons why I hold that bouillabaisse gave major inspiration to gumbo. First, is the time honored oral history attesting to that fact, as well as many historical studies which confirm it. Secondly, it just makes sense for a dish of such importance in French cooking, dealing with varieties of fresh fish, shellfish and vegetables to have an effect on some aspect of Creole and Cajun cookery. The third reason is the kicker. There is a Lenten variation of gumbo, not very well known outside of South Louisiana, called Gumbo Z' Herbs. This variation of gumbo is served on Good Friday and contains no meats or seafoods of any kind. This soup is chocked full of any number of greens including spinach, turnips, mustard or collard greens, scallions, parsley, cabbage, chicory, carrots, radishes and beet tops. Bouillabaisse also offers such a variation simply made with spinach. As with most arguments, the end result is really all that matters. After all, once conversation of any kind ceases and you dig into a bowl of that rich, roux based elixir with its seafood, meat, game, and vegetables which we call gumbo, you will probably care less about its origin and only long for more.

Everyone who settled in South Louisiana contributed to the origin of gumbo. In the African language the word for okra is "gumbo." The Africans brought the okra pod with them to Louisiana. This vegetable not only thickens and seasons the gumbo but also gives the soup its name. From Africa too, came the men and women who would contribute so much to Cajun cooking's development and continuing excellence in the world of cuisine. Earlier, I referred to the aspect of "the black hand in the pot" in Creole cooking. Now I must recognize and thank those early pioneers for their many influences and contributions to Cajun cookery and this influence only began with their contribution to our gumbo.

From the Choctaw Indians, we learned about sassafras leaves that were ground into gumbo file'. This herb was used to flavor and thicken gumbo when okra was not in season. Sassafras leaves were ground during the full moon, because no Cajun or Creole worth his salt would consider grinding at any other time. He knew full well that to harvest at any other moon stage would diminish the volume of spice in the hopper. Sassafras was also known for its medicinal properties. So, next time you eat file' gumbo, you will find that the main reason you "break out in a sweat" is not the heat of the gumbo or the spice in the soup, but the ground sassafras having its healing effect on your metabolism.

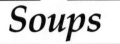

Soups

Everyone seemed to get into the act. From the Spanish came the rice used in our gumbo as well as the spice and the new world discovery of red pepper. Every nationality, including the West Indians, the Germans, and the Italians, had a bit of influence on the gumbos and soups of Cajun and Creole cooking.

By now everyone knows that "first you make a roux...". As is true with most dishes, if you know how to cook them, you don't need a recipe. It is also true that if you don't know how to cook a dish, a recipe won't do you much good without first understanding the basic principles and techniques of the dish. This is certainly the case with gumbo.

Hopefully after reading about the Cajuns and Creoles, their history and way of life, their trials and tribulations, and their love of good food, you will be primed and ready to proceed with our signature soups. The following is a compilation of carefully laid down rules and time honored principles that will assist you in working through the recipes in this chapter.

The section on rouxs should be carefully studied before beginning a Louisiana gumbo or soup. One factor to keep in mind is that the vegetables added to the roux arrest the browning process of the flour, for the most part. The moisture in the onion, celery and bell pepper will keep the roux from cooking to the point of burning but will allow it to continue to brown slightly. It is important to add the vegetables to the roux for that reason. Many people think that simmering the vegetables in liquid and adding the roux can produce the same effect. This is not true. The roux extracts the flavor from the vegetables and distributes it throughout the soup.

A portion of this mixture of roux and vegetables, spread on a little French bread crouton, was sometimes given to children in Cajun households to tide them over until the main meal was ready. I remember standing in line for this little treat, thinking it to be the best lagniappe in all of Cajun cooking. I have tried it again now that I am older and somehow, that great flavor seems to have diminished.

It is imperative to have all of your vegetables, spices and other ingredients ready so that no time will be lost and no attention drawn away from the preparation of your roux.

The order in which the vegetables are cooked is very important. Onions are always first. The flavor of the onion is transformed by long cooking.

Soups

In classical cuisine, all vegetables are cut in a uniform fashion. In order to achieve various flavors in the roux, cooks will prepare certain dishes with three different sizes of chopped onions; the first would become dark, sweet, and caramelized, the second would be translucent with a soft onion flavor, and the third would be lightly cooked with a crunchy texture and tangy onion bite.

In Cajun cuisine in particular, when cutting vegetables, there is no care taken for uniformity. The surprising end result is similar to the classical technique, without all the bother. Since some of the onion pieces are smaller, they cook quicker and take on a sweeter, deeper flavor while the larger ones retain their delicious onion bite. If you use a food processor, just make sure you don't over-chop. As a general rule, however, most vegetables in Cajun and Creole soup should be approximately 1/4 inch in size.

After the onions comes the celery. The proportion of celery to onions is always about one half. Cajun cuisine has no cream of celery soup, but if it did, I bet there still would be a larger amount of onions then celery in the recipe.

Next are bell peppers and garlic. Garlic cannot be added to hot oil alone, unless you remove it as it begins to brown, because it will turn bitter. If garlic is added to the roux however, after the onions, celery and bell pepper, there will be plenty of moisture from these vegetables to keep the garlic from burning. Don't ever "over-do" the amount of bell pepper or process it so fine that it becomes a mush. Remember that if more fresh bell pepper flavor is desired, a hand cut, fine mince of bell pepper may be added at the end of cooking. Onions, celery, and bell pepper are referred to as "the trinity" in Cajun and Creole cookery because of their presence in nearly every dish. Garlic, however, ranks right up there with them in my cooking and is only over-shadowed in importance by the noble onion.

Scallions or "shallots" are a story in themselves. The French cook with a little purplish bulb in the onion family called a shallot or "echalotte". It has a slight taste of garlic. When the French, particularly the Creoles, came to Louisiana, they could not find echalottes. However, the green onion, scallion or Louisiana shallot as we call it, was growing here wild in the bayous and proved to be an excellent substitute for the French shallot. Today in New Orleans and throughout South Louisiana, if you order shallots you will get scallions. In order to receive the little purplish bulb with the slight garlic taste, you must specify echalottes or "dry" shallots.

This confused nomenclature is unique to South Louisiana because of the adopting of new world ingredients to substitute for familiar friends left back home. Throughout my recipes, I will refer to "the Louisiana shallot" as green onions. If a more classical dish, such as beurre blanc, is being prepared and echalottes are needed, I will specify shallots.

Well, enough about the definition of a green onion, let's cook it! The green onion has two different parts, the sweet little white bulb and the long, tender, green shoots. In most cases the white of the green onion is put into the roux during the early stages of cooking along with the onions and celery. The sliced green tops are saved until later to be used with the chopped parsley. The green tops and the parsley are added after the liquid in order to maintain their freshness as they need no caramelizing. Curly parsley, stems removed and chopped, is used in abundance. In Creole cuisine, thanks to the Italian influence, some dishes utilize flat leaf Italian parsley. Before serving the gumbo, a small sprinkle of chopped green onions and parsley are added for zest and color.

Familiarize yourself with the section on stocks. If no stock is prepared, water will do; but stock, in my opinion, has a depth of flavor which will improve any recipe. Fish stock is often used in seafood gumbos, but I prefer shellfish stock. The flavor derived from the crustacean's skeleton (its shell and its natural "fat") is never omitted from my gumbo. Game, chicken, and shellfish stocks are also often utilized in my cooking of other soups and bisques.

Liquid should be added slowly to the roux and only after the vegetables have become translucent with a slight caramelized effect. The roux will have darkened slightly and developed a sheen as the mixtures have become one cohesive mass. There has been much discussion as to whether the stock should be added hot or cold to the roux. I have incorporated both hot and cold stocks under different circumstances and found very little difference. However, if you are one for rules, I should mention that cold liquids are normally added to a hot roux. They should be added in small amounts because they drop the cooking temperature and ensure slow cooking. This is believed essential in good gumbos by most Cajun and Creole cooks. Hot liquids are used when one is in a hurry to complete the project. One must take care when hot liquids are added to a hot roux as the splatter of hot roux could be quite harmful. In either case, once stocks are incorporated, continue adding the required liquid slowly, stirring constantly to ensure that the sauce that is developing remains smooth and the vegetables continue to cook.

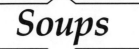

Chopped parsley, green onions and spices are normally added at this point. After the gumbo or soup has reached the proper consistency, seafood may be added, saving the oysters or lump crabmeat until right before serving.

If sausage or andouille is used in the recipe, it should be added immediately after the seasonings and directly into the roux. If poultry is utilized, it should be browned off in the oil prior to the addition of the flour. This process ensures even further flavor in the roux. If filé is used, it is always "steeped" or added at the end, before serving, after the gumbo is taken off the fire. If filé is added at a boiling point, it will become "ropey" and ruin the gumbo's texture. This is one reason why oysters and file' are matched so often in gumbos. Both are added at the end and are dual reminders not to boil after their addition.

You'll notice that the terminology "to taste" is used in reference to salt and pepper. You will also notice that in many recipes, I refer to a "dash" of Louisiana Gold Pepper Sauce. This wonderful pepper sauce is produced by a great supporter of Louisiana chefs and my close friend, Si Brown of Bruce Foods Corporation in New Iberia, Louisiana. Louisiana Gold is the only pepper sauce used in my cooking. Since each dish will be affected differently by the introduction of Louisiana Gold, I define a dash as whatever is necessary to season to your liking. The amount of salt and pepper added to foods in South Louisiana is that amount sufficient to bring out the natural flavors of the ingredients and produce a warm tang that "drags the flavor" down the back of the throat. The pepper, however, should never burn. This sensation may be a little dramatic for your uninitiated tastebuds, but it gives our cuisine a liveliness that is its trademark.

"Beautiful soup! Who cares for fish, game, or any other dish? Who would not give all else for two pennyworth only of beautiful soup?"

Lewis Carroll

Louisiana Seafood Gumbo

1 Hour   12 Servings

Comment:

The premier soup of Cajun country , seafood gumbo, is known worldwide as the dish to seek out when visiting South Louisiana. There are as many recipes for this soup as there are people who cook it. This however, is my favorite.

1 pound 35 count shrimp,
   peeled and deveined
1 pound jumbo lump crabmeat
2 dozen shucked oysters,
   reserve liquid
1 cup vegetable oil
1-1/2 cups flour
2 cups chopped onions
1 cup chopped celery

1 cup chopped bell pepper
1/4 cup diced garlic
1/2 pound sliced andouille sausage
1 pound claw crabmeat
3 quarts shellfish stock (see recipe)
2 cups sliced green onions
1/2 cup chopped parsley
salt and cayenne pepper to taste

In a two gallon stock pot, heat oil over medium high heat. Once oil is hot, add flour and using a wire whisk, stir constantly until brown roux is achieved. (see roux technique) Do not allow roux to scorch. Should black specks appear in roux, discard and begin again. Once roux is golden brown, add onions, celery, bell pepper and garlic. Saute approximately three to five minutes, or until vegetables are wilted. Add andouille, blend well into vegetable mixture and saute additional two to three minutes. Add claw crabmeat and stir into roux, as this will begin to add seafood flavor to the mixture. Slowly add hot shellfish stock, one ladle at a time, stirring constantly until all is incorporated. Bring to a low boil, reduce to simmer and cook approximately thirty minutes. Add additional stock if necessary to retain volume. Add green onions and parsley and season to taste using salt and cayenne pepper. Fold shrimp, lump crabmeat, oysters and reserved liquid into soup. Return to a low boil and cook approximately five minutes. Adjust seasonings and serve over cooked rice.

Changes

_____

_____

Shrimp and Okra Gumbo

1 Hour   12 Servings

Comment:

This is the only gumbo on the river road between Baton Rouge and New Orleans that incorporates okra into the recipe. Okra was considered a thickening agent as well as a vegetable and was only used during the summer growing months.

2 pounds 35 count shrimp,
   peeled and deveined
1 cup vegetable oil
1-1/2 cups flour
4 cups sliced okra
2 cups chopped onions
1 cup chopped celery

1 cup chopped bell pepper
1/4 cup diced garlic
3 quarts shellfish stock (see recipe)
2 cups chopped green onions
1/2 cup diced parsley
salt and cayenne pepper to taste

I must note at this time that in many cases the okra used in gumbos is first chopped and sauteed in oil until all of the stringy texture is removed and the vegetable is light brown. However, it is perfectly acceptable to add the uncooked okra into the dish. In a two gallon stock pot, heat oil over medium high heat. Once oil is hot, add flour and using a wire whisk, stir constantly until golden brown roux is achieved. (see roux technique) Do not allow roux to scorch. Should black specks appear, discard and begin again. When golden brown, reduce heat to simmer and saute okra approximately fifteen minutes. Add onions, celery, bell pepper and garlic and saute approximately three to five minutes or until vegetables are wilted. Add shellfish stock, one ladle at a time, stirring constantly until all is incorporated. Return to medium high heat, bring to a low boil and allow to simmer thirty minutes. Add shrimp, green onions and parsley and season to taste using salt and pepper. Allow to cook an additional five minutes. Serve over cooked rice.

Changes

_____

_____

_____

_____

Duck and Andouille Gumbo

1-1/2 Hours   12 Servings

Comment:

Almost every species of wild game in Louisiana has been used in the creation of gumbo. Since most Cajun men were hunters and trappers, it is not surprising that wild mallard duck and smoked andouille was the most popular of game gumbos.

2 mallard ducks, cut into
   serving pieces
1/2 pound sliced andouille
1 cup vegetable oil
1-1/2 cups flour
2 cups chopped onions
1 cup chopped celery
1 cup chopped bell pepper

1/4 cup diced garlic
3 quarts chicken stock (see recipe)
12 chicken livers
2 cups sliced green onions
1 cup chopped parsley
salt and cracked black pepper
   to taste

In a two gallon stock pot, heat oil over medium high heat. Once oil is hot, add flour and using a wire whisk, stir until roux is golden brown. (see roux technique) Do not scorch. Should black specks appear, discard and begin again. Add onions, celery, bell pepper and garlic and saute approximately three to five minutes or until vegetables are wilted. Add mallard duck and andouille and saute in roux approximately fifteen minutes. Add chicken stock, one ladle at a time, stirring constantly until all is incorporated. Bring to a rolling boil, reduce to simmer and add chicken livers. Cook until duck is tender, adding additional stock to retain volume of liquid. Once tender, approximately one hour, add green onions and parsley and season to taste using salt and pepper. Cook additional five minutes and serve over cooked rice.

Changes

_____

_____

_____

_____

Tasso and Okra Gumbo

1 Hour   12 Servings

Comment:

Tasso is used most often as a seasoning ingredient in vegetables and soups. Here I have elected to use tasso in a different fashion, a main ingredient in gumbo. I feel the flavor derived from this combination is unique to Cajun country.

2 pounds julienned tasso (see tasso recipe)	1 cup chopped bell pepper
4 cups sliced okra	1/4 cup diced garlic
1 cup oil	3 quarts chicken stock (see recipe)
1-1/2 cups flour	2 cups sliced green onions
2 cups chopped onions	1 cup chopped parsley
1 cup chopped celery	salt and cayenne pepper to taste

In a two gallon stock pot, heat oil over medium high heat. Once oil is hot, add flour and using a wire whisk, stir until roux is golden brown. (see roux technique) Do not scorch. If black specks should appear, discard and begin again. Add okra and saute in roux approximately fifteen minutes. Add onions, celery, bell pepper and garlic and saute approximately three to five minutes or until vegetables are wilted. Add tasso, blend well into vegetable mixture and cook additional two minutes. Add chicken stock, one ladle at a time, stirring constantly until all is incorporated. Bring to a rolling boil, reduce heat to simmer and cook approximately thirty minutes. Add green onions and parsley and cook additional five minutes. Season to taste using salt and cayenne pepper and serve over cooked rice.

HINT: You may wish to add left over chicken, turkey or seafoods to this gumbo.

Changes

_____

_____

_____

_____

Death By Gumbo

1 Hour   12 Servings

Comment:

This dish was created for Craig Claiborne of the New York Times. When asked to come to his home on Long Island to create a special dinner depicting the evolution of Cajun and Creole cuisine, I knew that this gumbo would be a natural.

FOR QUAIL:

12 partially deboned quail
12 1/8 inch slices of andouille
12 oysters poached in their own
    liquid
24 tbsps cooked white rice

1 tsp file powder
2 tbsps chopped parsley
salt and cracked black pepper
    to taste

Have your supplier debone the breast and backbone from twelve young Bob White quail. Season birds inside and out using salt and cracked black pepper. Season white rice with salt, pepper, file powder and chopped parsley. Open cavity of quail and begin by stuffing one tablespoon of cooked rice in front of cavity, one slice of andouille, one oyster and finally a second spoon of cooked rice in the rear, to hold all of the ingredients in place. Continue this process until all quails have been stuffed. Cover with clear wrap and set aside.

(Continued)

Changes

_____

_____

_____

_____

Soups

(*Death by Gumbo* continued)

FOR GUMBO:

12 stuffed and seasoned
  Bob White quail
1 cup vegetable oil
1-1/2 cups flour
2 cups chopped onions
2 cups chopped celery
1 cup chopped bell pepper
1/4 cup diced garlic

1 cup sliced mushrooms
1/2 cup sliced tasso
3 quarts chicken stock (see recipe)
1 tsp dry thyme
1 cup sliced green onions
1 cup chopped parsley
salt and cracked black pepper
  to taste

In a two gallon stock pot, heat oil over medium high heat. Add flour and using a wire whisk, stir constantly until roux is golden brown. (see roux technique) Do not scorch. If black specks should appear, discard and begin again. Add onions, celery, bell pepper and garlic. Saute three to five minutes or until vegetables are wilted. Add mushrooms and tasso and cook an additional three minutes. Add chicken stock, one ladle at a time, stirring constantly until all is incorporated. Add thyme, bring to a rolling boil, reduce to simmer and cook thirty minutes. Season to taste using salt and black pepper. Add stuffed quail into gumbo and allow to slowly simmer for thirty minutes. Once quail are tender and legs separate from the body easily, remove quail to a platter and keep warm. Strain all seasonings, tasso etc., from gumbo through a fine strainer and reserve gumbo stock. Return stock to the pot, add quail, green onions and parsley and bring to a low boil. When serving, place one quail in center of soup bowl and cover with gumbo.

Changes

_____

_____

_____

_____

Chicken and Oyster Gumbo

1-1/2 Hours   12 Servings

Comment:

Normally speaking, the Cajuns of South Louisiana would always include smoked sausage or andouille in this gumbo. However, when omitted, the oyster flavor is enhanced and the dish becomes a delicacy.

1 4-5 pound stewing hen, cut into serving pieces	1 cup chopped bell pepper
	1/4 cup diced garlic
4 dozen freshly shucked oysters, reserve liquid	3 quarts chicken stock (see recipe)
	24 fresh button mushrooms
1 cup vegetable oil	2 cups sliced green onions
1-1/2 cups flour	1 cup chopped parsley
2 cups chopped onions	salt and cracked black pepper
2 cups chopped celery	to taste

In a two gallon stock pot, heat oil over medium high heat. Once oil is hot, add flour and using a wire whisk, stir constantly until roux is golden brown. (see roux technique) Do not scorch. Should black specks appear, discard and begin again. Add onions, celery, bell pepper and garlic and cook approximately three to five minutes or until vegetables are wilted. Add hen, blend into vegetable mixture and saute fifteen minutes. Add chicken stock, one ladle at a time, stirring constantly until all is incorporated. Bring to a rolling boil, reduce to simmer and cook approximately one hour. Add mushrooms, oysters and liquid and cook an additional ten minutes. Blend in green onions and parsley and continue to simmer until oysters begin to curl at the edges. Season to taste using salt and pepper and serve over cooked rice.

Changes

_____

_____

_____

_____

Creole Oyster Soup

45 Minutes   12 Servings

Comment:

The Creoles of New Orleans were the aristocracy of the Old World and, likewise, maintained their finesse in cooking. Though the brown roux was common to Cajun country, the light butter roux was used by the Creoles in most soup recipes.

6 dozen freshly shucked oysters
1 quart oyster liquid
3/4 cup butter
1 cup chopped onions
1 cup chopped celery
1/2 cup chopped bell pepper
1/4 cup diced garlic

l/4 cup diced andouille sausage
1 cup flour
2 quarts heavy whipping cream
1 cup sliced green onions
1 cup chopped parsley
salt and Louisiana Gold
Pepper Sauce to taste

It is imperative to have your seafood supplier reserve one quart of fresh oyster liquid if this recipe is to be successful. In a two gallon stock pot, heat butter over medium high heat. Add onions, celery, bell pepper, garlic and andouille. Saute approximately three to five minutes or until vegetables are wilted. Sprinkle in flour and using a wire whisk, stir constantly until white roux is achieved in stock pot. (see roux technique) Add oyster liquid and heavy whipping cream, stirring to incorporate liquids into roux mixture. Bring to a low boil, reduce to simmer, and cook until cream is slightly reduced but of a soup like consistency. Hot water may be added should mixture become too thick. Add oysters, green onions and parsley and season to taste using salt and Louisiana Gold. Cook until edges of oysters begin to curl. Traditionally, a pat of sweet butter is placed in the center of each soup bowl prior to serving.

Changes

_____

_____

_____

_____

Oyster Rockefeller Soup

1 Hour   12 Servings

Comment:

This particular soup has become famous at Lafitte's Landing Restaurant and is requested on more occasions than all other soups combined. The concept to create a soup from the premier oyster dish of New Orleans was indeed a good idea.

6 dozen freshly shucked oysters
1 quart oyster liquid
1 cup melted butter
1 cup chopped onions
1 cup chopped celery
1/2 cup chopped bell pepper
1/4 cup diced garlic
1 10-ounce package cooked
　　frozen spinach (thawed)

1/2 cup finely diced
　　andouille sausage
1 cup flour
1-1/2 quarts chicken stock
　　(see recipe)
1 pint heavy whipping cream
1/2 cup sliced green onions
1/2 cup chopped parsley
salt and white pepper to taste
1/2 ounce Pernod or Herbsaint

In a two gallon stock pot, heat butter over medium high heat. Add onions, celery, bell pepper and garlic. Saute three to five minutes or until vegetables are wilted. Add spinach and andouille sausage. Using a metal spoon, chop spinach into vegetable mixture until all is well incorporated. Sprinkle in flour, blending well into spinach mixture. Stir constantly to avoid scorching. Add chicken stock and oyster liquid, one ladle at a time, until all is well blended. Bring to a low boil, reduce to simmer and cook thirty minutes. Add heavy whipping cream, oysters, green onions and parsley. Continue to cook until edges of oysters begin to curl. Season to taste using salt and white pepper. Stir in Pernod or Herbsaint. Adjust seasonings if necessary.

HINT: It is imperative that oyster liquid be used in this recipe if it is to be successful. Give your seafood supplier ample time to reserve this amount.

Changes

_____

_____

_____

Oyster and Artichoke Bisque

1 Hour   12 Servings

Comment:

Once again, Louisiana gulf oysters are used to create a masterpiece among cream based soups. This recipe is used on a weekly basis at Lafitte's Landing Restaurant. The great New Orleans chef, Warren LeRuth, introduced Cajuns to this dish.

6 dozen freshly shucked oysters
1 quart oyster liquid
8 fresh artichoke bottoms, sliced
    and uncooked
1 cup butter
1 cup chopped onions
1 cup chopped celery
1/2 cup chopped bell pepper

1/4 cup diced garlic
1 cup flour
1-1/2 quarts chicken stock
    (see recipe)
1 pint heavy whipping cream
1 cup sliced green onions
1 cup chopped parsley
salt and white pepper to taste

In a two gallon stock pot, melt butter over medium high heat. Add onions, celery, bell pepper, garlic and artichoke bottoms. Saute five to ten minutes or until vegetables are wilted and artichokes are tender. Remove all ingredients from stock pot and place in food processor equipped with a metal blade. Chop on high speed approximately one minute or until mixture is fairly well pureed. Return to stock pot and bring back to a simmer. Using a wire whisk, sprinkle in flour, stirring constantly until white roux is achieved. (see roux technique) Add chicken stock and oyster liquid, one ladle at a time, stirring constantly until all is incorporated. Bring to a low boil, reduce to simmer and cook thirty minutes. Add heavy whipping cream, oysters, green onions and parsley. Return to a boil, and cook until edges of oysters begin to curl. Season to taste using salt and white pepper.

HINT: It is imperative that oyster liquid be used in this recipe if it is to be successful. Give your seafood supplier ample time to reserve this amount.

Changes

_____

_____

_____

Oyster and Crab Bisque

1 Hour   12 Servings

Comment:

Combining the delicate flavors of oyster and lump crab isn't normally seen in Louisiana. However, this soup has proven time and again to be a favorite with our dining guests.

4 dozen freshly shucked oysters	1/2 tsp dry thyme
1 quart fresh oyster liquid	1 cup flour
1 pound jumbo lump crabmeat	1-1/2 quarts shellfish stock
1 cup butter	(see recipe)
1 cup chopped onions	1 pint heavy whipping cream
1 cup chopped celery	pinch of nutmeg
1/2 cup chopped red bell pepper	1/2 cup sliced green onions
1/4 cup diced garlic	1/2 cup chopped parsley
2 bay leaves	salt and white pepper to taste

In a two gallon stock pot, melt butter over medium high heat. Add onions, celery, bell pepper, garlic, bay leaves and thyme. Saute approximately three to five minutes or until vegetables are wilted. Sprinkle in flour and using a wire whisk, stir until white roux is achieved. (see roux technique) Add shellfish stock and oyster liquid, one ladle at a time, stirring constantly until all is incorporated. Bring to a low boil, reduce to simmer and cook thirty minutes. Add heavy whipping cream, nutmeg, oysters, green onions and parsley. Cook until edges of oysters begin to curl. Season to taste using salt and white pepper. Slowly fold in jumbo lump crabmeat, being careful not to break lumps. Adjust seasonings if necessary.

HINT: It is imperative that oyster liquid be used in this recipe if it is to be successful. Make sure you give your seafood supplier ample time to reserve this amount.

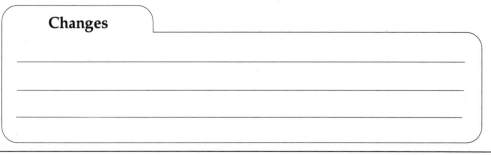

Changes

Cajun Crab Stew

1 Hour   12 Servings

Comment:

Other than gumbo, the crab stew is the most popular "soup" in the bayouland. Crabs were plentiful and this dish provided the creative Cajuns with yet another dish to whet their appetites.

12 whole crabs, cleaned
1 pound jumbo lump crabmeat
1 cup vegetable oil
1 cup flour
2 cups chopped onions
2 cups chopped celery
1 cup chopped bell pepper
1/4 cup diced garlic

2 bay leaves
1/2 tsp dry thyme
3 quarts shellfish stock (see recipe)
1 cup sliced green onions
1 cup chopped parsley
salt and Louisiana Gold
    Pepper Sauce to taste

In a two gallon stock pot, heat oil over medium high heat. Add flour and using a wire whip, stir constantly until roux is golden brown. (see roux technique) Do not scorch. Should black specks appear, discard and begin again. Add twelve clean crabs, stirring well into roux. Cook three to five minutes, then add onions, celery, bell pepper, garlic, bay leaves and thyme. Saute three to five minutes or until vegetables are wilted. Add shellfish stock, one ladle at a time, stirring constantly until all is incorporated. Bring to a low boil, reduce to simmer and cook thirty minutes. Add green onions and parsley and season to taste using salt and Louisiana Gold. Gently fold in jumbo lump crabmeat and adjust seasonings if necessary. Serve over cooked white rice.

Changes

_____

_____

_____

_____

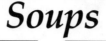

Soups

Corn and Crab Bisque

1 Hour   12 Servings

Comment:

Corn was growing wild here in 1755 when the Acadians arrived. They quickly married the flavor of Louisiana seafood to the sweet corn, and the rest is history. This soup is a gold medal winner in culinary competition.

3 cups whole kernel corn	1 cup flour
1 pound jumbo lump crabmeat	2-1/2 quarts shellfish stock
1 cup butter	(see recipe)
1 cup chopped onions	1 pint heavy whipping cream
1 cup chopped celery	1/2 cup sliced green onions
1/2 cup chopped red bell pepper	1/2 cup chopped parsley
1/4 cup diced garlic	salt and white pepper to taste

In a two gallon stock pot, melt butter over medium high heat. Add corn, onions, celery, bell pepper and garlic. Saute five to ten minutes or until vegetables are wilted. Add flour and using a wire whisk, stir until white roux is achieved. (see roux technique) Do not brown. Add stock, one ladle at a time, stirring constantly until all is incorporated. Bring to a low boil, reduce to simmer and cook thirty minutes. Add heavy whipping cream, green onions and parsley and continue cooking an additional three minutes. Gently fold in lump crabmeat, being careful not to break lumps. Season to taste using salt and white pepper.

HINT: Try making a stock with the corn cobs. Reduce it to one quart and add it into this soup in place of half the shellfish stock. This little extra work will be well worth it.

Changes

_____

_____

_____

_____

Veloute of Crawfish and Asparagus

1 Hour   12 Servings

Comment:

Though asparagus is not indigenous to our area, the availability of this vegetable in the markets has made it possible for a new creation to emerge from our table in the wilderness.

1 pound fresh crawfish tails
2 dozen trimmed asparagus
    spears
1 cup butter
1 cup chopped onions
1 cup chopped celery
1/2 cup chopped red bell pepper
1/4 cup diced garlic

1/2 tsp nutmeg
1 cup flour
2-1/2 quarts shellfish stock
    (see recipe)
1 pint heavy whipping cream
1 cup sliced green onions
1 cup chopped parsley
salt and white pepper to taste

You may wish to make one quart of asparagus stock by boiling the trimmed ends of the asparagus spears for thirty minutes. This will impart a concentrated asparagus flavor into the water and you may use this in place of one quart of the shellfish stock. In a two gallon stock pot, melt butter over medium high heat. Add onions, celery, bell pepper and garlic. Saute three to five minutes or until vegetables are wilted. Add nutmeg and flour and using a wire whisk, stir until white roux is achieved. (see roux technique) Do not brown. Add shellfish stock, one ladle at a time, stirring constantly until all is incorporated. Add asparagus and bring to a low boil, reduce to simmer and cook thirty minutes. Add heavy whipping cream, crawfish, green onions and parsley. Allow to cook an additional five minutes. Season to taste using salt and white pepper.

Changes

_____

_____

_____

_____

Creole Bouillabaisse

1-1/2 Hours   12 Servings

Comment:

There is no doubt in my mind that the Louisiana gumbo originated from the French bouillabaisse. The innovative Creoles, adapting to their new homeland in South Louisiana, created a new bouillabaisse by using what was available here in the bayous.

4 1-1/2 pound cleaned red snapper	3/4 cup tomato sauce
2 pounds head on 31-35 count shrimp	1/4 cup diced garlic
	4 whole bay leaves
2 pounds live crawfish	2 medium carrots, diced
12 fresh cleaned crabs	3 quarts shellfish stock (see recipe)
1 cup olive oil	2 cups dry white wine
2 cups chopped onions	1 tsp dry thyme
2 cups chopped celery	1 tsp dry basil
1 cup chopped red bell pepper	1 cup sliced green onions
4 whole diced tomatoes	1 cup chopped parsley
	salt and cayenne pepper to taste

Pour olive oil into a two gallon stock pot. Place in layers the onions, celery, bell pepper, tomatoes, tomato sauce, garlic, bay leaves and carrots. On top of vegetables, layer whole fish, shrimp, crawfish and crabs. Place on medium high heat covered and steam approximately three to five minutes. Add shellfish stock, white wine, thyme and basil. Bring to a low simmer, approximately 190 degrees F, or just below the boiling point. Top of stock should ripple but not boil. Cook thirty minutes and remove from heat. Carefully pour off all shellfish stock, and reserve for soup. Using a spatula remove all seafoods. Peel the shrimp, crawfish and crab. Debone all meat from the fish. Bring the stock back to a low boil and add all seafood. Reduce to a simmer and add green onions and parsley. Season to taste using salt and cayenne pepper. Serve by placing a generous amount of the seafoods in the center of a soup bowl and ladle over with hot soup.

Changes

_____

_____

Veloute of Crawfish and Crabmeat

1 Hour   12 Servings

Comment:

The two ruling factions of the Bayous come together in this soup. Again, the delicate flavors of crawfish and crab are combined with shellfish stock and cream to create a gold medal winner.

1 pound clean crawfish tails
1 pound jumbo lump crabmeat
1 cup butter
2 cups chopped onions
2 cups chopped celery
1 cup chopped red bell pepper
1/4 cup diced garlic
1 bay leaf

pinch of thyme
1 cup flour
2 ounces sherry wine
2-1/2 quarts shellfish stock
**   (see recipe)**
1 pint heavy whipping cream
1 cup chopped parsley
salt and white pepper to taste

In a two gallon stock pot, melt butter over medium high heat. Add onions, celery, bell pepper, garlic and bay leaf. Saute approximately three to five minutes or until vegetables are wilted. Add thyme and flour. Using a wire whisk, stir constantly until white roux is achieved. (see roux technique) Do not brown. Add sherry and shellfish stock stirring constantly until all is incorporated. Bring to a low boil, reduce heat to simmer and cook thirty minutes. Add heavy whipping cream, crawfish and parsley and continue to cook five additional minutes. Fold in lump crabmeat, being careful not to break lumps. Season to taste using salt and white pepper.

Changes

_____
_____
_____
_____

Squash and Shrimp Bisque

1 Hour   12 Servings

Comment:

Similar to corn and crab, our squash and shrimp soup combines a great seafood and vegetable to create a fabulous bisque. In no other part of America does a culture combine as many unlike ingredients to make use of all that God has given us.

1-1/2 cups diced yellow squash	1/2 cup chopped bell pepper
1-1/2 cups diced zucchini	1/4 cup diced garlic
3 dozen 50 count shrimp, peeled and deveined	1 cup diced tomatoes
	1 cup flour
1 cup butter	2-1/2 quarts shellfish stock (see recipe)
1 cup chopped onions	1 pint heavy whipping cream
1 cup chopped celery	salt and cayenne pepper to taste

In a two gallon stock pot, melt butter over medium high heat. Add squash, zucchini, onions, celery, bell pepper, garlic and tomatoes. Saute approximately five to ten minutes or until vegetables are wilted. Add flour and using a wire whisk, stir constantly until white roux is achieved. (see roux technique) Do not brown. Add shellfish stock, one ladle at a time, stirring constantly until all is incorporated. Add shrimp and heavy whipping cream and continue to cook approximately five additional minutes. Season to taste using salt and cayenne pepper.

Changes

_____

_____

_____

_____

Shrimp and Corn Soup, Maque Choux

1 Hour   12 Servings

Comment:

Maque, the Houmas Indian word for corn, is the main ingredient in this soup. Maque choux dates back to our early beginnings in Louisiana and was being prepared by the Indians upon the arrival of the Cajuns, in 1755.

4 dozen 50 count shrimp, peeled
   and deveined
3 cups whole kernel corn
1 cup oil
1 cup flour
2 cups chopped onions
2 cups chopped celery
1 cup chopped bell pepper
1/4 cup diced garlic

2 cups diced tomatoes
1/2 cup tomato sauce
2 whole bay leaves
1 tsp thyme
1 tsp basil
3 quarts shellfish stock (see recipe)
1 cup sliced green onions
1 cup chopped parsley
salt and cracked black pepper to taste

In a two gallon stock pot, heat oil over medium high heat. Add flour and using a wire whisk, stir constantly until roux is golden brown. (see roux technique) Do not scorch. Should black specks appear, discard and begin again. Add corn, onions, celery, bell pepper, garlic and tomatoes. Saute five to ten minutes or until vegetables are wilted. Add tomato sauce, bay leaves, thyme and basil. Add shellfish stock, one ladle at a time, stirring constantly until all is incorporated. Bring to a low boil, reduce to simmer and cook for thirty minutes. Add shrimp, green onions and parsley and continue to cook for ten additional minutes. Season to taste using salt and cracked black pepper. Here again, you may wish to make a corn cob stock in place of one quart of the shellfish stock. This will enhance the fresh corn flavor.

Changes

Veloute of Catfish and Brie

1 Hour   6 Servings

FOR STOCK:

3 5-8 ounce Catfish
    fillets
1 gallon cold water
2 small onions, diced

2 stalks celery, chopped
1 carrot thinly sliced
2 bay leaves
1 tbsp whole peppercorns

Place all of the above ingredients in a two gallon stock pot. Bring to a low boil, reduce to simmer and cook thirty minutes. Strain stock, remove all catfish pieces and discard all vegetables. Reserve hot stock and catfish for later.

FOR SOUP:

2 5-8 ounce Catfish
    fillets (cubed)
3/4 cup melted butter
1/2 cup diced onions
1/2 cup diced celery
1/2 cup diced red bell pepper

1/4 cup chopped garlic
3/4 cup flour
3 quarts reserved fish stock and fish
2 cups heavy whipping cream
6 ounces Brie cheese
salt and white pepper to taste

In a one gallon stock pot, heat butter over medium high heat. Saute onions, celery, bell pepper and garlic until vegetables are wilted, approximately three to five minutes. Blend in flour, stirring constantly until white roux is achieved. Do not brown. Using a wire whip, blend in hot fish stock and cooked fish pieces until smooth soup consistency is attained. Bring to a low boil, reduce to simmer and cook thirty minutes. Add heavy whipping cream and catfish cubes and continue to cook for approximately fifteen minutes. Fold in Brie cheese and continue to stir until cheese is melted and well blended. Season to taste using salt and pepper.

Changes

Cream of Catfish and Mushroom Soup

1 Hour   6 Servings

3 5-8 ounce Catfish
   fillets (cubed)
3/4 cup melted butter
1/2 cup diced onions
1/2 cup diced celery
1/2 cup diced bell pepper
1/4 cup chopped garlic

3/4 cup flour
3 quarts hot fish stock (see recipe)
3 cups sliced mushrooms
1 cup heavy whipping cream
pinch of thyme
pinch of basil
salt and white pepper to taste

In a one gallon stock pot, heat butter over medium high heat. Saute onions, celery, bell pepper and garlic until vegetables are wilted, approximately three to five minutes. Blend in flour, stirring constantly until white roux is achieved. Do not brown. (see roux technique) Using a wire whip, blend in fish stock until soup-like texture is attained. Add mushrooms and heavy whipping cream, bring to a low boil, reduce to simmer and cook thirty minutes. Add catfish cubes and season with thyme and basil. Continue to cook ten to fifteen additional minutes and season to taste using salt and pepper.

Changes

_____

_____

_____

_____

Cream of Eggplant Soup

1 Hour   12 Servings

Comment:

Eggplant stuffed with crabmeat and ground pork is one of the most common vegetables found in Louisiana. Incorporating eggplant into a soup is a new technique that is getting rave reviews.

2-3 medium eggplants, peeled
    and diced
1 cup butter
2 cups chopped onions
2 cups chopped celery
1 cup chopped bell pepper
1/4 cup diced garlic
1 cup diced tomatoes

1 cup flour
2-1/2 quarts chicken stock
    (see recipe)
1 pint heavy whipping cream
1 cup sliced green onions
1 cup chopped parsley
salt and white pepper to taste

In a two gallon stock pot, melt butter over medium high heat. Add eggplant, onions, celery, bell pepper, garlic and tomatoes. Saute five to ten minutes or until vegetables are wilted. Add flour and using a wire whisk, stir constantly until white roux is achieved. (see roux technique) Do not brown. Add chicken stock, one ladle at a time, stirring constantly until all is incorporated. Bring to a low boil and cook thirty minutes. Add heavy whipping cream, green onions and parsley, and cook for ten additional minutes. Season to taste using salt and white pepper. To create an interesting twist in this recipe, you may wish to add julienned andouille and any fresh shellfish such as crab or shrimp.

HINT: An old friend told me that one teaspoon of curry powder will make all the difference in the world in flavoring this dish. Should you want to experiment, give it a try.

Changes

_____

_____

_____

_____

Bisque of Three Lettuces

1 Hour   12 Servings

Comment:

The combination of these three lettuce flavors is incredible. This soup was created quite by accident, but has been one of the best creations to come out of our kitchen.

2 cups romaine lettuce
2 cups bibb lettuce
2 cups red leaf lettuce
1 cup butter
1 cup chopped onions
1 cup chopped celery
1/2 cup chopped bell pepper
1/4 cup diced garlic
1 cup sliced mushrooms

1/2 cup diced andouille sausage
1 cup flour
2-1/2 quarts chicken stock
   (see recipe)
2 ounces sherry
1 pint heavy whipping cream
1 cup sliced green onions
1 cup chopped parsley
salt and white pepper to taste

In a two gallon stock pot, melt butter over medium high heat. Add three lettuces, onions, celery, bell pepper, garlic, mushrooms and andouille. Saute and stir constantly until lettuces are wilted, approximately five to ten minutes. Remove ingredients from stock pot and place in food processor with metal blade. Chop on high speed until vegetables are pureed. Return mixture to pot, simmer and sprinkle in flour. Using a wire whisk, stir constantly until white roux is achieved. (see roux technique) Do not brown. Add chicken stock, one ladle at a time, stirring constantly until all is incorporated. Add sherry, heavy whipping cream, green onions and parsley, and cook an additional ten to fifteen minutes. Season to taste using salt and white pepper. If you wish, you may garnish with julienned pieces of the three lettuces.

Changes

_____

_____

_____

_____

Cream of Cauliflower and Duck Soup

1-1/2 Hours   12 Servings

Comment:

The recipe for this soup was given to me by Chef Paul Prudhomme. We spent an afternoon in his test kitchen as this soup was being prepared. After tasting it, I commented that I felt it was one of the finest soups I had ever eaten.

FOR DUCK STOCK:

1 Long Island duck	**2 cups diced carrots**
6 quarts cold water	**1 bay leaf**
2 cups diced onions	**1 tbsp black peppercorns**
2 cups diced celery	**1 cup dry white wine**

In a two gallon stock pot, place all of the above ingredients. Bring to a rolling boil and reduce to simmer. Cook until duck is tender and falling apart. Remove duck from stock and debone. Save skin for garnishing soup and dice the meat into one quarter inch cubes. Set aside. Reserve three quarts of duck stock for soup.

(Continued)

RMB9

Changes

_____

_____

_____

_____

Soups

(*Cream of Cauliflower and Duck Soup* continued)

FOR SOUP:

4 cups chopped cauliflower
cooked meat from duck
duck skin, baked in oven until
   crispy and brown
1 cup butter
2 cups chopped onions
2 cups chopped celery
1 cup chopped bell pepper
1/4 cup diced garlic

1 cup flour
2-1/2 quarts reserved duck stock
1 ounce brandy
1 pint heavy whipping cream
1 cup sliced green onions
1 cup chopped parsley
salt and cracked black pepper
   to taste

In a two gallon stock pot, melt butter over medium high heat. Add cauliflower, onions, celery, bell pepper and garlic. Saute approximately twenty-five minutes, stirring constantly until cauliflower can be mashed against bottom of pot. Allow to brown slightly. Add flour and stir, using a wire whisk, until white roux is achieved. (see roux technique) It is all right if flour browns slightly. Add duck stock, one ladle at a time, stirring until all is incorporated. Add brandy and whipping cream, bring to a rolling boil and reduce to simmer. Cook approximately thirty minutes. Add duck meat, green onions and parsley. Season to taste using salt and cracked black pepper. When serving, add a small amount of julienned duck skin to garnish soup.

Changes

Cream of Cauliflower Soup

1 Hour   12 Servings

Comment:

I can remember eating cauliflower only as a steamed cold vegetable salad, spiced with vinegar and cracked black pepper. My how times have changed! I haven't eaten cold cauliflower salad in a while but this cream soup is a regular on our menu.

4 cups chopped cauliflower
2 cups diced white meat of
   chicken
1 cup butter
1 cup chopped onions
1 cup chopped celery
1/2 cup chopped red bell pepper
1/2 cup chopped yellow bell
   pepper
1/4 cup diced garlic

1 cup diced tomatoes
1 cup flour
2-1/2 quarts chicken stock
   (see recipe)
1 ounce dry white wine
1 pint heavy whipping cream
1 cup sliced green onions
1 cup chopped parsley
salt and cracked black pepper
   to taste

In a two gallon stock pot, melt butter over medium high heat. Add cauliflower, chicken, onions, celery, bell peppers, garlic and tomatoes. Saute ten to fifteen minutes or until vegetables are wilted. Add flour and using a wire whisk, stir constantly until white roux is achieved. (see roux technique) Do not brown. Add chicken stock, one ladle at a time, stirring constantly until all is incorporated. Bring to a low boil and reduce to simmer. Cook approximately thirty minutes or until cauliflower is tender. Add white wine, heavy whipping cream, green onions and parsley. Cook for an additional fifteen minutes. Season to taste using salt and cracked black pepper. You may wish to add a sprinkle of finely diced fresh cauliflower to the center of each bowl when serving. This crispy texture will prove interesting in the soup.

Changes

_____

_____

_____

Cream of Cabbage Soup

1 Hour   12 Servings

Comment:

Here we took the traditional method of smothering cabbage with ham hocks and gave it a boost into the 1990's. I intended to capture the flavor I remembered so well but instead created a dish that was even better than the original.

4 pounds shredded cabbage
1/2 pound julienned andouille
　　sausage
1/2 pound julienned tasso
1 cup butter
2 cups chopped onions
2 cups chopped celery
1 cup chopped bell pepper
1/4 cup diced garlic
2 cups diced tomatoes

2 tbsps sugar
1 cup flour
1 tbsp lemon juice
1 ounce white wine
2-1/2 quarts chicken stock
　　(see recipe)
1 pint heavy whipping cream
1 cup sliced green onions
1 cup chopped parsley
salt and white pepper to taste

In a two gallon stock pot, melt butter over medium high heat. Add cabbage, andouille, tasso, onions, celery, bell pepper, garlic and tomatoes. Saute fifteen to twenty minutes or until cabbage is wilted. Add sugar and flour. Using a wire whisk, stir constantly until white roux is achieved. (see roux technique) Do not brown. Add lemon juice and white wine, blending well into the mixture. Add chicken stock, one ladle at a time, stirring constantly until all is incorporated. Bring to a rolling boil, reduce to simmer and cook thirty minutes. Add heavy whipping cream, green onions and parsley. Cook for ten additional minutes. Season to taste using salt and white pepper. This soup may be garnished with a few pieces of the shredded cabbage.

Changes

_____

_____

_____

_____

Cajun Vegetable Soup

1 Hour   12 Servings

Comment:

Vegetables were always canned or jarred during the spring months to ensure a good supply over the winter. Often, in the cold of January and February, I remember a huge pot of this vegetable soup on the stove available for tasting all day.

3 pounds bone-in soup meat
2 pounds cubed beef brisket
1 cup julienned andouille
   sausage
1 cup butter
1 cup coarsely chopped onions
1 cup coarsely chopped celery
1 cup coarsely chopped bell
   pepper
1 cup coarsely chopped carrots
1/4 cup diced garlic

1 cup flour
4 quarts chicken stock (see recipe)
6 diced tomatoes
6 cubed potatoes
1 cup whole kernel corn
1 cup lima beans
1 cup black-eyed peas
2 cups coarsely chopped cabbage
1 12-ounce package #4 thin spaghetti
salt and cracked black pepper
   to taste

In a two gallon stock pot, melt butter over medium high heat. Add onions, celery, bell pepper, carrots and garlic. Saute three to five minutes or until vegetables are wilted. Add flour and using a wire whisk, stir constantly until a white roux is achieved. (see roux technique) Do not brown. Add soup meat, cubed brisket and andouille. Saute three minutes and add chicken stock, one ladle at a time, stirring constantly until all is incorporated. Bring to a rolling boil and cook until brisket is tender, approximately forty-five minutes. Add tomatoes, potatoes, corn, beans, peas and cabbage. Cook an additional fifteen minutes. Add spaghetti and continue cooking until spaghetti is tender. Season to taste using salt and cracked black pepper. Additional chicken stock may be added to retain the volume of liquid. You may also wish to add any variety of your favorite vegetables to this recipe. On occasion, I have used smoked meats in this dish and boy, what a hit!

Changes

_____

_____

Cajun White Bean Soup

2 Hours   12 Servings

Comment:

As you have learned, white beans were brought to Louisiana by the Cajuns from Brittany. However, it was over 100 years later before some creative Cajun cook decided to create this white bean soup.

1 large package Great Northern beans	**2 cups chopped celery**
2 pieces heavy smoked ham hocks	**1 cup chopped bell pepper**
	1/4 cup diced garlic
	2 cups diced tomatoes
1 cup julienned tasso	**1 bay leaf**
3/4 cup Crisco oil	**salt and cracked black pepper**
2 cups chopped onions	**to taste**

It is best to pre-soak beans overnight in cold water. If this is done, discard the water and wash the beans before cooking. In a two gallon stock pot, melt Crisco over medium high heat. Add onions, celery, bell pepper, garlic and tomatoes. Saute three to five minutes or until vegetables are wilted. Add ham hocks and tasso, and continue to saute for an additional five minutes. Add white beans to the vegetable mixture and saute two minutes more. Add enough cold water to cover beans by two inches. Bring to a rolling boil, reduce to simmer and cook, stirring occasionally, for approximately one hour. Once beans begin to tender, mash against the side of the pot to create a creaming effect. Continue this process throughout the cooking period. Add bay leaf and season to taste using salt and cracked black pepper. Continue to cook, stirring occasionally to avoid scorching. Soup will be ready when texture is creamy white and the consistency of a cream of mushroom soup is achieved, approximately one and a half hours. Adjust seasonings if necessary.

HINT: A great variation to this soup is the use of red kidney beans in place of the white. Both of these soups may be made with the left over red or white beans from Monday lunch.

Changes

_____

_____

Creole Turtle Soup

2 Hours   12 Servings

Comment:

This Creole specialty is indeed a delicacy in the city of New Orleans. Though created in the bayous by the Cajuns, the original recipe has been changed and adapted to the Creole flavors and may be found in most restaurants in Louisiana today.

3 pounds cleaned snapping
    turtle
1/2 pound diced ham
1 cup vegetable oil
1 cup flour
2 cups chopped onions
2 cups chopped celery
1 cup chopped bell pepper
1/4 cup diced garlic
1 cup chopped tomato

4 quarts chicken stock (see recipe)
2 whole bay leaves
1/2 tsp thyme
1/2 tsp allspice
pinch of nutmeg
pinch of mace
6 whole cloves
1 tbsp lemon juice
1/2 cup madeira wine
3 grated boiled eggs
salt and cracked black pepper to taste

In a two gallon stock pot, heat oil over medium high heat. Add flour and using a wire whisk, stir constantly until roux is golden brown. (see roux technique) Do not scorch. Should black specks appear, discard and begin again. Add onions, celery, bell pepper, garlic and tomatoes. Saute three to five minutes or until vegetables are wilted. Add turtle and diced ham and stir well into mixture. Cook approximately ten minutes. Add chicken stock, one ladle at a time, stirring constantly until all is incorporated. Add bay leaf, thyme, allspice, nutmeg, mace, cloves and lemon juice. Bring to a low boil, reduce to simmer and cook approximately one to one and a half hours or until turtle is tender. Once the soup is cooked, add madeira wine and grated eggs. Season to taste using salt and cracked black pepper.

HINT: This soup may be made with equal success using alligator, ox tail or any other soup meat. The use of grated eggs in this recipe is a carryover from when we used the fresh turtle eggs in the dish.

Changes

Vegetables

Reba Meliet ©1989

Vegetables

On a first visit to South Louisiana everything seems bright green to the newcomer, and for a good reason. Our subtropical climate, coupled with the fertile fields topped with rich Mississippi River soil, provides an environment where just about any vegetable can grow and grow and grow.

Because of the vast number of vegetables found in South Louisiana, it is no wonder that the people of Bayou country create so many recipes using vegetables. Roadside produce stands dot the landscape with the freshest crops available daily. Even in supermarkets, vegetables are given top priority in presentation. The colorful red and yellow peppers, eggplants, sweet potatoes and a multitude of greens glisten along the aisles, unpackaged to allow the shoppers a chance to touch for themselves.

Vegetables are prepared smothered in sauces, quickly sauteed, topped with vinaigrettes or simply served fresh with salt, pepper and butter. Many times, two or more vegetables are diced and combined for a truly appetizing and delicious change of pace. Our Creole ratatouille is just one of the more popular multi-vegetable dishes created in New Orleans.

Cajun cooks are masters at stuffing vegetables with meat and seafood. Vegetables such as mirliton stuffed with shrimp, eggplant stuffed with crabmeat and tomatoes stuffed with okra are just a few examples of this tremendous technique.

"In the vegetable world, there is nothing so innocent, so confiding in its expression, as the small green face of a freshly shelled pea. Asparagus is pushy, lettuce is loud, radishes are gay, but the little pea is so helpless and friendly that it makes sensitive stomachs suffer to see how he is treated in the average home. Fling him into boiling water, and that's that."

William Irwin

Broccoli Casserole

1 Hour   6 Servings

Comment:

Broccoli was commonly found on the Creole tables of New Orleans. The Cajuns, however, did not actually use broccoli until the late 1950's when broccoli became available in the stores and markets around the bayous.

2 heads fresh broccoli
1/2 cup butter
1/4 cup chopped onions
1/4 cup chopped celery
1/4 cup red bell pepper
1/4 cup diced garlic
1/4 cup diced tasso
1/2 cup sliced mushrooms

1/2 cup flour
3 cups heavy whipping cream
salt and white pepper to taste
pinch of nutmeg
1/2 cup grated Parmesan cheese
1/2 cup seasoned Italian bread
**   crumbs**

Preheat oven to 375 degrees F. Cut broccoli into florets and boil in lightly salted water until tender but firm. Do not overcook. Remove and cool under tap water. Set aside. In a one quart sauce pot, melt butter over medium high heat. Saute onions, celery, bell pepper, garlic, tasso and mushrooms approximately five to ten minutes or until vegetables are wilted. Sprinkle in flour and using a wire whisk, stir until white roux is achieved. (see roux technique) Do not brown. Add heavy whipping cream, stirring constantly to form white cream sauce. Do not allow to scorch. Season to taste using salt, white pepper and nutmeg. Place cooked broccoli in baking dish and top with cream sauce. Sprinkle generously with Parmesan cheese and bread crumbs. Bake on center oven rack until casserole is bubbly and slightly brown on top. You may wish to use grated cheddar cheese in place of Parmesan for a milder taste.

Changes

_____

_____

_____

_____

Butter Beans with Ham

1 Hour   6 Servings

Comment:

Lima beans, or butter beans as they are known here in South Louisiana, are often cooked casserole style with different smoked meats. This recipe, however, is from my grandmother and she preferred to cook butter beans slowly, cream style.

1 pound fresh butter beans
1/2 cup Crisco or bacon
   drippings
1 cup chopped onions
1 cup chopped celery
1 cup chopped red bell pepper

1/4 cup diced garlic
1/2 pound smoked ham, cubed
2 smoked ham hocks
1 cup chopped green onions
1/2 cup chopped parsley
salt and cracked black pepper to taste

Rinse lima beans, removing any hard or discolored beans. The beans will cook faster if they are soaked in cold water overnight in the refrigerator. When ready to cook, rinse beans once again in cold water. In a two quart sauce pot, melt Crisco or bacon drippings over medium high heat. Add onions, celery, bell pepper, garlic and smoked ham. Saute approximately five minutes or until vegetables are wilted. Add ham hocks and cook five additional minutes. Add lima beans and enough cold water to cover beans by approximately two inches. Add green onions and bring to a rolling boil. Reduce to simmer and allow to cook thirty minutes, stirring occasionally to keep vegetables from scorching. Continue to cook, stirring occasionally, until beans are tender, approximately one hour. Season to taste using salt and pepper. Using a metal spoon, mash approximately one fourth of the beans against the side of the pot to create a creaming effect. Garnish with parsley. Beans should be tender and of a butter consistency when ready to serve. Butter beans may be served on top of cooked white rice or as a side vegetable.

Changes

_____

_____

_____

_____

Snap Beans with New Potatoes

1 Hour   6 Servings

Comment:

Green beans with new potatoes are probably the most frequently eaten vegetables in the homes of Cajun country. Potatoes were available year round and gave the dish more appeal to the traditional Cajun family when added to the snap beans.

1 pound fresh snap beans	**1/2 cup chopped red bell pepper**
10 peeled new potatoes	**1/4 cup diced garlic**
1/2 cup Crisco or bacon	**1/2 pound diced smoked ham**
drippings	**2 cups chicken stock (see recipe)**
1/2 cup chopped onions	**salt and cracked black pepper**
1/2 cup chopped celery	**to taste**

In a four quart sauce pot, melt Crisco or bacon drippings over medium high heat. Add onions, celery, bell pepper, garlic and smoked ham. Saute approximately three to five minutes or until vegetables are wilted. Add snap beans and new potatoes and stir fry for about three minutes in the vegetable mixture. Add chicken stock, cover the pot and reduce heat to simmer. Cook approximately thirty minutes or until potatoes are tender. The snap beans will be overcooked by most standards. However, this has been the chosen method of cooking snap beans by the Cajuns. Once tender, season to taste using salt and cracked black pepper. This vegetable may be served over cooked white rice as a side dish or as a vegetable.

Changes

_____

_____

_____

_____

Louisiana Red or White Beans

1-1/2 Hours   6 Servings

Comment:

When the French left Brittany for Nova Scotia in 1620, these Acadians, as they were to be known, brought with them these now famous beans. When exiled from Acadia, they left with few possessions but not without their beans.

1 pound dried navy or kidney
    beans
1/2 cup Crisco or bacon
    drippings
1 cup chopped onions
1 cup chopped celery
1/2 cup chopped bell pepper
1/4 cup diced garlic

1 cup sliced green onions
2 cups diced smoked ham
6 3-inch links andouille sausage
1/2 cup chopped parsley
1 cup sliced green onions
salt and Louisiana Gold
    Pepper Sauce to taste

The cooking time of white and red beans will be cut about one third if the beans are soaked overnight in cold water. This will help soften the outer shell and naturally the cooking time will be shortened. In a four quart sauce pot, melt Crisco or bacon drippings over medium high heat. Add onions, celery, bell peppers, garlic, green onions and smoked ham. Saute approximately five to ten minutes or until vegetables are wilted. Add andouille sausage and beans. Blend well with vegetables and cook two to three minutes. Add enough cold water to cover beans by approximately two inches. Bring to a rolling boil and allow to cook thirty minutes, stirring occasionally to avoid scorching. Reduce heat to simmer and cook approximately one hour or until beans are tender. Stir from time to time, as beans will settle to the bottom of the pot as they cook. Add chopped parsley and additional green onions. Season to taste using salt and Louisiana Gold Pepper Sauce. Using a metal spoon, mash approximately one third of the beans against the side of the pot to create a creaming effect. Once beans are tender and creamy, they are ready to be served. In order for the maximum flavor to develop, this dish should be cooked one day before it is to be served.

Changes

Smothered Cabbage and Andouille

1 Hour   6 Servings

Comment:

This dish may be found on the New Years Day table of every home in South Louisiana. Tradition has it that cabbage eaten on January 1st will ensure financial security in the upcoming year.

1 large head of cabbage	1/2 cup chopped bell pepper
1/2 pound sliced andouille sausage	1/4 cup diced garlic
1/2 cup bacon drippings	1 cup sliced green onions
1 cup chopped onions	1-1/2 cups chicken stock
1 cup chopped celery	salt and cracked black pepper to taste

Cut cabbage in quarters and discard the center heart and all large exterior leaves. Chop quarters into two or three pieces and separate the leaves. In a four quart sauce pot, melt bacon drippings over medium heat. Add onions, celery, bell pepper, garlic, green onions and andouille. Saute approximately five minutes or until vegetables are wilted. Add cabbage and blend well into vegetable mixture. Continue to stir fry until cabbage leaves are wilted. Add chicken stock and reduce heat to simmer. Cover pot and allow to cook, stirring occasionally, for approximately forty-five minutes. Season to taste using salt and pepper and continue cooking until cabbage is well smothered. This dish, similar to the snap beans, will be overcooked by most standards. However this is the method preferred by both Cajuns and Creoles.

Changes

_____

_____

_____

_____

Deep Fried Carrot Fritters

45 Minutes   6 Servings

Comment:

I can remember well dipping fresh fried carrot fritters in a bowl of Louisiana cane syrup and thinking all the time that I had been treated to a wonderful dessert.

10 medium size carrots, scraped
    and cleaned
1-1/2 quarts vegetable oil
2 eggs
3 tbsps flour
2 tbsps chopped pecans

1 tbsp sugar
1 tsp baking powder
salt and cracked black pepper
    to taste
1 cup plain flour

In a home style frying unit such as Fry Daddy or Fry Baby, preheat oil according to manufacturer's directions or to 375 degrees F. Boil carrots in a pot of lightly salted water until tender. Place boiled carrots in the bowl of a food processor with a metal cutting blade. Blend on high speed until carrots are pureed. Add eggs, flour, pecans, sugar and baking powder. Using the pulse button, blend five to ten seconds or until all ingredients are well incorporated and carrot mixture is smooth and fluffy. Season to taste using salt and pepper, and adjust sweetness to your personal taste. Remove mixture from the food processor and roll into three-inch oblong fritters. Dust in plain flour and deep fry, a few at a time, until fritters float to the surface. Remove to drain board or paper towels and keep warm. These fritters may also be pan fried in melted butter as a breakfast item, and served with Louisiana sugar cane syrup.

Changes

Buttered Grated Carrots

45 Minutes   6 Servings

Comment:

This is one of the most simple vegetables to prepare in the home kitchen. Since it has such a vivid color and unique taste, it should certainly become a favorite of yours.

1 pound carrots, scraped and
   cleaned
1/4 pound butter
1/4 cup chopped green onions
1 tbsp chopped parsley
1 tbsp diced garlic
1 tbsp brown sugar

1 ounce brandy
1 tbsp finely diced red bell pepper
1 tbsp finely diced yellow
   bell pepper
salt and cracked black pepper
   to taste

Using a grater, julienne carrots into thin strips. Depending on the size of the carrots, you may need to estimate if the quantity grated will be enough for six servings. It is best to have just a little extra, if you are unsure. In a ten inch heavy bottom saute pan, melt butter over medium high heat. Add carrots and stir fry until tender but not overcooked. Test for doneness by biting into one of the strips from time to time. When tender, add green onions, parsley, garlic and sugar. Stir fry these vegetables into the carrots for approximately five minutes. Remove saute pan from open flame and add brandy. Return to heat, but be cautious, as brandy will ignite for about five seconds. Add red and yellow bell peppers for color and saute two minutes. Season to taste using salt and cracked black pepper.

Changes

_____

_____

_____

_____

Baked Cauliflower and Crab

1 Hour   6 Servings

Comment:

Here, the normally bland taste of the cauliflower is overshadowed by the rich crabmeat mornay style sauce. This vegetable casserole will certainly be used time after time once you have tried the recipe.

1 large head of cauliflower	2 cups chicken stock (see recipe)
1/2 pound jumbo lump crabmeat	1 cup heavy whipping cream
1/2 cup butter	pinch of nutmeg
1/2 cup chopped onions	1 ounce dry white wine
1/2 cup chopped celery	1/2 cup grated cheddar cheese
1/2 cup diced red bell pepper	salt and cayenne pepper to taste
1/4 cup diced garlic	1/2 cup seasoned Italian
1/2 cup flour	bread crumbs

Preheat oven to 375 degrees F. Cut cauliflower into serving size pieces and boil in lightly salted water until tender but firm. Do not overcook. Remove cauliflower and cool under tap water. Set aside. In a two quart sauce pot, heat butter over medium high heat. Add onions, celery, bell pepper and garlic. Saute approximately three to five minutes or until vegetables are wilted. Sprinkle in flour and using a wire whisk, stir until white roux is achieved. (see roux technique) Do not brown. Add chicken stock, one ladle at a time, stirring constantly until all is incorporated. Bring to a low boil and add heavy whipping cream. Continue to stir as mixture will have a tendency to stick to the bottom of the pot. Reduce heat if necessary. Add nutmeg, white wine and blend in cheese, stirring as cheese is melting into sauce. Remove from heat and season to taste using salt and pepper. Gently fold in lump crabmeat, being careful not to break lumps. Place cauliflower in a baking dish and top with crabmeat cream sauce. Sprinkle with seasoned Italian bread crumbs. Bake fifteen to twenty minutes or until sauce is bubbly and bread crumbs are well browned.

Changes

_____

_____

Marinated Cauliflower

45 Minutes   6 Servings

Comment:

Of all the dishes I remember as a young boy growing up in the Bayous, marinated cauliflower comes to mind most often. Although this certainly was no delicacy then, it was simple to prepare and was always available.

1 large head cauliflower	1/4 cup diced garlic
2 cups coarsely chopped celery	1/2 cup olive oil
1 sliced sweet Vidalia onion	1 cup red wine vinegar
1 julienned red bell pepper	1/4 cup cracked black pepper
1 julienned yellow bell pepper	salt to taste

Cut cauliflower into bite-size pieces and boil in lightly salted water until tender but firm. Remove from pot and cool under tap water. Place cauliflower in two quart ceramic mixing bowl and add all other ingredients. Using your hands, continually mix vegetables with seasonings, olive oil, vinegar etc., until all is well incorporated and vegetables are well coated. Cover with clear wrap and allow to sit in the refrigerator a minimum of twenty-four hours. This colorful dish presents well on a vegetable tray for a cocktail event and is also a great diet food.

Changes

_____

_____

_____

_____

Maque Choux Corn

1 Hour   6 Servings

Comment:

Although Maque Choux is normally thought of as a corn soup, the Cajuns of River Road Louisiana cooked a similar vegetable flavored with the fresh water shrimp of the Mississippi River. Here is their version of that dish.

6 ears fresh corn
1 cup 150-200 count shrimp,
    peeled and deveined
1/2 cup bacon drippings
1/2 cup chopped onions
1/2 cup chopped celery
1/2 cup chopped red bell pepper

1/4 cup diced garlic
1/4 cup finely diced tasso
2 cups coarsely chopped tomatoes
2 tbsps tomato sauce
1 cup sliced green onions
salt and cracked black pepper
    to taste

Select tender, well-developed ears of corn and remove shucks and silk. Using a sharp knife, cut lengthwise through the kernels to remove them from the cob. Scrape each cob using the blade of the knife to remove all milk and additional pulp from the corn. This is important since the richness of the dish will depend on how much milk and pulp can be scraped from the cobs. In a four quart sauce pan, melt bacon drippings over medium high heat. Saute corn, onions, celery, bell pepper, garlic and tasso approximately fifteen to twenty minutes or until vegetables are wilted and corn begins to tenderize. Add tomatoes, tomato sauce and shrimp. Continue cooking until juice from the tomatoes and shrimp are rendered into the dish. Add green onions and season to taste using salt and pepper. Continue to cook an additional fifteen to twenty minutes or until full flavor of corn and shrimp is developed into the dish.

Changes

_____

_____

_____

_____

Corn Pudding

1 Hour   6 Servings

Comment:

Corn pudding was one of the many dishes given firsthand to the Cajuns and Creoles by the Indians living in South Louisiana. This dish is a Thanksgiving tradition on all tables in Bayou country.

3 cups whole kernel corn
1/2 cup bacon drippings or
    butter
1 cup chopped onions
1/2 cup chopped celery
1/2 cup finely diced red bell
    pepper
1/4 cup diced garlic

1/2 cup finely diced andouille
    sausage
1 tbsp sugar
salt and cayenne pepper to taste
4 egg yolks, well beaten
3/4 cup shredded cheddar cheese
4 egg whites, stiffly beaten

Preheat oven to 350 degrees F. In a ten inch heavy bottom saute pan, melt bacon drippings or butter over medium high heat. Saute corn, onions, celery, bell pepper, garlic and andouille approximately ten to fifteen minutes or until vegetables are wilted. Season to taste using sugar, salt and cayenne pepper, and allow to cook an additional ten minutes. Add a small amount of chicken stock, should mixture become too dry. Remove from heat and allow to cool approximately thirty minutes, stirring occasionally. Fold beaten egg yolks and cheddar cheese into corn mixture. Once well blended, gently fold in stiffly beaten egg whites. Pour mixture into a well-oiled casserole dish. Place in water bath and bake on the center oven rack for approximately one hour. This recipe may be enhanced by adding shrimp or lump crabmeat after the beaten eggs. I have also seen this recipe prepared for Sunday brunch.

Changes

Baked Cushaw

1-1/2 Hours   6-10 Servings

Comment:

Cushaw is truly one of the great gifts given South Louisiana by the Indians. There has been much debate over whether it is a squash or a pumpkin, but who cares! When cooked with brown sugar and cinnamon, it becomes a masterpiece.

1 medium size cushaw pumpkin	**2 tbsps vanilla**
3/4 pound butter	**pinch of cinnamon**
1 cup brown sugar	**pinch of nutmeg**
1/2 cup Louisiana cane syrup	**pinch of clove**
1/2 cup chopped pecans	**pinch of salt**

For those not familiar with the cushaw of South Louisiana, I should mention that this vegetable is a green and white striped crooknecked pumpkin. Since the outer shell of the cushaw is somewhat unmanageable, I suggest that you have someone chop the cushaw into two inch squares, leaving the shell intact. Using a teaspoon, scrape all seeds from the center of the cushaw. Place cubed cushaw into a pot of lightly salted boiling water and cook until meat is tender, approximately thirty minutes. Test to be sure that the meat will scrape away from the shell with ease before removing it from the boiling water. When tender, remove from pot and cool under tap water. Scrape all meat from the shell and set aside. In a four quart sauce pot, heat butter over medium high heat. Saute cushaw, mashing well into the hot butter. Add all remaining ingredients and continue to cook, stirring occasionally to avoid scorching. Cook until cushaw is smooth and slightly browned. Adjust seasonings if necessary and serve as you would candied yams. This dish was served in the fall and winter months in place of sweet potatoes.

Changes

_____

_____

_____

_____

Eggplant Casserole

1-1/2 Hours   6 Servings

Comment:

Typical of most vegetables served in South Louisiana, the eggplant is also prepared casserole style. By combining meats, seafoods and vegetables, the Cajuns and Creoles are able to create a much heartier dish for the table.

**4 medium size eggplants,
   peeled and cubed**
1/2 pound ground beef
**1/2 pound 150-200 count shrimp,
   peeled and deveined**
1/4 pound butter
1 cup chopped onions

1 cup chopped celery
1/2 cup chopped bell pepper
1/4 cup diced garlic
1 cup rich chicken stock (see recipe)
**salt and cracked black pepper
   to taste**
2 cups seasoned Italian bread crumbs

Preheat oven to 375 degrees F. Boil eggplant in lightly salted water until very tender and to the point of being mushy. Drain and set aside. In a four quart sauce pot, melt butter over medium high heat. Saute onions, celery, bell pepper and garlic approximately three to five minutes or until vegetables are wilted. Add ground beef and slowly cook until golden brown and each grain of meat is totally separated, approximately twenty-five to thirty minutes. Once mixture is browned, add chicken stock, a little at a time, if the meat has become too dry during cooking. Add cooked eggplant and shrimp and continue cooking approximately thirty minutes longer or until all vegetables, meat and eggplant are well blended. Season to taste using salt and cracked black pepper. Remove from heat and sprinkle in one cup of bread crumbs to absorb most of the liquid. Place eggplant mixture in a baking dish and top with remaining bread crumbs. Bake until bread crumbs are golden brown.

Changes

_____

_____

_____

_____

Stuffed Eggplant with Crab

1-1/2 Hours   6 Servings

Comment:

This dish is most commonly eaten as an entree. However, try cutting it into vegetable size portions and serving in place of a potato dish.

3 medium size eggplants, split
   lengthwise
1 eggplant, peeled and cubed
1/2 pound white crabmeat
1/2 pound ground pork
1/4 pound butter
1 cup chopped onions
1/2 cup chopped celery
1/2 cup chopped red bell pepper
1/4 cup diced garlic

1/2 cup diced tomatoes
1/2 cup ground andouille sausage
1 cup rich chicken stock
   (see recipe)
salt and cracked black pepper
   to taste
1-1/2 cups seasoned Italian
   bread crumbs
3/4 cup grated Parmesan cheese

Preheat oven to 375 degrees F. Boil all eggplant in lightly salted water until tender. Remove and cool under tap water. Using a metal spoon, scrape meat from inside of the halved eggplants, being careful not to tear the shell. Save the shells to be stuffed later. Add this scraped meat to the uncooked cubed eggplant and set aside. The cubed eggplant has been added to ensure that enough vegetable will be available at the time of stuffing. In a four quart sauce pot, melt butter over medium high heat. Saute onions, celery, bell pepper, garlic, tomatoes and andouille approximately ten to fifteen minutes or until vegetables are wilted.

(Continued)

Changes

(*Stuffed Eggplant with Crab* continued)

Add ground pork and slow cook until golden brown and each grain of meat is well separated. Add small amounts of chicken stock, should the meat mixture become too dry during cooking. When mixture is browned, add eggplant, and continue to cook an additional thirty minutes until vegetables, meat and eggplant are well blended. Remove from heat and season to taste using salt and cracked black pepper. Gently fold in crabmeat and sprinkle bread crumbs into the mixture to absorb most of the liquid. Using a metal cooking spoon, stuff shells with cooked eggplant mixture, dividing equally between the six shells. Sprinkle additional bread crumbs and Parmesan cheese on top of stuffed eggplant and place on baking pan. Bake until bread crumbs and cheese are golden brown.

Changes

_____

_____

_____

_____

Sweet Pickled Mirliton

1 Hour   2 Jars

Comment:

Often during the mirliton season, one would simply grow more than he could eat. Sweet pickling of the vegetable seemed to be the answer to this dilemma.

4 medium size mirlitons   **1 stick of cinnamon**
1/2 cup vinegar   **6 whole cloves**
1/3 cup sugar   **pinch of salt**
1/4 cup beet juice   **1/2 tsp whole black peppercorns**
1/4 tsp whole allspice

Place two jars along with lids in a 212 degree bath, and allow to sterilize for thirty minutes. Cut mirlitons into one-half inch thick pickle slices, removing seeds from the center of the vegetables. Boil mirliton slices in lightly salted water for approximately five minutes. Remove and cool under tap water. This fast blanching will slightly tenderize the pickle but will not overcook it. In a saute pan over medium high heat, combine all remaining ingredients. Bring to a low boil and simmer for five minutes. Pack cooked mirliton into hot sterilized jars, dividing them equally between the two jars. Pour sweetened vinegar mixture in equal amounts into the two jars. Add plain vinegar to cover mirlitons should there not be enough hot liquid. Quickly seal, and allow to set at room temperature until caps seal.

Changes

138

Shrimp Stuffed Mirliton

1 Hour   6 Servings

Comment:

The Chiote squash or vegetable pear, as some may know it, is known here in South Louisiana as mirliton. It was brought here by the Cajuns from South America in 1755. Today, it is the premier vegetable of the Cajuns and Creoles.

3 mirlitons, sliced lengthwise
1 cup 150-200 count shrimp,
    peeled and deveined
1/4 pound butter
1 cup chopped onions
1 cup chopped celery
1/2 cup chopped bell pepper
1/2 cup sliced green onions
1/4 cup diced garlic

1/2 pound diced ham
1 cup rich chicken stock (see recipe)
salt and cracked black pepper
    to taste
1/4 cup chopped parsley
1-1/2 cups seasoned Italian
    bread crumbs
6 pats chipped butter

Preheat oven to 375 degrees F. Boil mirlitons in lightly salted water until meat is tender enough to scoop from the shells. Once tender, remove and cool under tap water. Using a metal spoon, remove seeds from the center of the mirlitons and gently scoop all meat out of the shells. Reserve meat and save shells for stuffing later. In a four quart sauce pot, melt butter over medium high heat. Saute onions, celery, bell pepper, green onions, garlic and diced ham. Cook approximately fifteen minutes or until vegetables are wilted. Add chicken stock should vegetable mixture become too dry during cooking. Add mirlitons and shrimp, and continue cooking approximately twenty-five to thirty minutes or until mixture is well incorporated. Remove from heat and season to taste using salt, cracked black pepper and parsley. Sprinkle in seasoned bread crumbs to absorb any excess liquid. Stuff mirliton mixture into the shells, dividing equally into six portions. Place stuffed mirlitons on a baking pan and top with one pat of chipped butter and remaining bread crumbs. Bake until golden brown.

Changes

_____

_____

Smothered Okra

1-1/2 Hours   6-8 Servings

Comment:

Okra was brought to Louisiana by the Africans in the early 1700's. In fact, most people do not realize that the African word for okra is gumbo. The okra is sometimes smothered and frozen to keep on hand for shrimp and okra gumbo.

2 quarts fresh sliced okra
1/4 cup vegetable oil
1 cup chopped onions
1 cup chopped celery
1/2 cup chopped bell pepper
1/4 cup diced garlic

3 cups diced tomatoes
1/2 cup hot water
salt and cracked black pepper
**   to taste**
dash of Louisiana Gold
**   Pepper Sauce**

It is important to select only the young and tender okra for smothering. As the season progresses, the okra hardens and is no longer prime for smothering. In a four quart sauce pan, heat oil over medium high heat. Saute okra, onions, celery, bell pepper and garlic approximately thirty minutes or until okra stops stringing. The okra will become slimy during this process and should be stirred constantly until the stringing ceases. Add tomatoes and hot water, bring to a low boil and cook approximately one hour, stirring occasionally. Season to taste using salt and cracked black pepper and a dash of Louisiana Gold. You may wish to add lump crabmeat or shrimp into the okra at the end of the cooking and serve as a side vegetable. Many people will saute a large batch of okra and divide it into smaller portions to freeze for later use.

Changes

_____

_____

_____

_____

Okra Stuffed Tomatoes

45 Minutes   6 Servings

Comment:

This is an interesting side dish incorporating okra. Since it is difficult to find dishes that may be prepared readily with okra, this is one presentation that will quickly win praise.

2 cups smothered okra (see
   recipe)
1/2 cup lump crabmeat
6 medium size tomatoes
1/4 pound butter
1 cup chopped onions
1/2 cup chopped celery
1/4 cup diced garlic

3/4 cup diced ham or andouille
   sausage
salt and cracked black pepper
   to taste
1/2 cup Parmesan cheese
1/2 cup seasoned Italian
   bread crumbs

Preheat oven to 375 degrees F. Smother okra according to the previous recipe. This may be a great time to smother a little extra for the freezer. While okra is cooking, core out center of tomatoes and reserve all of the pulp. You may wish to peel the skin from the tomatoes, however, this is not necessary. When cored, rinse and set aside. In a ten inch heavy bottom saute pan, melt butter over medium high heat. Add onions, celery, garlic, diced ham or andouille sausage and tomato pulp. Saute approximately ten to fifteen minutes or until vegetables are wilted. Add smothered okra and chop well into the vegetable mixture. Continue to saute ten to fifteen minutes longer, until all seasonings are well incorporated. Season to taste using salt and cracked black pepper. Gently fold in the lump crabmeat. Stuff tomatoes with the sauteed okra mixture, and top with Parmesan cheese and bread crumbs. Place on a baking pan and bake until bread crumbs are golden brown. Serve immediately. This dish may be served as an interesting side vegetable or as a light lunch entree.

Changes

_____

_____

_____

Old Fashion Potato Stew

1 Hour   6 Servings

Comment:

As common as red beans and rice, potato stew cooked with river shrimp became a pleasant substitution on that Monday wash day in Louisiana. Both dishes could be cooked in the black iron pot next to the wash kettle, making lunch a little easier.

4 large potatoes, peeled and
    cubed
2 cups 150-200 count shrimp,
    peeled and deveined
1/2 cup vegetable oil
1/2 cup flour
1 cup chopped onions
1/2 cup chopped celery

1/2 cup chopped bell pepper
1/4 cup diced garlic
4 cups chicken stock (see recipe)
1/2 cup sliced green onions
1/2 cup chopped parsley
salt and cracked black pepper
    to taste

In a two quart sauce pot, heat oil over medium high heat. Add flour and using a wire whisk, stir constantly until golden brown roux is achieved. (see roux technique) Do not scorch. Should black specks appear, discard and begin again. Add onions, celery, bell pepper and garlic. Saute approximately five to ten minutes or until vegetables are wilted. Add potatoes and continue to saute three to five minutes. Add chicken stock, one ladle at a time, until all has been incorporated. Bring to a low boil, add green onions and reduce to simmer. Cook until potatoes are tender, approximately twenty to thirty minutes. Once tender, add shrimp and parsley and season to taste using salt and cracked black pepper. Continue cooking until shrimp are pink and curled. Do not overcook. This dish makes a wonderful breakfast hash when combined with leftover roast beef or turkey. For an interesting flavor twist, add one quarter inch slices of heavy smoked sausage when the chicken stock is added.

Changes

Spinach Marguerite

1 Hour   6 Servings

Comment:

This particular recipe is a spicy rendition of the more traditional Spinach Madeline. Spinach is found in abundance here in South Louisiana and this recipe gives us a pleasant option when considering it as a side dish.

2 10-ounce packages, cooked
    frozen spinach (thawed)
1/2 cup melted butter
1/2 cup chopped onions
1/2 cup chopped celery
1/2 cup chopped bell pepper
1/4 cup diced garlic
1 cup finely chopped ham or
    tasso

1/2 cup flour
3-1/2 cups heavy whipping cream
1/2 cup diced tomatoes
1/2 cup grated cheddar cheese
1/4 cup finely diced jalapeno
    peppers
salt and cracked black pepper
    to taste

Preheat oven to 375 degrees F. In a four quart sauce pan, melt butter over medium high heat. Add onions, celery, bell pepper, garlic and chopped ham or tasso. Saute approximately five to ten minutes or until vegetables are wilted. Sprinkle in flour and using a wire whisk, stir constantly until white roux is achieved. (see roux technique) Do not brown. Slowly add heavy whipping cream, stirring constantly until all is incorporated. Add tomatoes, cheddar cheese and jalapeno peppers. Continue cooking for an additional five to ten minutes, stirring constantly, as mixture will tend to stick. Add a small amount of heavy whipping cream should mixture become too thick. Season to taste using salt and cracked black pepper. Remove from heat and add cooked spinach, stirring well into the seasoned white sauce. Place mixture in baking dish, cover and bake until bubbly, approximately twenty-five to thirty minutes. Serve immediately. This spinach casserole doubles nicely as a hot hors d'oeuvre when served with garlic croutons.

Changes

_____

_____

Summer Squash Pecan Saute

45 Minutes   6 Servings

Comment:

This is a wonderful and quick stir-fried vegetable to have as a side dish when eating salad or pasta as an entree.

10 summer squash, diced
1/2 cup chopped pecans
1/4 pound butter
1/2 cup chopped onions
1/2 cup chopped celery
1/2 cup diced red bell pepper
1/4 cup diced garlic

1/4 cup diced smoked ham
1/4 cup diced tomato
salt and cayenne pepper to taste
1/4 cup seasoned Italian
    bread crumbs
1/4 cup grated Parmesan cheese

In a ten inch heavy bottom saute pan, melt butter over medium high heat. Saute pecans until golden brown and pecan flavor has spiced the butter. Using a slotted spoon, remove the pecans and set aside for later. Into the saute pan add diced summer squash, onions, celery, bell pepper, garlic and ham. Saute approximately five to ten minutes or until squash becomes tender. Add tomato and season to taste using salt and cayenne pepper. Continue cooking until tomato is heated thoroughly and squash is tender throughout. Remove from heat and stir in Italian bread crumbs, Parmesan cheese and pecans. Serve immediately. For additional color, you may consider dicing an array of garden vegetables available in your area. Add these to the saute pan at the same time as the squash and other vegetables.

Changes

_____

_____

_____

_____

White Squash with Shrimp

1 Hour   6 Servings

Comment:

The white squash is similar to the patty pan squash found throughout America. It is grown in abundance here in the Bayous, and is normally the only squash seen on the tables in South Louisiana.

5 medium size white squash	1/2 cup chopped red bell pepper
1 cup 150-200 count shrimp, peeled and deveined	1/4 cup diced garlic
	1/4 cup sliced green onions
1/4 pound butter	salt and cracked black pepper to taste
1 cup chopped onions	1/4 cup chopped parsley
1 cup chopped celery	1 cup seasoned Italian bread crumbs

Preheat oven to 375 degrees F. Peel squash and remove all seeds from the center. Dice squash and boil in lightly salted water until tender, approximately fifteen to twenty minutes. When tender, remove and cool under tap water. Set aside. In a ten inch heavy bottom saute pan, melt butter over medium high heat. Add onions, celery, bell pepper, garlic, green onions and shrimp. Saute approximately five to ten minutes or until vegetables are wilted and shrimp are pink. Add squash, stirring well into vegetable seasonings, and continue to cook approximately fifteen minutes longer. Remove from heat and season to taste using salt and cracked black pepper. Add parsley and sprinkle in seasoned Italian bread crumbs to absorb excess liquids. Place cooked squash in baking dish and top with remaining bread crumbs. Bake until golden brown.

Changes

_____

_____

_____

_____

Turnip Casserole

1 Hour   6 Servings

Comment:

Turnips are normally found stewed in the same fashion as potatoes with shrimp. From time to time we will create a turnip casserole and present it in the following manner:

**8-10 medium size turnips,
    peeled**
1-1/2 cups diced ham
1/2 cup crumbled bacon
1/4 pound butter
1 cup chopped onions
1/2 cup chopped celery
1/2 cup red bell pepper

1/4 cup diced garlic
1/4 cup sliced green onions
1/4 cup chopped parsley
**1/2 cup seasoned Italian
    bread crumbs**
**salt and cracked black pepper
    to taste**
1 cup grated cheddar cheese

Preheat oven to 375 degrees F. Cube turnips and boil in lightly salted water until tender. Do not overcook. Once tender, remove and cool under tap water. In a heavy bottom ten inch saute pan, melt butter over medium high heat. Add onions, celery, bell pepper, garlic, green onions, ham and bacon. Saute approximately five to ten minutes or until vegetables are wilted. Add cubed turnips and slowly saute until turnips are reheated and well incorporated into the seasoning mixture. Fold in parsley and sprinkle with seasoned Italian bread crumbs. Season to taste using salt and cracked black pepper. Place turnip mixture in a baking dish and top with grated cheddar cheese. Cover and bake on center oven rack until cheese is melted and casserole is bubbly.

Changes

_____

_____

_____

_____

Cajun Black Eyed Peas

1-1/2 Hours   6 Servings

Comment:

Black eyed peas may sometimes be referred to in the South as field peas. Whatever you may wish to call them is fine with me, but I suggest you try cooking them in the following fashion for a truly new experience.

1 pound dried black eyed peas
1 pound heavy smoked pork
  sausage
1/2 pound cubed smoked ham
1/2 cup Crisco or bacon
  drippings
1 cup chopped onions
1 cup chopped celery

1 cup chopped bell pepper
1/4 cup diced garlic
1 tsp dry basil
1 bay leaf
1 cup sliced green onions
1/2 cup chopped parsley
salt and cracked black pepper
  to taste

It is always best to presoak any hard-shell bean in cold water overnight before cooking. This will cut the cooking time by one third. Drain peas from soaking water and rinse in cold tap water. In a one gallon stock pot, melt Crisco or bacon drippings over medium high heat. Add onions, celery, bell pepper, garlic, basil, ham and smoked sausage. Saute approximately ten to fifteen minutes or until vegetables are wilted. Add bay leaf and peas. Add enough cold water to cover peas by two inches and bring to a low boil. Cook for thirty minutes, stirring occasionally. Reduce heat to simmer and continue cooking approximately forty-five minutes or until tender. Stir from time to time, as peas will settle to the bottom of the pot and tend to stick. Once tender mash about one third of the peas on the side of the pot using a metal cooking spoon. This will give the peas a creamy texture. Season to taste using salt and cracked black pepper. Add green onions and parsley and continue cooking until peas are tender and creamy.

Changes

Cajun Candied Yams

1 Hour   6 Servings

Comment:

Here is another of the true delicacies of Louisiana cooking given to us by the native Indians. Though originally sweetened with the natural sugars of wild persimmons and muscadines, today we substitute apples and red seedless grapes.

8 medium Louisiana yams	1/2 tsp nutmeg
1 red apple, sliced and cored	1 tbsp lemon juice
1 green apple, sliced and cored	1 ounce brandy
1 cup red seedless grapes	2 tbsps corn starch, dissolved
3 cups reserved yam liquid	in 1/2 cup cold water
1/2 cup brown sugar	1/2 cup chopped pecans
1/2 cup Louisiana cane syrup	marshmallows (optional)
1/2 tsp cinnamon	

Preheat oven to 375 degrees F. Peel yams and slice into one inch thick pieces. Boil yams in lightly salted water until tender, approximately thirty minutes. When tender, remove yams, set aside and reserve three cups of the boiling liquid. In a two quart sauce pan, bring yam liquid to a rolling boil. Add sugar, cane syrup, cinnamon, nutmeg, lemon juice and brandy. Cook approximately five minutes. Add sliced apples and red grapes and return to a low boil. Reduce heat to simmer, add dissolved corn starch and continue cooking as mixture thickens. Adjust sweetness to your liking by adding additional sugar or syrup. Place yams in baking dish and top with cooked syrup. Sprinkle with pecans and add marshmallows if desired. Bake until bubbly hot and marshmallows are melted. This is the traditional yam dish for a Louisiana Thanksgiving.

Changes

_____

_____

_____

_____

Poultry

Reba Meliet © 1989

Poultry

The popularity of chicken in Cajun and Creole recipes stems directly from the German, French and Spanish influence in the early 1700's. Chicken was one of the few animals that the early settlers were able to raise successfully and easily in the Bayous of South Louisiana. Therefore, it is easy to understand the proliferation of poultry recipes which exist today.

Chicken Sauce Piquante was given to us by the Spanish who made "sauce piquante" a household word. Baked Garlic Chicken was created by the Italians in the French Market of New Orleans. Chicken and Burgundy Wine undoubtedly had its roots in the French Coq au Vin. Chicken Maque Choux was a gift from the Indians living in the swamplands of Bayou country.

So as you can readily see, great poultry dishes, whether baked, broiled, braised or smothered, are served on the tables in South Louisiana in many unique ways. In most cases, these incredible poultry dishes can be found only in Cajun and Creole cooking.

"Poultry is to the cook what a canvas is to the painter."
Brillat-Savarin

RM 89

Chicken Stew Cabanocey

1 Hour   6 Servings

Comment:

The fricassee or stewed chicken has been the most popular poultry dish among the Cajuns and Creoles. The traditional chicken stew was always prepared on Sunday in our home and is still today a family favorite.

1 6 pound stewing hen	2 cups sliced mushrooms
1/2 cup vegetable oil	6 cups chicken stock (see recipe)
1/2 cup flour	6 fresh chicken livers
1 cup chopped onions	1 cup sliced green onions
1 cup chopped celery	1 cup chopped parsley
1 cup chopped bell pepper	salt and cracked black pepper
1/4 cup diced garlic	to taste

Cut stewing hen into serving pieces. Depending on the size, some of the larger cuts, such as the breasts, may be cut into two pieces. In a two gallon heavy bottom sauce pot, heat oil over medium high heat. Add flour and using a wire whisk, stir constantly until light brown Cajun roux is achieved. (see roux technique) Do not scorch. Should black specks appear, discard and begin again. When browned, add onions, celery, bell pepper, garlic and mushrooms. Saute approximately ten to fifteen minutes or until vegetables are wilted. Add hen pieces and saute in roux mixture for five to ten minutes. Slowly add chicken stock, one ladle at a time, stirring constantly until all is incorporated. Bring to a rolling boil, reduce to simmer and cook for one hour or until hen is tender. Add chicken stock if necessary to retain volume of liquid. Add chicken livers, green onions and parsley and season to taste using salt and cracked black pepper. Continue cooking an additional thirty minutes.

Changes

_____

_____

_____

_____

Chicken Sauce Piquante

1-1/2 Hours   6 Servings

Comment:

The sauce piquantes were brought to Louisiana by the Spanish in 1690. It was the innovative Cajuns, however, who made "sauce piquante" a household word. Today, any wild game or domestic meat may be found in a pot of sauce piquante.

1 5-pound stewing hen	1 cup diced tomatoes
1/2 cup oil	1/2 cup tomato sauce
1/2 cup flour	2 tbsps diced jalapenos
1 cup chopped onions	6 cups chicken stock (see recipe)
1 cup chopped celery	1 cup sliced mushrooms
1/2 cup chopped bell pepper	1 cup sliced green onions
1/4 cup diced garlic	1/2 cup chopped parsley
2 whole bay leaves	salt and cracked black pepper
1/2 tsp basil	to taste
1/2 tsp thyme	

Cut stewing hen into serving pieces. Depending on the size, some of the larger cuts, such as the breasts, may be cut into two pieces. In a two gallon sauce pot, heat oil over medium high heat. Add flour and using a wire whisk, stir constantly until light brown Cajun roux is achieved. (see roux technique) Do not scorch. Should black specks appear, discard and begin again. When brown, add onions, celery, bell pepper, garlic, bay leaves, basil and thyme. Saute approximately five to ten minutes or until vegetables are wilted. Add tomatoes, tomato sauce and jalapenos and continue to cook an additional three to five minutes. Add hen pieces and blend well into seasoning mixture. Add chicken stock, one ladle at a time, stirring constantly until all is incorporated. Bring to a rolling boil, reduce to simmer and allow to cook for forty-five minutes. Add mushrooms, green onions and parsley and season to taste using salt and cracked black pepper. Continue cooking, stirring occasionally, until meat is tender and sauce piquante is thickened, approximately thirty minutes. In addition to white rice, the sauce piquante may also be served over spaghetti or any other pasta.

Changes

Smothered Chicken

1 Hour   6 Servings

Comment:

Here is another of the traditional South Louisiana chicken dishes. Unlike the more complex chicken stew, this dish was quicker to make and was cooked more often.

1 3-pound fryer chicken	**1 tbsp diced garlic**
1/2 cup flour	**2 cups chicken stock (see recipe)**
3/4 cup vegetable oil	**salt and cracked black pepper**
1/2 cup chopped onions	**to taste**
1/2 cup chopped celery	**1/2 cup sliced green onions**
1/4 cup chopped bell pepper	**1/4 cup chopped parsley**

Cut fryer into serving pieces and season well using salt and cracked black pepper. Dust chicken pieces in flour until lightly coated and set aside. In a one gallon dutch oven, heat oil over medium high heat. Saute chicken pieces, a few at a time, until golden brown on all sides. Remove pieces from dutch oven and continue frying until all pieces are done. Using the same oil, add onions, celery, bell pepper and garlic. Saute approximately three to five minutes or until vegetables are wilted. Return chicken pieces to dutch oven, placing them on top of the sauteed vegetables. Add one cup of chicken stock and reduce heat to simmer. Cover dutch oven and slowly cook chicken approximately forty-five minutes, stirring occasionally, and adding additional chicken stock as necessary. Season to taste using salt and cracked black pepper and add green onions and parsley. Continue to cook for an additional five minutes or until chicken is totally tender. The smothered chicken may be served over jambalaya (see recipe) or as an entree.

Changes

_____

_____

_____

_____

Baked Garlic Chicken

1-1/2 Hours   6 Servings

Comment:

One of the largest settlements in the city of New Orleans is that of "Little Italy." The Italians operated the produce and truck farming industry in Louisiana and garlic chicken is a favorite in the market area of New Orleans.

2 young baking hens
salt and cracked black pepper to
   taste
16 cloves garlic

1/2 pound butter
1 small onion, quartered
1 celery stalk, halved
2 small carrots

Preheat oven to 350 degrees F. Season baking hens generously inside and out using salt and cracked black pepper. I suggest overseasoning the inside of the cavity since only a small amount of these spices will affect the taste of the hen. Place four cloves of garlic and one eighth pound of butter inside the cavity of each hen. Into each cavity add one half of the onions, celery and carrots. Place the two hens side by side in a deep roasting pan. Rub each breast with remaining butter, and place eight cloves of garlic in the bottom of the roasting pan. Cover and bake for one hour, basting occasionally. Once hens are tender, remove cover and allow to brown, approximately fifteen minutes.

Changes

_____

_____

_____

_____

Baked Chicken with Oysters

1-1/2 Hours   6 Servings

Comment:

Once again, we see the marriage of meat and seafood on the Louisiana table. Chicken seems to play a major part in keeping this marriage of two different food groups alive and well.

1 3-pound fryer
2 dozen fresh oysters, reserve
   liquid
1 cup flour
1/2 cup vegetable oil
2 cups chicken stock (see recipe)
1/2 cup butter
1/2 cup chopped onions
1/2 cup chopped celery

1/2 cup chopped red bell pepper
1/4 cup diced garlic
1/2 cup flour
2 cups chicken stock (see recipe)
1 cup heavy whipping cream
1/2 cup sliced mushrooms
1/2 cup sliced green onions
salt and cayenne pepper to taste

Preheat oven to 375 degrees F. Cut chicken into serving size pieces and season well using salt and pepper. Dust in flour until evenly coated. In a one gallon dutch oven, heat oil over medium high heat. Saute chicken well on all sides until golden brown. Add two cups of chicken stock, reduce heat to simmer and cook covered approximately thirty minutes. Remove chicken and keep warm. Remove juices from dutch oven and reserve for sauce. In the same dutch oven, melt butter over medium high heat. Add onions, celery, bell pepper and garlic. Saute approximately three to five minutes or until vegetables are wilted. Add flour and using a wire whisk, stir constantly until a white roux is achieved. (see roux technique) Do not brown. Add juices from chicken, chicken stock and heavy whipping cream, a little at a time, stirring constantly until all is incorporated. Bring to a low boil, reduce to simmer and add mushrooms, green onions, oysters and oyster liquid. Continue cooking until edges of oysters begin to curl. Season to taste using salt and cracked black pepper. Place chicken pieces in baking dish and top with oyster cream sauce. Bake thirty additional minutes and check for doneness. This dish is excellent when served over pasta.

Changes

_____

Chicken in Burgundy Wine

1-1/2 Hours   6 Servings

Comment:

A classical Creole dish of the city of New Orleans, this recipe undoubtedly has its roots in French Coq au Vin. The introduction of fresh vegetables and the trinity of Cajun seasonings makes this a true Louisiana dish.

1 3-pound fryer, cut into serving pieces	1 cup diced new potatoes
3/4 cup bacon drippings	2 cups small button mushrooms
1 cup flour	1 cup diced tomatoes
2 cups chopped onions	1 whole bay leaf
1 cup chopped celery	1/2 tsp dry thyme
1 cup chopped bell pepper	1/2 tsp dry basil
1/4 cup diced garlic	salt and cracked black pepper to taste
2 cups sliced carrots	3 cups burgundy wine

Preheat oven to 375 degrees F. In a heavy bottom dutch oven, melt bacon drippings over medium high heat. Season chicken well using salt and cracked black pepper and dust lightly in flour. Saute chicken pieces, a few at a time, until all are golden brown. Remove and keep warm. Place all remaining ingredients, except burgundy wine, in dutch oven. Stir fry five to ten minutes until vegetables are wilted. Return chicken to dutch oven and place on top of sauteed vegetables. Add burgundy wine and season to taste with salt and black pepper. Cover and bake for forty-five minutes, stirring occasionally. Add a small amount of chicken stock, should ingredients become too dry during cooking. This dish may be served with cooked white rice but is also excellent on fettuccine noodles.

Changes

Cajun Chicken Cordon Bleu

1 Hour   6 Servings

Comment:

Here, we have taken a traditional French dish and given it a South Louisiana twist. Stuffing the breast with tasso not only spices it just a little, but also gives the guest a pleasant surprise when biting into his entree.

6 boneless breasts of chicken
6 slices hot pepper cheese
12 thin slices smoked tasso
1 cup flour
1/4 pound butter
1 cup chopped onions
1/2 cup chopped celery
1/2 cup chopped bell pepper

1/4 cup diced garlic
1 cup sliced mushrooms
12 tiny pearl onions
1/4 cup sliced green onions
1 cup chicken stock (see recipe)
1 cup dry white wine
salt and cracked black pepper
   to taste

Pound chicken breasts lightly to flatten and tenderize. Place one piece of pepper cheese in the center of each breast and top with tasso. Roll breasts into a turban shape and secure with toothpicks. Season lightly using salt and cracked black pepper. Dust generously in flour, shaking off all excess. Set aside. In a ten inch heavy bottom saute pan, melt butter over medium high heat. Saute chicken breasts slowly on all sides until golden brown. Remove breasts and keep warm. Into the same saute pan add onions, celery, bell pepper, garlic, mushrooms, pearl onions and green onions. Quickly stir fry until vegetables are wilted, approximately five to ten minutes. Return chicken breasts to saute pan and pour in chicken stock and white wine. Bring to a low boil, reduce heat to simmer, cover and cook chicken breasts about thirty minutes. Season to taste using salt and pepper. Serve each breast with generous serving of sauteed vegetables and sauce.

Changes

_____

_____

_____

Chicken and Yams Point Houmas

1-1/2 Hours   6 Servings

Comment:

Once again, we see the use of Louisiana yams as a main ingredient in the recipe. While the Indians used yams mainly as a full course entree, the Cajuns and Creoles adapted the yams into many innovative dishes. Here is one such dish.

1 3-pound fryer	1/4 cup Creole mustard
4 large yams	1/2 cup Louisiana sugar cane syrup
1 sliced sweet Vidalia onion	1 cup chicken stock
1/4 cup pecan halves	1 cup orange juice
1/2 pound melted butter	salt and cracked black pepper to taste

Preheat oven to 375 degrees F. Cut fryer into serving pieces, season with salt and pepper and set aside. Peel yams and slice into one quarter inch slices. Rinse under cold water and arrange yams and onions across the bottom of a four quart baking dish. Season lightly with salt and pepper. Place chicken pieces on top of yams and sprinkle with pecan halves. In a small saute pan, heat butter over medium high heat. Add mustard, cane syrup, chicken stock and orange juice, bring to a light boil and season with cracked black pepper. Generously spoon sauce over chicken and potatoes. Cover baking dish, place in oven and bake approximately one hour. Remove cover and bake an additional fifteen minutes or until chicken is brown and tender.

HINT: You may wish to par boil the yams slightly and use a smaller bird such as cornish hen, which will cook a little quicker. By the way, Point Houmas was the home camp of the Houmas Indians and is located ten miles East of Donaldsonville, Louisiana.

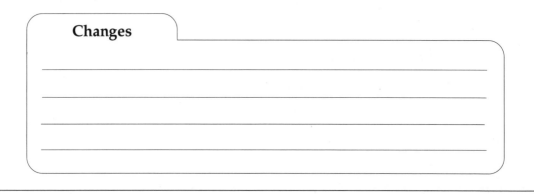

Changes

_____

_____

_____

_____

Chicken Provencal

1-1/2 Hours   6 Servings

Comment:

The Provencal style comes from the southern part of France bordering the Mediterranean Sea. However, dishes reflecting the flavor of Provence often find their roots in the northern part of Spain. This is one such dish.

1 3-pound fryer	1 cup sliced mushrooms
1 cup flour	2 cups tomato sauce
3/4 cup olive oil	1 cup chicken stock (see recipe)
1 cup chopped onions	pinch of dry basil
1 cup chopped celery	pinch of dry thyme
1/2 cup chopped bell pepper	1 whole bay leaf
1/4 cup diced garlic	salt, cracked black pepper and
1/4 cup chopped green onions	cayenne pepper to taste
1/2 cup sliced black olives	2 ounces burgundy wine
1/2 cup sliced green olives	

Cut chicken into serving pieces and season lightly using salt and cracked black pepper. Dust lightly in flour and set aside. In a heavy bottom dutch oven, heat olive oil over medium high heat. Saute chicken on all sides, a few pieces at a time, until golden brown. Remove chicken from pot and keep warm. In the same oil saute onions, celery, bell pepper, garlic, green onions, black olives, green olives and mushrooms. Stir fry quickly until vegetables are wilted. Add tomato sauce and chicken stock, bring to a low boil and reduce heat to simmer. Season sauce with basil, thyme and whole bay leaf. Return chicken to Provencal sauce, mix well and cover. Slow simmer until chicken is tender, approximately forty-five minutes. Season to taste using salt and cayenne pepper and finish with burgundy wine.

Changes

_____

_____

_____

_____

Chicken Bayou Lafourche

1 Hour   6 Servings

Comment:

This recipe works especially well as a cocktail party appetizer. You may try breading the stuffed breast in flour and deep frying. Once cooked, slice into one fourth inch slices and serve with your favorite sauce.

FOR STUFFING:
6 boneless chicken breasts
1/2 pound chopped crawfish
  tails
1/4 cup finely diced onions
1/4 cup finely diced celery
1/4 cup finely diced red bell
  pepper

1 tsp finely diced garlic
1/4 cup finely chopped green onions
1/2 tsp Pernod or Herbsaint
1 tbsp sherry
1/2 cup Bechamel Sauce (see recipe)
salt and cracked black pepper
  to taste
1/2 cup flour

Pound chicken breasts lightly to flatten and season with salt and cracked black pepper. In a one quart mixing bowl combine all remaining ingredients except flour. Blend well to incorporate all seasonings and adjust if necessary. Place an equal amount of the stuffing in the center of each breast, roll into a turban shape and secure with toothpicks. Dust lightly in flour and set aside.

(Continued)

Changes

_____

_____

_____

_____

Terrine of Smoked Catfish

Stuffed Shrimp Viala

Crawfish Bisque

Chicken Bayou Lafourche

Cajun Stuffed Rack of Lamb

Catfish in Oyster Andouille Butter

Stuffed Leg of Rabbit

Dessert table: Foreground, Caramel Custard, far right, Bread Pudding, far left, Cajun Fig and Pecan Pie.

Poultry

(*Chicken Bayou Lafourche* continued)

FOR SAUCE:

3/4 cup butter
1/2 cup chopped onions
1/2 cup chopped celery
1/4 cup chopped red bell pepper
1/4 cup diced garlic
1/4 cup sliced green onions
1/2 pound crawfish tails

1/2 cup sliced mushrooms
1 ounce dry white wine
1/2 cup flour
3 cups shellfish stock (see recipe)
1/2 cup heavy whipping cream
salt and Louisiana Gold
    Pepper Sauce

In a one quart heavy bottom sauce pan, melt butter over medium high heat. Saute chicken on all sides until golden brown. Adjust heat if necessary to keep from burning butter. When browned, remove and keep warm. In the same butter saute onions, celery, bell pepper, garlic and green onions, approximately three to five minutes or until vegetables are wilted. Add crawfish and mushrooms and continue to saute for an additional three minutes. Deglaze with white wine. Add flour and using a wire whip, stir constantly until white roux is achieved. (see roux technique) Add shellfish stock and heavy whipping cream, a little at a time, stirring constantly until all is incorporated. Bring to a low boil, reduce to simmer and cook three minutes, stirring constantly. Season to taste using salt and Louisiana Gold. Return chicken breasts to sauce, turning occasionally. Cook until done, approximately ten to fifteen minutes. Adjust seasonings if necessary. A small amount of shellfish stock or whipping cream may be added should sauce become too thick.

Changes

Chicken Maque Choux

1 Hour   6 Servings

Comment:

This is just one more attempt by the Cajuns to create a dish using two ingredients available most of the year. Maque Choux has been seen as a soup, vegetable and now as an entree. This proves that when we like a flavor, we create a dish.

1 3-pound fryer	2 cups chopped tomato
8 ears young tender corn	2 tbsps tomato sauce
1 cup flour	1 cup sliced mushrooms
3/4 cup vegetable oil	2 cups chicken stock (see recipe)
1 cup chopped onions	salt and cracked black pepper
1 cup chopped celery	to taste
1/2 cup chopped red bell pepper	dash of Louisiana Gold
1/4 cup diced garlic	Pepper Sauce
1/4 cup sliced green onions	

Cut chicken into serving size pieces. Season well with salt and cracked black pepper. Dust pieces in flour on all sides until well coated. In a heavy bottom dutch oven, heat oil over medium high heat. Saute chicken and brown well on all sides. When browned, remove from pot and keep warm. In the same oil add corn, onions, celery, bell pepper, garlic, green onions and tomatoes. Saute three to five minutes or until vegetables are wilted. Add tomato sauce and mushrooms, return chicken to the pot and stir well into the vegetables. Add chicken stock, cover, reduce heat to simmer and cook until chicken is tender, approximately forty-five minutes. Season to taste using salt, cracked black pepper and a dash of Louisiana Gold Pepper Sauce.

Changes

_____

_____

_____

_____

Chicken Creole Style

1 Hour   6 Servings

Comment:

This recipe is in some ways similar in flavor to the sauce piquante. The difference, however, is that almost every culture in early New Orleans seems to have added their own flavor to this recipe.

1 5-pound stewing hen
1/2 cup vegetable oil
1/2 cup flour
2 cups chopped onions
1 cup chopped celery
1/2 cup chopped bell pepper
1/4 cup diced garlic
1 dozen button mushrooms
2 cups diced tomatoes
1 tbsp finely diced jalapenos
1/2 cup tomato paste

1 tsp crushed oregano
1/2 tsp dry thyme
pinch of marjoram
1/2 tsp basil
1 cup dry red wine
4 cups chicken stock (see recipe)
salt and cracked black pepper
  to taste
dash of Louisiana Gold
  Pepper Sauce

Cut hen into serving size pieces. Some of the larger pieces, such as the breasts, may be cut into two pieces. In a two gallon dutch oven, heat oil over medium high heat. Add flour and using a wire whisk, stir constantly until golden brown roux is achieved. (see roux technique) When browned add onions, celery, bell pepper, garlic, mushrooms, tomatoes and jalapenos. Saute approximately five to ten minutes or until vegetables are wilted. Add chicken and blend well into vegetable mixture. Continue cooking an additional three minutes. Add tomato paste, oregano, thyme, marjoram and basil and blend well into roux mixture. Add wine and chicken stock, a little at a time, stirring constantly until all is incorporated. Bring to a low boil and reduce to simmer. Allow to cook, stirring occasionally, approximately one hour. Add small amounts of chicken stock should the mixture become too thick. Season to taste using salt, pepper and Louisiana Gold. Continue cooking until chicken is tender. This dish may be served over white rice or as a side dish with jambalaya.

Changes

_____

Breast of Chicken Orleans

1 Hour   6 Servings

Comment:

It is easy to notice in this recipe, that chicken in Louisiana is removing itself from the sauce piquantes and brown roux type dishes. Here is a more classical presentation using all of the same ingredients seen in the older dishes.

FOR MARINADE:

6 boneless chicken breasts
1/4 cup olive oil
1/4 cup red wine vinegar
1 small onion, cubed
1 stalk of celery, cubed

1 small carrot, cubed
1/2 tsp dry thyme
1/2 tsp dry basil
1/2 tsp cracked black pepper

Mix all marinade ingredients together in a one quart ceramic mixing bowl. Once well blended, add chicken breasts and coat well with marinade. Allow to sit in marinade at room temperature for thirty minutes.

(Continued)

Changes

_____

_____

_____

_____

Poultry

(*Breast of Chicken Orleans* continued)

FOR SAUCE:

1/2 cup butter
1/2 cup diced onions
1/2 cup diced celery
1/4 cup diced red bell pepper
1/4 cup diced garlic
1/4 cup sliced mushrooms

1 cup crawfish tails or
   small shrimp
1/2 cup flour
1 ounce sherry
2 cups chicken stock (see recipe)
1 cup heavy whipping cream
salt and white pepper to taste

In a two quart heavy bottom sauce pot, melt butter over medium high heat. Saute chicken breasts three minutes on each side. Remove and keep warm. In the same butter add onions, celery, bell pepper, garlic and mushrooms. Saute approximately three to five minutes or until vegetables are wilted. Add crawfish tails and sprinkle with flour. Using a wire whip, stir constantly until light roux is achieved. (see roux technique) Add sherry, chicken stock and heavy whipping cream. Bring to a low boil, reduce heat to simmer and cook five minutes, stirring constantly. Return chicken breasts to sauce and season to taste using salt and pepper. Allow to cook ten to fifteen minutes or until chicken is done. Add small amounts of chicken stock should sauce become too thick.

Changes

_____

_____

_____

_____

Chicken Paella

1 Hour   6 Servings

Comment:

The one dish that influenced Louisiana cooking more than any other is Paella. Not only was it the forefather of our present day jambalaya, it was also the hearty dish that kept many Cajun and Creole families alive during lean times.

1 3-pound fryer
1/2 cup olive oil
1/2 cup diced onions
1/2 cup diced celery
1/2 cup diced red bell pepper
1/2 cup diced green onions
1/4 cup diced garlic
1/2 cup sliced mushrooms
1/2 cup diced ham
1/2 pound sliced andouille
   sausage

1 cup cooked black eyed peas
1 cup diced tomatoes
3 cups long grain rice (Uncle Ben's)
4 cups chicken stock (see recipe)
1 tsp dry thyme
1 tsp dry basil
salt and cracked black pepper
   to taste
dash of Louisiana Gold
   Pepper Sauce

Cut chicken into serving pieces and season well using salt, black pepper and Louisiana Gold. Set aside. In a four quart dutch oven, heat olive oil over medium high heat. Brown chicken well on all sides, a few pieces at a time, until all are done. Remove and keep warm. In the same oil add onions, celery, bell pepper, green onions, garlic, mushrooms, ham, andouille, black eyed peas and tomatoes. Saute approximately three to five minutes or until vegetables are wilted. Add rice and stir fry into the vegetables for three additional minutes. Add chicken stock, thyme and basil. Season to taste using salt, pepper and Louisiana Gold. Bring to a low boil and cook for three minutes, stirring occasionally. Add chicken, blend well into rice and vegetable mixture, and reduce heat to very low. Cover pot and allow rice to cook thirty to forty-five minutes, stirring at fifteen minute intervals.

Changes

_____

_____

Chicken and Andouille Pasta

30 Minutes   6 Servings

Comment:

This dish reflects the many cultures which contributed to the cooking of South Louisiana. Chicken came with the Spanish and Germans in the late 1600's, andouille with the French in the mid 1700's and pasta with the Italians in the 1800's.

5 boneless chicken breasts	1/2 cup sliced mushrooms
1 cup diced andouille	1/4 cup diced garlic
3/4 cup flour	pinch of dry thyme
1/2 cup olive oil	pinch of dry basil
1/4 cup diced onions	1 ounce dry white wine
1/4 cup diced celery	4 cups heavy whipping cream
1/4 cup diced red bell pepper	salt and cayenne pepper to taste
1/4 cup diced yellow bell pepper	1/4 cup chopped parsley
1/2 cup diced tomatoes	3 cups cooked rotini pasta

Cut chicken breasts into one inch cubes and season with salt and pepper. Dust lightly with flour and set aside. In a ten inch heavy bottom saute pan, heat olive oil over medium high heat. Saute chicken until lightly browned on all sides. Add andouille, onions, celery, bell peppers, tomatoes, mushrooms and garlic. Saute approximately three to five minutes or until vegetables are wilted. Add thyme and basil and deglaze with white wine. Add heavy whipping cream and bring to a low boil. Stirring occasionally, allow cream to reduce and thicken until approximately one half in volume. Season to taste using salt and pepper. Add parsley and cooked pasta. Blend well into sauce and serve immediately.

Changes

_____

_____

_____

_____

Smoked Chicken Louisianne

2 Hours   6 Servings

Comment:

Smoking was at one time the most common cooking technique used along the Bayous. Fish and wild game were smoked on a daily basis to ensure a good steady supply. Here, we incorporate the technique to produce a light lunch or dinner.

FOR MARINADE:

6 boneless breasts of chicken   1 tbsp Louisiana Gold Pepper Sauce
1 cup olive oil   1 tsp diced garlic
1/2 cup Louisiana cane syrup   1 tsp cracked black pepper
3 tbsp Worcestershire sauce   1 ounce dry red wine

Combine all marinade ingredients and using a wire whisk, stir to ensure that all seasonings are well blended. Add chicken breasts and cover with the marinade. Allow to sit at room temperature for thirty minutes.

FOR SMOKING:

Prepare home style smoker according to manufacturer's instructions. Have available chips of pecan wood and sugar cane if possible. In the water pan, place one quart of water and two cans of Barq's root beer. The root beer will give the chicken a taste that is certainly unique. Once smoker is ready, place water pan in position and add small amounts of pecan wood and sugar cane to hot coals. Place chicken breasts on middle smoker rack and cook according to directions. Check for doneness at one hour. The chicken breasts may be eaten warm on colored lettuces as an entree salad or sliced cold and served with sweet mustard as an appetizer.

Changes

_____

_____

_____

_____

Hot Chicken Salad Casserole

1 Hour   6 Servings

Comment:

This is another great idea for a light lunch dish. You may wish to try your own variation of this casserole for your next hors d'oeuvre party. Either way it is a different presentation of a very light chicken idea.

1 3-pound fryer
1/2 cup butter
1 cup finely diced onions
1-1/2 cups diced celery
1/4 cup diced red bell pepper
1/4 cup diced garlic
1/2 cup sliced green onions
1/2 cup flour
2 cups chicken stock (see recipe)

1 cup heavy whipping cream
salt and cayenne pepper to taste
2 cups chopped pecans
1 cup mayonnaise
1 tbsp lemon juice
6 chopped hard boiled eggs
1-1/2 cups seasoned Italian
    bread crumbs

Preheat oven to 350 degrees F. Using a sharp knife, totally debone fryer. This should give approximately four cups of chicken meat. In a two quart sauce pot, melt butter over medium high heat. Add onions, celery, bell pepper, garlic and green onions. Saute approximately three to five minutes or until vegetables are wilted. Add flour and using a wire whisk, stir constantly until white roux is achieved. (see roux technique) Add chicken stock and heavy whipping cream, stirring constantly until all is incorporated. Reduce heat to simmer and allow to cook ten to fifteen minutes. Add small amounts of chicken stock or cream should sauce become too thick. Season to taste using salt and cayenne pepper. In a four quart casserole dish, place chicken and top with pecans, mayonnaise, lemon juice and hard boiled eggs. Add white sauce and blend into chicken mixture until all is well incorporated. Top casserole with seasoned Italian bread crumbs and bake for approximately forty-five minutes.

Changes

_____

_____

_____

Cajun Baked Chicken

1-1/2 Hours   6 Servings

Comment:

I can remember vividly my grandmother hand cleaning young chickens to bake for a holiday table. Her recipe was simple but very seldom have I had that flavor duplicated. This recipe is the closest I have come to recreating that great memory.

2 2-1/2 pound fryers
salt to taste
cracked black pepper to taste
granulated garlic to taste
1/2 pound butter
2 small onions, halved

2 stalks celery, halved
2 small carrots
6 cloves garlic
paprika for color
2 cups chicken stock (see recipe)

Preheat oven to 350 degrees F. Wash chickens well inside and out. Generously season with salt, black pepper and granulated garlic. I suggest overseasoning the inside of the cavity, as only a portion of this seasoning will affect the meat. In the cavity of each chicken place one heaping tablespoon of butter, followed by one onion, one celery, one carrot and three cloves of garlic. Thoroughly coat the outside of each chicken with remaining butter and adjust seasonings. Sprinkle each chicken generously with paprika to ensure even color. Place the chicken in a roasting pan with one inch lip, and add chicken stock to the bottom of the pan. Cover chickens with a tent made of aluminum foil to protect the breasts from browning too quickly. Bake on center rack of oven, basting after thirty minutes of cooking. Continue basting every fifteen minutes for one and a half hours. Remove aluminum foil and allow breasts to brown evenly. Chicken will be cooked when leg quarters can be pulled away easily from the sides of the chicken. Simple but wonderful.

Changes

Oven Barbecued Chicken

1-1/2 Hours   6 Servings

Comment:

If done properly, no one will be able to tell the difference between pit barbecue and this recipe. This technique was originally given to me by an old chef who loved barbecue. When his health did not permit him to cook outdoors, this resulted.

2 2-1/2 pound fryers
1/2 cup melted butter
1/2 cup Worcestershire sauce
1/4 cup Louisiana Gold Pepper
    Sauce
1/4 cup liquid smoke
3/4 cup brown sugar

salt to taste
cracked black pepper to taste
granulated garlic to taste
chili powder to taste
2 cups cold water
1-1/2 cups barbecue sauce

Preheat oven to 350 degrees F. Cut chicken into serving pieces, rinse under cold water and set aside. In a large baking pan, with one inch lip, space chicken evenly, skin side up. Coat on all sides with the above ingredients except water and barbecue sauce. Once well coated on all sides, return to the skin side up position. Add water into the bottom of the baking pan and place on center rack of oven. Bake approximately one hour or until chicken is well browned. Using a one inch brush, coat chicken well with barbecue sauce and allow to cook an additional ten to fifteen minutes. Remove and serve.

Changes

_____

_____

_____

_____

Southern Fried Chicken

45 Minutes   6 Servings

Comment:

Though southern fried chicken is more indigenous to the Virginias and Carolinas, I would be remiss not to include a recipe for this infamous dish. I suggest making this a patio event with the family involved.

2 2-1/2 pound fryers	salt to taste
1 quart peanut oil	cracked black pepper to taste
2 cups milk	4 cups flour
1 cup water	3 cups heavy whipping cream
3 eggs	1/2 cup chicken stock

Cut chicken into serving pieces. Using the sharp end of a paring knife, stick the blade numerous times into the heavy parts of the chicken such as breasts and thighs. This will allow the hot oil to penetrate the meat and cooking time will be reduced. In a twelve inch black iron skillet, preheat oil over medium high heat. I have selected peanut oil because it has a much higher burning point and should be considered whenever frying is called for. Combine milk, water and eggs in a one quart mixing bowl. Whisk well using a wire whip until a nice smooth eggwash is achieved. Season to taste using salt and black pepper. In an 8-1/2 x 11" baking pan, season three and one half cups of flour with salt and black pepper. Dust chicken lightly in flour, dip in eggwash and return to the flour for a second coating. Shake off all excess flour. Fry larger pieces first, skin side down, turning occasionally, and allow to cook until clear juices flow from the meat. This should take approximately twenty to thirty minutes. Once cooked, remove to drain board or paper towels and keep warm. Continue until all pieces are done. Pour off all but one half cup of oil. Using a wire whisk, blend in remaining one half cup of flour, stirring constantly until light roux is achieved. Add heavy whipping cream and chicken stock and continue stirring until milk gravy is smooth and bubbly. Correct seasonings if necessary. Serve chicken with generous serving of milk gravy.

Changes

Cornish Hens Des Allemands

45 Minutes   6 Servings

Comment:

Most people don't realize that the Germans were among the first to settle South Louisiana. The original settlement was in present day St. Charles Parish, west of New Orleans. The following was a favorite dish of the Germans in Louisiana.

6 Cornish game hens
salt to taste
cracked black pepper to taste
granulated garlic to taste
6 tsps green peppercorns
6 tsps Worcestershire sauce

3 tsps Louisiana Gold Pepper Sauce
1/2 pound melted butter
1 tsp dry thyme
1 tsp dry basil
paprika
1 oz dry white wine
1/4 cup chopped parsley

Preheat oven to 350 degrees F. Split Cornish hens in two and remove back bone and wing tips. Season hens well on all sides using salt, pepper and granulated garlic. Using a sharp paring knife, cut small pockets in breasts and thighs of each hen. Insert green peppercorns in each pocket and place on baking sheet skin side up. Coat each bird well with Worcestershire, Louisiana Gold, melted butter, thyme, basil and paprika. Add additional salt and pepper if necessary. Pour excess butter and white wine in bottom of baking pan and place in oven. Bake for thirty minutes, basting occasionally with drippings. Hens will be cooked when legs separate easily from thighs. Remove from oven, place hens on serving platter and keep warm. Add chopped parsley to pan drippings, blend well into sauce and pour over Cornish hens.

Changes

_____

_____

_____

_____

Breast of Duck Lafitte

1-1/2 Hours   6 Servings

Comment:

Our family sugar plantation was called Cabanocey. The name came from a Houmas Indian word meaning, "Where Mallards Roost." It got the name from the mallard duck breeding area on our property. This dish originally used mallard ducks.

FOR MARINADE:

6 boneless breasts of duck	1 tsp dry basil
1/2 cup vegetable oil	1/2 tsp coriander
1/2 cup dry red wine	1 tsp black peppercorns
2 tbsps Louisiana cane syrup	1/2 cup diced onions
2 bay leaves	1/2 cup diced celery
1 tsp dry thyme	1/2 cup diced carrots

In a one quart ceramic mixing bowl combine all marinade ingredients. Using a wire whisk, stir well until all spices are incorporated. Add duck breasts, cover with marinade and allow to sit at room temperature for one hour.

FOR SAUCE:

1/4 cup vegetable oil	1 tsp green peppercorns
1/4 cup sliced green onions	2 oz brandy
1/4 cup sliced mushrooms	2-1/2 cups heavy whipping cream
1 tsp diced garlic	salt and white pepper to taste

In a ten inch heavy bottom saute pan, heat oil over medium high heat. Remove duck breasts from marinade and reserve one half cup of the marinade for sauce. Place duck breasts in saute pan and cook three to four minutes on each side. Once all breasts are browned, remove from pan and keep warm. In same oil saute green onions, mushrooms, garlic and peppercorns. Cook until vegetables are wilted, about three minutes. Remove pan from open flame, add brandy and return to heat. Brandy will flame about two minutes when ignited. Add whipping cream and reserved marinade, bring to a low boil and allow cream to reduce by one half volume. Return breasts to sauce and adjust seasonings with salt and pepper. Cook in sauce about five to ten minutes and serve.

Changes

Baked Long Island Duck

2 Hours   6 Servings

Comment:

This is the best recipe available for baked Long Island Duck. Once you cook it this way, you will continue to cook duck over and over again. In fact, all chefs working at Lafitte's Landing must cook our duck in this fashion.

2 Long Island ducklings	**paprika for color**
salt to taste	**2 medium onions, halved**
cracked black pepper to taste	**2 medium carrots, halved**
granulated garlic to taste	**2 stalks celery, halved**

Preheat oven to 475 degrees F. Wash ducks inside and out with cold tap water. Remove necks, livers and gizzards from cavity and place in a roasting pan with a two inch lip. Season ducks well inside and out using all dry seasonings. I suggest over-seasoning the inside of the ducks, as only a small amount of this seasoning will affect the taste. Stuff the cavity of each duck with one half of all fresh vegetables and place ducks in roasting pan breast side up. Surround ducks with necks, liver and gizzards. Do not put water or butter in the pan because ducks will baste themselves during cooking. Cover pan tightly with aluminum foil and bake ducks for one and a half hours. Remove foil and bake uncovered for thirty minutes more. The secret here lies in covering the ducks. The steam created in the tightly covered pan creates a condition that not only tenderizes the ducks but ensures that all fat is cooked away from under the skin. When done, the ducks are perfectly tender and the skin is crisp to the touch. The ducks will be cooked when the legs separate easily from the body.

Changes

_____

_____

_____

_____

Roasted Turkey Cajun Style

2-1/2 Hours   6 Servings

Comment:

You may wish to cook capon in this fashion also. When cooked this way, the bird will remain moist and juicy. Try replacing a baked chicken with either of these two birds and I think you will cook turkey and capon more often.

1 8-10 pound turkey or capon	2 stalks celery, halved
salt to taste	6 laurel leaves
cracked black pepper to taste	4 apples, halved
granulated garlic to taste	4 Louisiana yams, halved
1/2 pound butter	paprika for color
2 medium onions, halved	2 strips raw bacon
2 medium carrots, halved	

Preheat oven to 475 degrees F. Remove neck, liver and gizzard from inside cavity of bird. Wash bird inside and out using cold tap water. It may be more convenient to use your sink as the place to season the bird. When using the sink, all drippings and running of water will simply go down the drain. Season the bird well inside and out using salt, cracked black pepper and granulated garlic. I suggest over-seasoning the inside cavity, as only a small amount of this seasoning will actually affect the final taste. If you prefer a particular spice common to your area, please feel free to use it at this time. Once well seasoned, place bird in large baking pan with a two inch lip. Place one fourth pound of butter inside cavity toward the neck of the bird. This butter will melt and baste the bird during cooking. Add onion, carrots and celery to inside cavity and push well into place. If cooking a turkey, return legs into flap of skin at rear of cavity, as this will hold them in place nicely. Using your finger tips, slide your hand between breast of bird and breast skin. Open a pocket all the way from the rear cavity to the neck.

(Continued)

Changes

_____

_____

Poultry

(*Roasted Turkey Cajun Style* continued)

Into this pocket, place the remaining fourth pound of butter, mashing it well into place. Position three of the laurel leaves in a decorative manner under the skin on each side of the breasts. Once the bird is cooked, these leaves will show beautifully from under the skin. Place apples and yams around bird in baking pan. Sprinkle breasts evenly with paprika and top with two bacon strips in a criss-cross pattern across the breasts. Cover pan tightly with aluminum foil and place in oven. Cook thirty minutes, turn temperature down to 425 degrees F. and cook one and one half hours. Since every bird as well as every oven is different, I suggest checking the bird for tenderness after one hour. You surely don't want to overcook your centerpiece. Remove foil and allow bird to brown evenly. Bird will be cooked when legs separate easily from body.

Changes

_____

_____

_____

_____

Deep Fried Turkey

Comment:

Yes, I was just as shocked the first time I heard of deep fried turkey. However, there are those in Louisiana who would cook it no other way. I have eaten it many times and must admit, it's hard to beat. So quit laughing and start frying.

1 15-pound turkey
5 gallons peanut oil
Louisiana Gold Pepper Sauce to taste
Worcestershire sauce to taste
salt to taste

black pepper to taste
cayenne pepper to taste
onion powder to taste
garlic powder to taste
celery salt to taste

There is a company here in Louisiana that produces a fried turkey seasoning blend and markets it under the trade name "Cajun Injector". I have found the spice blend in this injector to be very good. They have made the work of injecting spices into the breasts of the turkey quite easy. Ask your grocer for this device by name. In a ten gallon stock pot, heat oil over a propane burner outdoors. Using a candy thermometer, preheat oil to 325 degrees F. Season the turkey generously using all of the above spices. You must remember that the majority of the seasonings will simply be washed away from the bird so, please, over-season inside and out. Once the oil is hot, lower the turkey into the pot and cook for twenty-five minutes. Carefully turn the bird and cook an additional fifteen to twenty minutes. It is important that you watch the bird carefully during the last twenty minutes of cooking to prevent burning. Test for doneness with a meat thermometer. The outside of the bird will look slightly overcooked, however, it will be wonderfully moist inside.

HINT: Since so much oil is required to fry the turkey, I suggest waiting for a large family outing and using the same oil to fry fish, chicken or other items. When done, simply allow oil to cool and ladle clean oil from pot into one gallon containers.

Changes

Meats

SPECIAL: 7 STEAKS 69¢

L. Folse & Son
FRESH MEATS

PECANS

BEEF
PORK

Reba Meliet
© 1989

Meats

The Germans, who arrived in Louisiana in 1690, brought the first beef cattle to Cajun country. Until that time, cattle was not found anywhere around New Orleans. Due to the small amount of fresh beef available, the Cajun and Creole cooks were creatively spurred on. They created many interesting ways to make a small amount of beef go a long way. Attempts were also made to disguise the poor quality of cheaper grades of beef. What the early Cajun and Creole cooks came up with were well-seasoned, creative versions of meat that still abound today. From a simple pork chop to a savory steak, South Louisianians love to pile vegetables and spicy sauces on meat and then serve it over a bed of hot rice. Another method for using less desirable cuts and organ meats was to make a stew with brown roux and wild mushrooms that we know today as "debris".

Pork was plentiful and very popular in both the Creole and Cajun kitchens. The Cajuns used every bit of the pig in boudin, sausage, cracklings, hogs head cheese and andouille. Boudin, a Cajun delicacy, is a white sausage made with rice, ground pork, and vegetables. In one dish using boudin, the casing is over-cooked allowing it to break, creating a spicy rice stew. Andouille, the premier sausage of Cajun country, is made with lean pork and lots of garlic. It is smoked up to seven hours with pecan wood and sugar cane and is popular as both an appetizer and a seasoning for vegetables and soups.

Today, such meats as veal and lamb have taken their place in the repertoire of Louisiana meat recipes. We find such classical meat dishes as tournedos being Cajunized by topping them with crawfish, crabmeat or shrimp and a touch of Cajun butter. Rack of lamb stuffed with crawfish has caused many a gourmet to return to Lafitte's Landing Restaurant.

"I have no idea what's the fuss about cooking. If you throw a lamb chop into the oven, what's to keep the thing from getting done?"

Joan Crawford

The Boucherie

From birth until death, every event in the life of a Cajun and Creole revolves around food. Whether visiting with friends and family, celebrating the birth of a new born child or mourning the passing of a loved one, every event involves eating. It is easy to understand how the community butchering or "la boucherie de cochon", became the main social event of the fall and winter. The Acadians in bayou country were comprised of an extended family unit. To aid in the tremendous task of butchering and processing a pig or calf, this extended family gathered together along with other friends and family living in the area.

"La boucherie de compagnie" was a community society made up of twenty families in each area. On the coldest days of winter, the families of la boucherie would gather to preserve the valuable assets of a fattened hog or calf and make it possible for each family to enjoy a steady supply of fresh meat in those days prior to refrigeration. The boucherie was also a day of close fellowship and was usually culminated with a culinary feast and traditional music and dancing.

The anticipated event really began the evening before as the men and boys would gather in the barn yard. As the men sipped muscadine wine and chewed on a handful of salted "graton" or crackling, from a previous boucherie, they would plot the course of the next day's event. Everyone reported on his family's needs as the strategy of what would be prepared was planned. One would need smoked bacon, another would need andouille, while yet a third was short on tasso.

The boys would gather firewood in the early evening, stock piling the wood close to where the pots would stand. They worked quickly, knowing quite well that if they were slack in their duties tonight, they would miss the conversation of the men who would cook throughout the next day. This conversation was sprinkled with stories, jokes, vital cooking tips and laughter. This expectation would quicken their steps, for the pot still had to be set up.

The well-oiled, well-seasoned black iron pots were arranged in a neat row six inches off of the ground, standing on bricks saved from boucherie to boucherie. This height insured that the fire could breath and give sufficient heat to boil the many gallons of water needed for the boucherie. These black iron caldrons stood like sentrys in a row, lined up, at guard, awaiting the first light of day. The huge number forty pots were set in place and filled with water from the cistern. This boiling water would be used to scald the bristles from the hog and sterilize the meat.

Meats

It was difficult to go to sleep at 6:00 p.m. with the anticipation of the next day's event in mind. However, the men and boys knew they must sleep, for the work that faced them was extraordinarily intense and they needed a good night's rest. Grandmere would say, "fait do do, ma chere", as the little ones were tucked in for the night.

The pigs designated for butchering had been sectioned off two to three weeks earlier to dine on a feast of straight corn. This diet not only gave the meat a delicious flavor, but cleaned the entrails and made the task of cleaning the intestines for sausages more palatable. One important point to keep in mind was that there was no waste. Everything but the oink was needed, used and made into something tasty, nutritious and vital for the Cajuns.

The men began to arrive before dawn to light the fires and kill the hogs. The children slept as the mules were hitched and awaited that moment when a nudge and pat would hoist the hogs over the branch of an oak tree and onto the tables for cleaning. A hog could weigh as much as five hundred pounds and it was not uncommon to kill three or four at a time with as many as six being butchered in one day.

With twenty families working hand in hand, there could be as many as twenty men and women, forty boys and girls, forty grandparents and any number of willing friends. One hundred to one hundred fifty workers gathered for a boucherie was not uncommon. In a group of this size, there would be ten black families of the area, well versed in the art of the boucherie, who, because of their skill and experience, would share equally in the division of meats.

I am reminded of an occasion during my childhood concerning two black men who would help my grandfather at the boucheries each year. I would walk to the train depot each morning to sit next to Shank and Pelenk, two brothers, who would watch the train go by before starting the day's work. I would sit with a broom straw in my mouth, duplicating their posture, and listening to the stories they shared back and forth. One morning Pelenk said to his brother as the train went by, "One day, I'm going to buy this railroad." To which Shank replied, without a shift of expression, " No way...I'll never sell!" Imagine my surprise as I ran home with the exciting news of my friends' incredible possession, only to find out that my leg had been expertly pulled.

Meats

As the dull "thud" was heard from the single shot of the twenty-two caliber rifle used to kill the pig, the women would approach the dead animal and, with razor sharp knives, cut the jugular and catch the blood in number three wash tubs. Immediately, vinegar and salt would be added to prevent coagulation and the blood would be taken into the house. Clean white sheets covered these tubs, filled with the "sang de porc", and awaited the preparation of the boudin rouge. This Cajun blood sausage was made with cooked pork and rice and had been savored by the ancestors of the Acadians in the coastal regions of France. Today, these regions in the northern part of France are renowned for their boudin rouge.

The water in the number forty pots would be boiling at a fierce rate as it was poured over the pig. The skin would be scraped free of bristles and washed clean with the hot liquid. With this task completed, the hogs would be hung by their back legs as the mules hoisted them up for further cleaning.

The pigs would be slit from the tail to the jaw as women would gather entrails in washtubs and immediately separate the intestines from the "hook-up". The hook-up consisted of the kidneys, liver, heart, lungs and tongue and was referred to as such because it formed a uniform train, which remained in tact to await preparation of the "debris." This soul-satisfying dish included all of the above ingredients, slowly simmered in a rich brown gravy and seasoned with onions, celery, bell pepper, garlic and green onions. This dish, when served over rice, became the mainstay for the hard-working Acadian butchers. The ladies would split up into their usual teams. One such team would clean the intestines. They were cleaned by hand, thoroughly washed inside and out, scraped until clear and soaked in a solution of baking soda and iced water. These would become the receptacles for such delights as andouille, boudin and saucisse.

Another team would be busy for most of the day washing and chopping the onions, celery, bell pepper, garlic, green onions and parsley. These mountains of seasoning would be needed in many dishes before the day was done. Wash tubs, brimming with these vegetables, would be carried out to the men who manned the pots. The boucherie was a grand opportunity to catch up on local events and chat about family and friends. "The Blanchard girl is marrying that Landry boy. Do you think that is a good match?" The conversation between the ladies continued as they "passed a good time" preparing ingredients for the boucherie.

The head and feet were first cut from the animal and, after proper cleaning, would go into the number twenty-five pot for hours of simmering. Lean trimmings were added to the pot, from time to time, along with vegetable seasonings and spices. As the meat in the pot became tender and fell from the bones, the mixture was ready for the final step in making the hogs head cheese. The meat was removed from the pot, finely diced by the ladies and placed in the molds. The boiling liquid was reduced even further and seasoned with salt and cracked black pepper. Fresh green onions and parsley were then added and the final flavors adjusted. The seasoned liquid was then poured over the meat and refrigerated until jelled. Hogs head cheese is as much a delicacy in Cajun and Creole cuisine today as it was then. This delicious gelatinous loaf is served in the same fashion as a pate or terrine.

A one inch layer of fat and skin was then removed from the carcass of the pig. The fat was cut into one inch squares and placed into number twenty-five pots along with a few cups of cold water. As the water began to boil, the lard was rendered from the fat in the pot. The longer it cooked, the more brown the gratons or crackling became. When golden brown, the crackling was removed from the hot lard, squeezed of all excess grease and placed on sheets of newspaper to drain and cool. Once lightly salted, it was ready to be enjoyed as the favorite snack of bayou country. The lard was then placed in five gallon cans and allowed to cool. This lard was essential for all baking and frying done by the Cajuns and Creoles.

Armed with their "boudinieres", four inch cow horns used for stuffing, those skilled at charcuterie would make up the boudins and sausages. In order to preserve them, a string of the boudins and sausages would be placed in the five gallon cans of hot lard from the gratons. When the lard cooled, the sausages were sealed from the air, preserved, and thoroughly cooked.

Thin slices of lean meat were trimmed from the neck and backbone during butchering and cooked down with vegetables and wild Louisiana mushrooms. The grillades, as they were known, were allowed to simmer all day in a small black iron pot so that the cooks and butchers could have lunch at their disposal. Depending on their needs, tasso was smoked, hams were curred and meat was salted and put away. Fresh pork was cut into roast chops and ribs and divided equally among the assembly.

Meats

As the last of the projects was finished, the evening meal was prepared. The men cooked pork and andouille jambalaya and grillades. The women stirred large pots of white beans with smoked ham hocks. Small round meat patties, seasoned with salt, pepper, garlic, green onions and parsley, and wrapped in caul fat, were fried in a black iron skillet. These platines were served on top of the jambalaya. Of course, everyone had individual brown bags with salted gratons, with a little extra slice of meat left on the crackling just for this special night.

After dinner, the Cajuns would put away their knives and pick up squeeze boxes, fiddles, scrub boards and triangles to produce the distinctive sounds characteristic of Cajun music. Songs were sung in French and everyone danced to celebrate the success of the boucherie.

It was late in the evening when the weary butchers made their way home with a child in one arm and the bounty of the boucherie in the other. Tired from their work, they were full of stories and gossip but refreshed by the dancing and sounds of laughter which faded into the night.

Andouille Sausage

6 Hours   5 12-inch links

Comment:

Andouille is the Cajun smoked sausage so famous nationally today. Made with pork butt, shank and a small amount of pork fat, this sausage is seasoned with salt, cracked black pepper and garlic. The andouille is then slowly smoked over pecan wood and sugar cane. True andouille is stuffed into the beef middle casing which makes the sausage approximately one and a half inches in diameter. When smoked, it becomes very dark to almost black in color. It is not uncommon for the Cajuns to smoke andouille for seven to eight hours at approximately 175 degrees.

Traditionally, the andouilles from France were made from the large intestines and stomach of the pig, seasoned heavily and smoked. In parts of Germany, where some say andouille originated, the sausage was made with all remaining intestines and casings pulled through a larger casing, seasoned and smoked. It was served thinly sliced as an hors d'oeuvre.

It is interesting to note that the finest andouille in France comes from the Brittany and Normandy areas. It is believed that over half of the Acadian exiles who came to Louisiana in 1755 were originally from these coastal regions.

5 pounds pork butt
1/2 pound pork fat
1/2 cup chopped garlic
**1/4 cup cracked black
    peppercorns**

2 tbsps cayenne pepper
1 tbsp dry thyme
4 tbsps salt
**6 feet beef middle casing (see
    butcher or specialty shop)**

(Continued)

Changes

_____

_____

_____

_____

(*Andouille Sausage* continued)

Cube pork butt into one and a half inch cubes. Using a meat grinder with four one quarter inch holes in the grinding plate, grind pork and pork fat. If you do not have a grinding plate this size, I suggest hand cutting pork butt into one quarter inch square pieces. Place ground pork in large mixing bowl and blend in all remaining ingredients. Once well blended, stuff meat into casings in one foot links, using the sausage attachment on your meat grinder. Tie both ends of the sausage securely using a heavy gauge twine. In your homestyle smoker, smoke andouille at 175-200 degrees F for approximately four to five hours. The andouille may then be frozen and used for seasoning gumbos, white or red beans, pastas or grilling as an hors d'oeuvre.

Changes

_____

_____

_____

_____

Chaurice Sausage

1 Hour   9 12-inch links

Comment:

Chaurice is a spicy pork sausage used extensively in Creole cooking. One of the few sausages seasoned with fresh vegetables, it is seen time and time again in different presentations on the Creole table. It is related to the Spanish chorizos which is commonly used in paella, the forefather of our own jambalaya. We found chorizos was also commonly used to flavor garbanzo beans. Today in South Louisiana, chaurice is seen most often as a pan-fried side dish for white or red beans. Although much more common in Creole cooking, the chaurice is used from time to time by the Cajuns as well.

4 pounds pork butt
2 pounds pork fat
2 cups finely diced onions
1 cup finely diced celery
1/2 cup finely diced garlic
2 cups finely chopped green
     onions

1/2 cup finely chopped parsley
1 tbsp dry thyme
1/4 cup cracked black pepper
2 tbsps cayenne pepper
3 tbsps salt
12 feet pork or sheep casing

Cut pork butt into one and a half inch pieces. Using a meat grinder with a coarse chopping plate, grind pork and pork fat. In a large mixing bowl, combine all remaining ingredients. Blend well to ensure that all spices are evenly distributed throughout the sausage. Once ingredients are well blended, use the sausage attachment on your meat grinder to stuff into the casings. You should section the sausage at one foot intervals by twisting the casing as it fills. Tie off the sausage at each end using a heavy gauge twine. The sausage may then be frozen. To cook, place chaurice in a heavy bottom saute pan with approximately one fourth cup cold water. Bring to a low simmer and cover. Cook approximately thirty minutes adding water if necessary. Uncover pan and raise temperature to medium high. Continue cooking until sausage is well brown on all sides, approximately fifteen minutes.

Changes

Smoked Tasso

2-1/2 Hours   3 pounds

Comment:

Tasso is yet another example of the Cajun and Creole desire for unique flavor in a recipe. Tasso is a dried smoked product that is seasoned with cayenne pepper, garlic and salt and heavily smoked. The word tasso is believed to have come from the Spanish word "tasajo" which is dried, cured beef. Although this delicacy is often thinly sliced and eaten alone, it is primarily used as a pungent seasoning for vegetables, gumbos and soups.

Today in South Louisiana, tasso is becoming a popular seasoning for new and creative dishes. It has also gained wide acclaim as an hors d'oeuvre served with dipping sauces or fruit glazes.

At Lafitte's Landing Restaurant, we have incorporated tasso into our cream sauces and compound butters to create a new taste unheard of in classical cooking.

4 pounds pork butt
1/2 cup Worcestershire sauce
1 tbsp Louisiana Gold Pepper
 Sauce
1/2 cup granulated garlic

1/4 cup fresh cayenne pepper
1/4 cup cracked black pepper
1/4 cup salt
1/4 cup brown sugar

Cut pork butt into one half inch thick strips. Place on a baking pan and season with Worcestershire and Louisiana Gold sauces. Once liquids are well blended into meat, add all remaining ingredients. Mix well into meat to ensure that each piece is well coated with the seasoning mixture. Cover with clear wrap and refrigerate overnight. Using a home style smoker, and using briquettes flavored with pecan wood and sugar cane strips if possible, smoke tasso at 175-200 degrees F for two and a half hours. Once cooked, tasso may be frozen or used to season gumbos, vegetables, or a great pot of white or red beans.

Changes

_____

_____

_____

Boudin Blanc

3 Hours   8-10 pounds boudin

Comment:

Boudin blanc, the Cajun pork and rice sausage, is without a doubt the best known sausage in South Louisiana. Its less famous sister, boudin rouge, though made in the same fashion, is colored by the addition of pork blood into the dish and is considered a rare delicacy. The boudin blanc of Louisiana is quite different from the milk based boudin of France. The Louisiana version is much more spicy and normally includes rice as a main ingredient. Boudin rouge originated from the boudin noir or blood pudding of France and was particularly enjoyed around Christmas time. These well seasoned by-products of the boucherie are a delight to savour and well worth the extra effort. The boudins are normally served cold as a Cajun canopy, however, in our house it was best eaten hot as a breakfast item.

FOR STOCK:

1 large hog head, split and cleaned	4 stalks celery, halved
3 pig feet	12 heads garlic
5 pounds pork butt	12 sprigs parsley
1-1/2 pounds pork liver	1/2 cup black peppercorns
6 onions, quartered	4 gallons cold water

Place all of the above ingredients in a ten gallon stock pot. Bring to a rolling boil and cook until meat is tender, approximately two hours. Continue to add water as necessary to keep meat from sticking. Remove the liver from the pot after one and a half hours and cut into one inch pieces. Once pork butt is tender and the meat is falling from the head bones, remove all ingredients from the pot. Reserve all liquid. When meat is cool, pull from the bones and set aside for later.

(Continued)

Changes

_____

_____

(*Boudin Blanc* continued)

FOR SEASONINGS:

2 cups finely diced onions
2 cups finely diced celery
1 cup finely diced bell pepper
2 cups finely diced green onions
1/2 cup finely diced garlic

2 cups finely chopped parsley
7 cups cooked rice (see recipe)
salt and cracked black pepper to taste
1 hank of sausage casing

In a large mixing bowl, combine all seasoning ingredients with pork mixture except cooked rice and casing. Using a meat grinder with a fine cutting blade, grind all meats and vegetables. Use a small amount of reserved cooking liquid to keep ingredients moist. Mix white rice thoroughly with ground pork mixture and season to taste using salt and cracked black pepper. Once seasonings are evenly distributed throughout the meat, stuff into casings using the sausage attachment on your meat grinder. Boudin should be sectioned off in six to eight inch links. You may do so by twisting the casing as it is being filled. To cook boudin, simply poach in 190 degree F water. Do not allow water to boil. Cook approximately thirty minutes.

Changes

_____

_____

_____

_____

Cajun Stuffed Chaudin

1-1/2 Hours   6 Servings

Comment:

Just about every culture on earth has found some interesting method of stuffing the stomach of a butchered animal. Possibly none is more famous than the haggis of Scotland, but having eaten both haggis and chaudin, I'll take chaudin any day!

1 medium size chaudin
   (pork stomach)
2 quarts cold water
4 tbsps soda
1/2 cup vinegar
1/2 cup butter
1 cup chopped onions
1/2 cup chopped celery
1/4 cup diced red bell pepper
1/4 cup diced garlic
1/2 cup sliced mushrooms
1/2 cup ground andouille
   sausage
1/2 pound ground beef
3 pounds ground pork

1 cup seasoned Italian
   bread crumbs
2 eggs
1/2 cup chopped green onions
1/2 cup chopped parsley
salt and cracked black pepper
   to taste
1/2 cup vegetable oil
2 small sliced onions
1 cup diced celery
1/2 cup chopped bell pepper
1/4 cup diced garlic
2 cups diced carrots
2 cups sliced mushrooms
3 cups chicken stock
salt and cayenne pepper to taste

(Continued)

Changes

_____

_____

_____

_____

(*Cajun Stuffed Chaudin* continued)

Have your butcher clean one chaudin properly for you. Place chaudin in a large bowl with water, soda and vinegar. Allow to set for one hour. In a heavy bottom saute pan, heat butter over medium high heat. Add onions, celery, bell pepper, garlic, mushrooms and andouille and saute three to five minutes or until vegetables are wilted. Add ground beef and pork. Continue to cook until meat is well browned and separated, about forty-five minutes. Once browned, add bread crumbs, eggs, green onions and parsley. Cook an additional three minutes and season to taste using salt and cracked black pepper. Remove from heat and set aside. Remove chaudin from soda water and rinse under tap two or three times. Using a large metal spoon, stuff chaudin with ground meat dressing until completely full. Secure open ends with toothpicks and heavy gauge twine. In a heavy bottom dutch oven, heat oil over medium high heat. Saute onions, celery, bell pepper, garlic, carrots and mushrooms approximately two minutes or until vegetables are wilted. Add chaudin and brown well on all sides. Add chicken stock, bring to a low boil and reduce heat to simmer. Cover dutch oven and allow chaudin to cook approximately one hour turning occasionally. Season to taste using salt and cayenne pepper. Once cooked, slice into one half inch slices and serve with natural sauce.

Changes

_____

_____

_____

_____

Hogs Head Cheese

3 Hours   4 one pound trays

Comment:

Many cooks today feel that hogs head cheese is a county rendition of the more classical daube glace. Though similar in nature, I feel head cheese is the by product of sausage making such as boudin and has been around for hundreds of years.

FOR STOCK:

1 hog head, split and cleaned
4 pig feet, scraped and cleaned
4 pounds pork butt
3 cups finely diced onions
3 cups finely diced celery
2 cups finely diced bell pepper
1/2 cup finely diced garlic
2 whole bay leaves
1 tsp dry thyme

1/4 cup whole peppercorns
1/2 cup finely sliced green onions
1/2 cup finely diced parsley
1/2 cup finely diced red bell pepper
1/2 cup finely diced carrots
salt and cracked black pepper
    to taste
3 envelopes unflavored gelatin,
    dissolved

In a four gallon stock pot, place all of the above ingredients up to and including the whole peppercorns. Add enough water to cover the contents by three inches and bring to a rolling boil. Using a ladle, skim all foam and other impurities that rise to the surface during the first half hour of boiling. Continue to cook until meat is tender and pulling away from the bones, approximately two and one half hours. Remove all meat from stock pot and lay out on a flat baking pan to cool. Reserve ten cups of the cooking stock and return to a low boil. Add all remaining ingredients, except gelatin and salt and pepper, boil for three minutes and remove from heat. Season to taste using salt and cracked black pepper. Add dissolved gelatin and set aside. Once meat has cooled, remove all bones and finely chop in a food processor. Place equal amounts of the meat in four trays and ladle in hot seasoned stock. The mixture should be meaty with just enough stock to gel and hold the meat together. Cover with clear wrap and place in refrigerator to set overnight. Head cheese is best eaten as an appetizer with croutons or crackers.

Changes

Grillades

1 Hour   6 Servings

Comment:

The origin of grillades has been the subject of many arguments in Bayou country. It is believed that the dish originated when the country butchers preparing the boucherie sliced thin pieces of fresh pork and pan-fried these with sliced onions. The cooking took place, most feel, in black iron pots over the boucherie fires. The grillades were then eaten over grits or rice throughout the day. Today, grillades and grits are a tradition on many Sunday brunch menus. Most recipes call for veal round pounded lightly and smothered in its natural juices. One of the things I find most interesting about grillades is that it's one of those dishes that has a place on all rungs of the social ladder. Grillades may be eaten on the sharecroppers breakfast table or on the grand buffets of New Orleans.

2 medium size round steaks	1 cup diced tomatoes
1 cup flour	1 cup finely sliced green onions
1/4 cup Crisco or bacon drippings	1/4 cup diced garlic
	3 cups beef stock (see recipe)
1 cup finely diced onions	1 cup sliced mushrooms
1 cup finely diced celery	1/4 cup parsley
1/2 cup finely diced bell pepper	salt and cracked black pepper to taste

Cut round steak into three inch square cubes. Season to taste using salt and cracked black pepper. Dust pieces generously in flour and set aside. In a heavy bottom dutch oven, heat oil or bacon drippings over medium high heat. Saute round steak until brown on all sides. Add onions, celery, bell pepper, tomatoes, green onions and garlic. Saute until vegetables are wilted, approximately three to five minutes. Add beef stock, bring to a low boil and reduce heat to simmer. Cover dutch oven and allow grillades to cook slowly for approximately forty-five minutes. Stir occasionally to keep seasonings from scorching. Once tender, add mushrooms and parsley, adjust seasonings if necessary and cook ten additional minutes. Serve over grits as a breakfast item or over rice as an entree.

Changes

_____

Pork and Sausage Jambalaya

1 Hour   6 Servings

Comment:

Jambalaya has become the best known rice dish in America. The origin of this dish cannot be disputed. When the early Spanish settlers came to New Orleans, in the early 1700's, they brought with them the recipe for their famous paella. Since the ingredients for paella were not to be found in South Louisiana, their recipe was quickly adapted to the products at hand. Oysters and crawfish replaced clams and mussels in the recipe. Andouille took the place of ham and the new dish emerged from the paella pans of the Spanish. Since the main ingredient in the dish was rice, the dish was named "Jambon a la yaya". Yaya is the African word for rice and there is no argument that the "black hand in the pot" had a tremendous influence on our jambalaya. Today, the dish is made with many variations and with whatever is available. The most popular combination, however, is pork, chicken and andouille.

2 pounds cubed pork
1 pound sliced andouille
1/4 cup Crisco or bacon
   drippings
2 cups chopped onions
2 cups chopped celery
1 cup chopped bell pepper
1/4 cup diced garlic
7 cups beef or chicken stock
   (see recipe)

2 cups sliced mushrooms
1 cup sliced green onions
1/2 cup chopped parsley
salt and cayenne pepper to taste
dash of Louisiana Gold
   Pepper Sauce
4 cups Uncle Ben's
   Long Grain Rice

(Continued)

Changes

_____
_____
_____
_____

(Pork and Sausage Jambalaya continued)

In a two gallon dutch oven, heat Crisco or bacon drippings over medium high heat. Saute cubed pork until dark brown on all sides and some pieces are sticking to the bottom of the pot, approximately thirty minutes. This is very important as the brown color of jambalaya is derived from the color of the meat. Add andouille and stir fry an additional ten to fifteen minutes. Tilt the pot to one side and ladle out all oil, except for one large cooking spoon. Add onions, celery, bell pepper and garlic. Continue cooking until all vegetables are well caramelized, however, be very careful as vegetables will tend to scorch since the pot is so hot. Add beef stock, bring to a rolling boil and reduce heat to simmer. Cook all ingredients in stock approximately fifteen minutes for flavors to develop. Add mushrooms, green onions and parsley. Season to taste using salt, cayenne pepper and Louisiana Gold. I suggest that you slightly over-season since the rice tends to require a little extra seasoning. Add rice, reduce heat to very low and allow to cook thirty to forty-five minutes, stirring at fifteen minute intervals.

Changes

_____

_____

_____

_____

Meats

The Cochon de Lait

The Cochon de lait is described as the art of cooking a pig before an open hardwood fire. Although the origin of this social event in Louisiana is obscure, it is known that the custom began at least a century ago and that the cochon de lait was popular throughout Cajun country. The people of St. James Parish were known for their knowledge of the art of cochon de lait. The Germans, having settled in St. James Parish in 1690, brought with them the pigs and skilled butchers. The Germans could have introduced this art here in Cajun country, however, local legend gives a different account. History tells us that the traditional preparation of cochon de lait, French for suckling pig, came to South Louisiana in the early 1800's with veterans of Napoleon's army who settled in and about the region. Local historians contend that the legend may be correct, since feasting on roasted suckling pigs was a great tradition in Europe.

Years ago, church fairs in South Louisiana specialized in what was called "cochon a la broche" or spit roasted pig. Though the preparation was generally the same, a much larger pig was used in spit roasting. The cochon de lait uses a pig thirty pounds or less which is normally cooked as a table centerpiece for holiday family gatherings. Many homes cooked the pig hanging from a fireplace in the kitchen, but most roasted the pig outdoors over a pecan wood and sugar cane fire.

Since that time, the practice has undergone many changes but remains basically the same today. Much larger pigs are being cooked to feed groups of people, with pigs up to 200 pounds regarded as excellent for open-fire cooking. The town of Mansura, Louisiana, in Avoyelles Parish, which was first settled by some of Napoleon's soldiers and so named because the area reminded them of Mansura, Egypt, one of their campaign grounds, holds a cochon de lait festival each year. Mansura has been designated by the Louisiana legislature as "La Capital du Cochon de Lait."

Meats

When cooking the suckling pig over an open fire, I normally season the pig well inside and out with salt, cracked black pepper, granulated garlic and brown sugar. Using a meat saw, I cut through the backbone at the neck and tail and lay the pig open, flat. I then wrap the pig in a wire mesh and secure it with wire to hold it in proper form during the long cooking process. The pig is then slowly rotated in front of the hardwood fire, which is built three to four feet away from the pig. The fire, constantly maintained, cooks the pig in four to six hours. Normally, I use the ratio of one hour for every five pounds of weight, although not all pigs will cook at the same rate. After each hour of cooking, I flip the pig head side down, to ensure even cooking overall. The cochon de lait is indeed a Louisiana tradition and one of the main social events of the Cajuns and Creoles. In fact, I do so much cochon de lait cooking that I have constructed my "cochon de lait factory", an open pit oven holding 18 thirty pound pigs for cooking at one time.

Cajun Cochon de Lait (Oven Style)

Select a suckling pig approximately five to six weeks old. This pig should weigh about 15 to 20 pounds. Have your butcher clean the pig thoroughly, removing all entrails, tongue, eyes, etc. Season the pig inside and out well using salt, cracked black pepper, granulated garlic, thyme, basil and sage. Over-season the outside of the pig. Due to thickness of the skin, only a portion of this seasoning will affect the taste. Wrap the pig in aluminum foil and place in the refrigerator overnight. Remove pig from refrigerator and stuff with pecan rice dressing. (see recipe) Do not over-stuff, as stuffing will expand slightly during cooking. Using four inch skewers, truss belly cavity, tying securely with butcher's twine. Turn the pig over and place the front feet under its head and the back feet under its belly. Using a very sharp paring knife, cut slits diagonally at two inch intervals in the skin from head to tail. Make these cuts approximately 1/8 inch deep. Make one incision from the back of the neck to the top of the tail along the backbone. These cuts will enhance cooking and carving and will allow the fat to escape and baste the pig during cooking. Place the large end of a carrot or a small block of wood in the pig's mouth to keep it open during cooking. This will permit garnishing later. Place the pig feet down in a roasting pan and brush lightly with butter. Wrap ears, nose and tail in aluminum foil to prevent burning. Place four large quartered onions, three whole garlics sliced in half (peelings need not be removed), one bunch of celery and six halved apples in bottom of the roasting pan. Cover pan tightly with aluminum foil. Place the pig in a preheated 350 degree oven, basting every thirty to forty-five minutes with natural drippings. Cook approximately twelve to fifteen minutes per pound. When internal temperature reaches 150 degrees F. and the skin is brown and crisp, the cochon de lait is ready for serving. Remove the aluminum foil and allow the pig to brown completely. Place the pig on a large carving board and reserve all pan juices. Take roasting pan with reserved juices, tilt and skim off excess fat. Place pan on stove top on high heat and bring juices to a boil. Deglaze with two cups of red wine and add one quart of demi-glace. (see recipe) Scrape bottom of pan well and reduce to four cups. Season to taste using salt and cracked black pepper and serve in a gravy boat. Place suckling pig on a large silver tray or serving platter and garnish with oven browned potatoes and carrots. For additional color, you may wish to add a few bunches of whole parsley, tomatoes and orange slices. Place a cherry in each eye and an apple in the mouth. To carve, remove rear ham and front legs first. Slice all meat from these pieces. Insert carving knife in slit along the backbone, remove loins and slice accordingly. Serves 10.

Meats

Smothered Pork Chops with Oyster Mushrooms

1 Hour   6 Servings

Comment:

Oyster mushrooms are found growing wild all over South Louisiana. Today, they may be purchased from any specialty food shop. As a young boy growing up in Cajun country, we had oyster mushrooms deep fried in corn meal as a real special treat.

12 thinly cut pork chops	1/2 pound oyster mushrooms
1 cup flour	3 cups beef or chicken stock
1/2 cup Crisco or bacon	(see recipe)
drippings	1 bay leaf
2 cups chopped onions	1/2 tsp dry thyme
2 cups chopped celery	1/2 tsp dry basil
1 cup chopped bell pepper	1/2 cup chopped green onions
1/4 cup chopped garlic	1/2 cup chopped parsley
1 cup diced tomatoes	salt and cracked black pepper to taste

Season pork chops well using salt and cracked black pepper. Dust generously in flour and set aside. In a heavy bottom dutch oven, heat oil or bacon drippings over medium high heat. Saute pork chops until golden brown on all sides. Once browned, remove and keep warm. In the same oil, saute onions, celery, bell pepper, garlic, tomatoes and mushrooms. Cook until vegetables are wilted, approximately three to five minutes. Add beef stock, bay leaf, thyme and basil. Bring to a low boil, reduce to simmer and cook three to five minutes. Add green onions and pork chops. Cover dutch oven and allow pork chops to cook approximately thirty minutes. Season to taste using salt and cracked black pepper. Add parsley and continue cooking until pork chops are completely tender.

Changes

Smothered Pork with Turnips

1 Hour   6 Servings

Comment:

During the winter season, turnips were plentiful and the boucheries were being performed all along the River Road. It is no wonder that these two ingredients came together in the black iron pot to become a common dish on the Cajun table.

2-1/2 pounds cubed pork
4 turnips, peeled and diced
1/2 cup vegetable oil
1/2 cup flour
1 cup chopped onions
1 cup chopped celery

1/2 cup chopped bell pepper
1/4 cup diced garlic
4 cups beef or chicken stock (see recipe)
1 cup chopped green onions
1/2 cup chopped parsley
salt and cracked black pepper to taste

In a heavy bottom dutch oven, heat oil over medium high heat. Add flour and using a wire whisk, stir constantly until light Cajun roux is achieved. (see section on roux technique) Add cubed pork and stir fry well into roux. Add onions, celery, bell pepper and garlic. Continue cooking until vegetables are wilted, approximately three to five minutes. Add turnips and blend well into roux mixture. Add beef stock, a little at a time, stirring constantly into roux. Bring to a low boil, reduce to simmer and cook forty-five minutes. Add green onions and parsley. Season to taste using salt and cracked black pepper. Continue to cook until pork is tender.

Changes

Medallions of Pork in Fig Glaze

1 Hour   6 Servings

Comment:

In the evolution process, it seems quite natural that we Cajuns continue to combine ingredients at hand. Sauteing pork medallions and flavoring the sauce with Louisiana figs could not be more natural.

12 3-ounce medallions of pork
1/2 cup fig preserves
1/4 cup vegetable oil
1 cup flour
1/2 cup sliced green onions
1/2 cup sliced mushrooms

1 tbsp diced garlic
1 ounce port wine
2 cups demi-glace (see recipe)
1 tbsp chopped parsley
salt and cayenne pepper to taste

In a ten inch saute pan, heat oil over medium high heat. Season pork to taste using salt and cayenne pepper. Dust lightly in flour and saute until medium rare and brown on both sides. Once browned, add green onions, mushrooms and garlic. Saute until vegetables are wilted, approximately one to two minutes. Deglaze with port wine and add fig preserves and demi-glace. Continue cooking until sauce is slightly thickened and meat is cooked to your liking. Add parsley and season to taste using salt and cayenne pepper. Serve two medallions per person and a generous serving of fig demi-glace.

Changes

_____

_____

_____

_____

Cajun Glazed Ham

1 Hour   6 Servings

Comment:

This is a wonderful recipe to create your own special holiday ham. It is quite simple to accomplish, but I guarantee you will receive rave reviews with this dish. Try adding a few of your own secret spices.

1 5-pound cured ham
1 cup Creole mustard
1 cup brown sugar
1/2 cup Louisiana cane syrup
1/4 cup pineapple juice

1/4 cup cracked black pepper
pinch of cinnamon
pinch of nutmeg
pinch of allspice
pinch of ground clove

Preheat oven to 350 degrees F. In a ceramic mixing bowl, combine all of the above ingredients, except ham. Using a wire whisk, blend all spices into the mustard-sugar mixture until well incorporated. Place ham in center of dutch oven and coat completely with the sweet mustard mixture. Bake uncovered for one hour. You may wish to decorate the ham for the table centerpiece. If so, use a sharp paring knife to cut slits one eighth inch deep diagonally across the ham. Continue in the same pattern from the opposite side until even triangles appear from the cuts. Stuff with cloves and, using toothpicks, secure pineapple slices or fresh strawberries to the top of the ham before baking.

Changes

_____

_____

_____

_____

Daube

3 Hours   6-8 Servings

Comment:

Although a less tender, inexpensive cut of beef, daube is commonly found on the tables in South Louisiana. The slow cooking process combined with the many vegetable seasonings tends to make this dish a very full flavored entree.

1 5-pound beef shoulder roast
1/4 pound salt pork fat
1/4 cup salt
1/4 cup cracked black pepper
1/4 cup finely diced garlic
1/2 cup bacon drippings or
    vegetable oil
2 cups chopped onions
2 cups chopped celery

1 cup chopped bell pepper
1/4 cup diced garlic
1/4 cup tomato sauce
2 cups diced carrots
1 cup dry red wine
1 quart beef stock (see recipe)
salt and cracked black pepper
    to taste

Cut the salt pork fat into one fourth inch strips about two inches long. Combine one fourth cup salt and one fourth cup cracked black pepper. Using a sharp paring knife, cut six to eight one-inch deep slits into the shoulder roast. Open these slits with two fingers and stuff with generous amounts of garlic, salt, pepper and pork fat. Continue until all slits have been stuffed. Season roast well on all sides using salt and cracked black pepper. In a heavy dutch oven, heat bacon drippings over medium high heat. Brown roast well on all sides. When golden brown, add onions, celery, bell pepper and garlic. Saute until vegetables are wilted, approximately three to five minutes. Add tomato sauce, carrots and red wine, blending well into the vegetable mixture. Add beef stock, bring to a rolling boil and reduce heat to simmer. Cover dutch oven and allow roast to simmer two and a half hours. Season to taste using salt and cracked black pepper and continue to cook until roast is tender. Slice and serve with natural sauce.

Changes

_____

_____

_____

Meats

Daube Glace

2 1/2 Hours   2 4x8 inch terrine pans

Comment:

Daube glace is the most classical of the Creole hors d'oeuvres. Usually made with leftover daube, further cooked with additional seasonings, this dish is also found in most retail markets around the city of New Orleans.

1 3-pound cooked daube (see recipe)
2 quarts beef stock (see recipe)
sauce from pre-cooked daube
1/2 cup finely diced onions
1/2 cup finely diced celery
1/2 cup finely diced bell pepper
1/4 cup diced garlic
1/2 cup finely diced red bell pepper
1/2 cup finely diced carrots
1/2 cup finely minced parsley
salt and cayenne pepper to taste
3 envelopes gelatin, dissolved

Cut cooked daube into one inch cubes. In a heavy dutch oven, bring beef stock and sauce from daube to a light boil. Add cooked meat, onions, celery, bell pepper and garlic. Reduce heat to simmer and allow to cook until meat begins to string apart. Strain all ingredients from liquid through a fine sieve and set aside. Return liquid to heat and reduce to one and a half quarts. Add red bell pepper, diced carrots and parsley. Season to taste using salt and cayenne pepper. Using a wire whisk, blend dissolved gelatin into sauce. Remove from heat. Break the meat into small pieces and place equal amounts in two terrine molds. Include all cooked vegetables from the original sauce. Ladle stock over the meat, cover with clear wrap and allow to gel in refrigerator. Daube glace is best when allowed to sit over twenty-four hours for flavors to develop. The daube glace should be sliced and served with garlic croutons.

Changes

_____

_____

_____

_____

Tournedos Bayou Lafourche

30 Minutes   6 Servings

Comment:

The filet mignon is the most tender of all cuts of meat. Though found in many variations in South Louisiana, this particular version, named after the most famous of Louisiana bayous, is a favorite of ours.

12 3-ounce medallions of
     tenderloin
1/4 cup bacon drippings or
     vegetable oil
1/4 cup finely diced onions
1/4 cup finely diced celery
1 tbsp finely diced garlic

1/4 cup sliced mushrooms
1/4 cup finely sliced green onions
2 ounces dry red wine
3 cups beef demi-glace (see recipe)
salt and cracked black pepper
     to taste

In a ten inch heavy bottom saute pan, heat bacon drippings or oil over medium high heat. Season medallions using salt and cracked black pepper. Saute beef in hot oil until golden brown on all sides and medium rare. Add onions, celery, garlic, mushrooms and green onions. Saute until vegetables are wilted, approximately two to three minutes. Deglaze with red wine, allow to reduce to one ounce and add demi-glace. Continue to cook until beef is done to your liking. Season to taste using salt and cracked black pepper. Serve two medallions per person and top with generous serving of Sauce Bayou Lafourche.

Changes

Filet of Beef Viala

30 Minutes   6 Servings

Comment:

The present home of Lafitte's Landing Restaurant is the Old Viala Plantation, reputed to have been the home of the pirate, Jean Lafitte, from 1799 to 1804. The Vialas were a prominent family in early Louisiana, hence the name of this dish.

6 8-ounce filet mignons
1/2 pound lump crabmeat
1/2 cup bacon drippings or
**   vegetable oil**
1/2 cup finely diced onions
1/2 cup finely diced celery
1 tbsp finely diced garlic
1/4 cup sliced mushrooms
1/4 cup finely sliced green
**   onions**

2 ounces marsala wine
3 cups beef demi-glace (see recipe)
1/4 cup chopped parsley
1/4 pound butter
1/4 cup chopped parsley
1/4 cup chopped red bell pepper
1 ounce white wine
salt and cracked black pepper
**   to taste**

Preheat oven to 350 degrees F. In a ten inch heavy bottom saute pan, heat bacon drippings or oil over medium high heat. Season filets using salt and cracked black pepper. Saute beef until golden brown on all sides. Remove from saute pan and place on a baking sheet and set aside. In the same saute pan, add onions, celery, garlic, mushrooms and green onions. Saute until vegetables are wilted, approximately two to three minutes. Deglaze with marsala wine. While wine is reducing, place filets in oven to continue cooking. They should remain in oven approximately ten to fifteen minutes to cook medium. Once wine is reduced, add demi-glace and parsley. Season to taste using salt and black pepper. Remove from heat and keep warm. In a nine inch saute pan, melt butter over medium high heat. Add parsley, red bell pepper and lump crabmeat. Saute two to three minutes or until crabmeat is hot. Do not overcook. Add white wine, bring to a low boil and season to taste using salt and pepper. Remove filets from oven when done to your liking. Top with generous serving of the Viala sauce and sauteed lump crabmeat.

Changes

Medallions of Beef Marchand De Vin

45 Minutes   6 Servings

Comment:

The Wine Merchants Sauce is the best known of the New Orleans classical sauces made famous at Antoine's Restaurant in the French Quarter. The original version included bone marrow as a main ingredient.

12 3-ounce medallions filet
   mignon
1 cup peeled crawfish tails
1/4 cup butter
1/2 cup unseasoned flour
1/4 cup chopped onions
1 cup sliced mushrooms
1/2 cup diced tomato

1/2 cup sliced green onions
1 tbsp diced garlic
1 tbsp finely diced ham
1/2 cup dry red wine
2 cups demi-glace (see recipe)
salt and cracked black pepper
   to taste
1 tbsp chopped parsley

In a heavy bottom saute pan, melt butter over medium high heat. Dust medallions of beef in flour, shaking off all excess. Place in hot butter and saute until golden brown on each side or to desired doneness. Add onions, mushrooms, tomato, green onions, garlic and ham and saute three to five minutes or until vegetables are wilted. Add crawfish tails, deglaze with red wine and add demi-glace. Bring to a rolling boil and continue to cook until sauce is slightly reduced but meat is not overcooked. Season to taste using salt and black pepper and garnish with parsley. Serve two medallions in center of serving plate and top with generous serving of Merchand De Vin sauce.

Changes

_____

_____

_____

_____

Roasted Tenderloin in Cane Syrup

1-1/2 Hours   6 Servings

Comment:

Here again, we combine meat with the sugar cane syrup of Louisiana as a natural marinade. In this case, however, the syrup will assume a two-fold purpose. First, as a tenderizer, and second, as a wonderful flavoring device.

1 special trimmed beef tenderloin	1 tbsp salt
1/2 cup port wine	1 tbsp dried thyme
1/4 cup Louisiana cane syrup	1 tbsp dried basil
1/2 cup cracked black pepper	1 tbsp dried tarragon

Preheat oven to 400 degrees F. In a baking pan with one inch lip, place tenderloin and cover with port wine, rubbing well into the meat. Allow excess wine to remain in bottom of baking pan. Using the same technique, add the cane syrup, making sure the beef is well coated. Season meat completely using all of the remaining ingredients. Allow to set at room temperature for one hour. Place baking pan in center of oven and cook uncovered approximately twenty-five minutes for medium rare. For accuracy, a meat thermometer may be used. This dish may be served hot or cold. For variation, grill or smoke meat on an outdoor pit and top roasted tenderloin with a Marchand De Vin sauce.

Changes

_____

_____

_____

_____

Smoked Loin of Lamb

1-1/2 Hours   6 Servings

Comment:

Though lamb was not commonly found in South Louisiana cooking until the late 1960's, today it has a prime spot on Louisiana tables. At Lafitte's Landing, we have a reputation for the finest variations of lamb recipes in the state.

3 4 rack lamb loins (deboned)
4 cans Barq's Root Beer or
    Dr. Pepper (optional)
1/2 cup dry red wine
3/4 cup brown sugar
1/4 cup diced garlic

1/4 cup chopped rosemary
1/4 cup dried thyme
1/4 cup dried basil
salt and cracked black pepper
    to taste

Preheat home style smoker according to manufacturer's directions. Pre-soak pecan or hickory chips in cold water. In the water pan, place root beer or Dr. Pepper. The use of these liquids instead of water will impart a special flavor to the meat that will surely be a hit. On a large sheet pan, place lamb loins and top with red wine. Moisten lamb loins well with the wine to ensure that all seasonings will adhere to the meat. Generously coat with all remaining ingredients and allow to sit at room temperature for one hour. Place water pan in smoker and put lamb loins on top rack. Place wood chips on coals and smoke, covered, approximately forty-five minutes. Check for doneness and use the scale provided with your smoker to ensure proper cooking. The lamb may be served hot but is also excellent served cold and thinly sliced with Creole mustard.

Changes

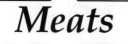
Cajun Stuffed Rack of Lamb

1 Hour   6 Servings

Comment:

By stuffing the lamb rack with Louisiana seafoods, we give this earthy flavored meat a new dimension. This dish has won gold medals in culinary competitions and will certainly be a winner on your table.

FOR STUFFING:

6 4-bone lamb racks
1 cup cooked shrimp, chopped
1 cup claw crabmeat
1/4 cup finely diced onions
1/4 cup finely diced green
    onions

1 tbsp diced garlic
1 tbsp diced red bell pepper
1/2 cup bechamel sauce (see recipe)
1/2 cup seasoned Italian
    bread crumbs
salt and cayenne pepper to taste

Have your butcher select six choice lamb racks and special trim each rack. In a one quart mixing bowl, combine all of the remaining ingredients, blending well to ensure that all seasonings are evenly mixed. Season to taste using salt and pepper. Stuffing should be moist but stiff enough to stand on its own. Add more bread crumbs or bechamel if necessary. Using a six inch paring knife, cut a three quarter inch slit in the center of the lamb loin. Be sure not to cut completely through the meat. The pocket should be large enough to hold a generous portion of the stuffing. Lightly season the inside of the pocket with salt and pepper. Stuff each loin with an equal amount of the seafood stuffing. Set aside.

(Continued)

Changes

_____

_____

_____

_____

Meats

(*Cajun Stuffed Rack of Lamb* continued)

FOR COOKING:

1/4 cup melted butter

2 tbsps dried thyme

2 tbsps dried basil

1 tbsp dried tarragon

1 tbsp crushed rosemary

2 tbsps diced garlic

salt and cracked black pepper
   to taste

1 cup dry red wine

3 cups demi-glace (see recipe)

Preheat oven to 400 degrees F. On a large baking pan with a one inch lip, place stuffed lamb racks. Moisten with melted butter and season generously with thyme, basil, tarragon, rosemary and garlic. Season to taste using salt and cracked black pepper. Place the racks on the baking pan, bone side up, and bake approximately twenty-five minutes for medium rare. Remove from oven and deglaze the baking pan with red wine, making sure to scrape bottom well. Pour these ingredients into a ten inch saute pan and add demi-glace. Bring to a boil and reduce until slightly thickened. Using a sharp knife, slice lamb racks into four chops each and top with a generous portion of demi-glace.

Changes

_____

_____

_____

_____

Baked Rack of Lamb St. James

1 Hour   6 Servings

Comment:

As a young boy growing up in St. James Parish, Louisiana, one of my favorite pastimes was picking blackberries. The blackberries were not only sold to make spending money, but were used to produce a beautiful glaze for meats and game.

6 4-bone lamb racks	salt and cracked black pepper
1/2 cup melted butter	to taste
1/4 cup dried thyme	1/2 cup blackberry liqueur
1/4 cup dried basil	1 cup fresh blackberries
1/4 cup dried tarragon	(or other berries)
1/4 cup crushed rosemary	3 cups demi-glace (see recipe)
3 tbsps diced garlic	

Preheat oven to 400 degrees F. Place lamb racks in a large roasting pan with a one inch lip. Moisten racks with a small amount of the melted butter to ensure that seasonings will adhere to the meat. Season generously with thyme, basil, tarragon, rosemary and garlic. Season to taste using salt and cracked black pepper. Roast approximately twenty-five minutes for medium rare. When done, remove racks from baking pan and deglaze with blackberry liqueur. Scrape bottom of roasting pan well and pour drippings into a ten inch saute pan. Bring to a rolling boil and add blackberries and demi-glace. Cook until sauce is slightly thickened. Using a sharp boning knife, cut each rack into four chops. Place on a ten inch serving plate and top with generous portion of blackberry glaze. Any other fresh fruit or berry and its comparable liqueur may be substituted. I personally prefer strawberries or blueberries to any other.

Changes

_____

_____

_____

_____

Medallions of Veal Ponchatoula

1 Hour   6 Servings

Comment:

Ponchatoula is considered by most the strawberry capital of Louisiana. We have seen many innovative recipes using this summer fruit emerge from this tiny village. Here is one such recipe.

6 6-ounce veal medallions
1/2 cup melted butter
1 cup unseasoned flour
1/2 cup sliced mushrooms
1/2 cup sliced green onions
1 tbsp diced garlic

1/2 cup dry white wine
1 cup sliced strawberries
2 cups demi-glace (see recipe)
1/2 cup heavy whipping cream
salt and cayenne pepper to taste

In a ten inch saute pan, heat butter over medium high heat. Dust veal medallions in flour and saute in butter three to five minutes on each side. Since veal cooks quickly, be careful not to overcook. Remove medallions from saute pan and add mushrooms, green onions and garlic. Saute three to five minutes or until vegetables are wilted. Deglaze with white wine and add strawberries and demi-glace. Bring to a rolling boil and cook until sauce is slightly thickened. Add heavy whipping cream and season to taste using salt and pepper. Once sauce is thick enough to coat the back of a cooking spoon, remove from heat. Place veal medallion in center of dinner plate and top with generous serving of strawberry sauce.

Changes

_____

_____

_____

_____

Veal Birds with Oyster Stuffing

1 Hour   6 Servings

Comment:

Veal was another meat seldom seen in South Louisiana. The Cajuns and Creoles preferred to allow their calves to mature to the full grown state, so veal was seldom available. Today, however, it is used extensively.

FOR STUFFING:

1 pound bulk pork sausage
1 pint fresh shucked oysters
1/4 pound butter
1/2 cup diced onions
1/2 cup diced celery
1/2 cup diced red bell pepper
2 tbsps diced garlic

1/4 cup chopped green onions
1 egg
1/2 cup seasoned Italian
   bread crumbs
salt and cracked black pepper
   to taste

In a ten inch saute pan, melt butter over medium high heat. Add bulk sausage and chop well in the skillet. Cook until sausage is golden brown. Add oysters, onions, celery, bell pepper, garlic and green onions and saute until vegetables are wilted. Remove from heat, add egg and blend well into mixture. Sprinkle in bread crumbs, a little at a time, blending well until consistency is tightened but not too dry. Season to taste using salt and cracked black pepper. Set aside.

(Continued)

Changes

_____

_____

_____

_____

(Veal Birds with Oyster Stuffing continued)

FOR COOKING:

6 6-ounce veal cutlets
1 cup unseasoned flour
1/2 cup vegetable oil
1/2 cup dry white wine

2 cups demi-glace (see recipe)
1 cup heavy whipping cream
salt and white pepper to taste

Preheat oven to 350 degrees F. Have your butcher tenderize the veal cutlets by pounding gently or running through a meat tenderizer. Place cutlets on a large baking sheet with a one inch lip. Place an equal amount of stuffing in the center of each cutlet, roll into a turban shape and secure with toothpicks. Dredge each veal bird in flour and lightly season with salt and white pepper. In a ten inch heavy bottom saute pan, heat oil over medium high heat. Saute veal until lightly browned on all sides. Remove to baking pan and bake fifteen to twenty minutes for medium rare. Meanwhile, discard excess oil from saute pan, deglaze with white wine and add demi-glace. Bring to a rolling boil, reduce to one half volume and add heavy whipping cream. Season to taste using salt and pepper. Remove veal from baking pan and place in saute pan of sauce for three to five minutes. Serve each veal bird with generous portion of cream sauce.

Changes

_____

_____

_____

_____

Veal with Yams in Port Wine

1 Hour   6 Servings

Comment:

Time and time again we continue to see the marriage of meat and vegetables or meat and seafoods. This technique, although not unique to Louisiana, is certainly more recognized here than in any other part of America.

6 6-ounce veal medallions
1 cup cubed yams
1 cup unseasoned flour
1/2 cup melted butter
1/2 cup sliced mushrooms
1/2 cup chopped green onions

1 tbsp chopped garlic
1/2 cup port wine
2 cups demi-glace (see recipe)
salt and cracked black pepper
   to taste

The yams should be diced into one half inch cubes. Place yams into a pot of lightly salted water and boil until tender but not overcooked. Cool and set aside. Dust veal medallions in flour, shaking off all excess. In a ten inch heavy bottom saute pan, heat butter over medium high heat. Saute veal medallions three to five minutes on each side making sure not to overcook. Remove medallions and keep warm. Add mushrooms, green onions and garlic and saute two to three minutes or until vegetables are wilted. Add yams and deglaze with port wine. Reduce to one half volume. Add demi-glace, bring to a rolling boil and season to taste using salt and cracked black pepper. Once sauce is thickened, place veal in center of serving plate and top with generous serving of yam sauce.

Changes

_____

_____

_____

_____

Medallions of Veal and Shrimp

1 Hour   6 Servings

Comment:

Since shrimp are one of the main commodities to come from the Gulf of Mexico, it seems obvious that they should be found in the saute pan with veal. A good hearty shrimp stock will improve the flavor of this dish tremendously.

6 6-ounce veal medallions
24 jumbo shrimp (peeled and
    deveined, reserve shells)
1/2 cup melted butter
1 cup unseasoned flour
1/2 cup sliced mushrooms
1/2 cup chopped green onions
1/2 cup diced red bell pepper

1 tbsp chopped garlic
1 tbsp green peppercorns (optional)
1/2 cup dry white wine
1 cup shellfish stock (see recipe)
2 cups heavy whipping cream
salt and white pepper to taste
2 tbsps chopped parsley
1 tbsp paprika

A hearty shrimp stock may be made by boiling the shrimp shells and heads in two to three cups of shellfish stock or water. (see stock technique) This stock will improve the flavor of this dish, however, chicken stock may be substituted. In a heavy bottom saute pan, heat butter over medium high heat. Dust veal medallions in flour, shaking off all excess, and saute three to five minutes on each side being careful not to overcook. Remove medallions from saute pan and add mushrooms, green onions, red bell pepper, garlic and peppercorns. Saute three to five minutes or until vegetables are wilted. Deglaze with white wine and add shrimp and shellfish stock. Bring to a rolling boil and reduce to one half volume. Add heavy whipping cream and season to taste using salt and pepper. Reduce cream until sauce is thickened. Return veal medallions to hot sauce. Serve one medallion in the center of the plate with a generous serving of sauce. Top with four jumbo shrimp and garnish with chopped parsley and paprika.

Changes

_____

_____

_____

Calves Liver River Road Style

1 Hour   6 Servings

Comment:

Since the River Road area was settled by the Germans in 1690, it is no wonder that organ meats such as liver are used extensively in dishes here. Liver is often used in grillades and boudins, however, this recipe is a personal favorite.

6 6-ounce calves liver slices
18 bacon slices
1 cup unseasoned flour
1 large onion (thinly sliced)
1 cup sliced mushrooms

1 cup chopped green onions
1 tbsp chopped garlic
2 cups demi-glace
salt and cracked black pepper
    to taste

Have your butcher hand select six slices of veal or calves liver. This will ensure the best possible product for the saute pan. In a heavy bottom saute pan over medium high heat, cook bacon. Once bacon is well browned, remove from pan and set aside. Make sure all bacon drippings remain in the saute pan. Dust liver in unseasoned flour until well coated. Saute in hot bacon drippings over medium high heat until golden brown, three to five minutes on each side. Remove and keep warm. Saute sliced onions, mushrooms, green onions and garlic until sliced onions are transparent and wilted. Add demi-glace and season to taste using salt and pepper. Return liver to the hot sauce and cook two to three minutes. Place cooked liver in center of dinner plate and top with generous serving of demi-glace. Garnish with three slices of cooked bacon.

Changes

Seafood

Seafood

One of the most prevalent aspects of the South Louisiana landscape is water. Everywhere you look there is water in the form of bayous, swamps, bays, rivers, lakes and the Gulf of Mexico.

Each area features its own variety of fish or shellfish. In the swamps and bayous we find crawfish, one of the most popular forms of shellfish in Louisiana, and fresh water fish such as bass and catfish. In bays along the riveted coastline are the oyster beds which produce the tastiest, juiciest oysters in the world. One couple from California, who has traveled the world many times over, returns each year to Lafitte's Landing just for the oysters, which they claim are by far the best in the world.

From the rivers, fishermen pull in catfish, which enjoys a popularity in Louisiana unlike any other state. The Gulf of Mexico, off the Louisiana coast, is a department store for seafood lovers. Shrimp, pompano, red snapper, redfish, lemon fish, scallops, speckled trout, mackerel, and swordfish are just a part of the bounty Louisiana fishermen deliver to coastal fish markets daily. Crabs are found in many types of inland waterways from rivers and bayous to lakes and bays.

Although the seafoods found in South Louisiana were not the same as what was available in the Old Country, early settlers did not have any trouble adapting their recipes to what was pulled from the waters. In fact, seafood is probably the most important aspect of Cajun and Creole cuisine today because of its great variety and availability.

South Louisianians are very creative in preparing seafood dishes. They love to show off each dish like a newborn baby. Whether boiled, broiled, steamed, stewed, baked, fried, or au gratin, Cajun and Creole seafood dishes exemplify the true nature of our culture.

"They fried the fish with bacon and were astonished; for no fish had ever seemed so delicious before. They finally learned that the quicker a fresh water fish is on the fire after he is caught, the better he is."

Mark Twain

Farm Raised Catfish

"The Domesticated Fish Gone Wild"

Catfish has rapidly become the new fillet on America's dinner tables. Though once thought of as a Southern fried delicacy only, today catfish has assumed its rightful position on the menus of fine restaurants nationwide.

One reason for this exciting image change, with chefs and homemakers alike, is farm raised catfish. This new product of aquaculture not only guarantees the highest quality of fresh product nationwide, but place a steady ongoing supply in America's supermarkets. Though Mississippi leads the nation in farm raised catfish production, Louisiana, Texas, Alabama and a host of other states have entered into catfish production as well as processing of the finished product.

I have worked with the catfish industry over the past few years developing new and interesting recipes. Here are some of my latest creations.

223

Grilled Catfish Salad

1 Hour   6 Servings

FOR MARINADE:

3 5-8 ounce catfish fillets   1 tbsp dried basil
1/4 cup melted butter   1 tbsp cracked black pepper
1/4 cup Louisiana cane syrup   salt to taste
1 tbsp dried thyme

In a mixing bowl combine all of the above ingredients and mix well to ensure that spices are well blended. Allow fillets to set in marinade approximately thirty minutes. Charbroil the fillets on a hot barbecue grill three to five minutes on each side or until fish is cooked to desired doneness. Remove and keep warm.

FOR SALAD:

6 leaves red leaf lettuce   1 cup high quality blue cheese
6 leaves romaine lettuce   dressing
6 leaves mache lettuce   6 cherry tomatoes sliced
6 leaves curly endive   cracked black pepper to taste
1/2 cup crumbled blue cheese

On a six inch salad plate, place one piece of red leaf lettuce as a base. In a large mixing bowl, combine the other three lettuces and break into appropriate size serving pieces. Place one handful of mixed lettuces on top of red leaf lettuce. Using a sharp knife, cut grilled catfish into one inch slices. Place an equal number of slices on top of each salad, sprinkle with blue cheese crumbles and top with salad dressing. Garnish each salad with tomato circles and cracked pepper.

Changes

Catfish Pasta

1 Hour   6 Servings

3 5-8 ounce catfish fillets
3/4 cup melted butter
1 cup unseasoned flour
1/4 cup diced onions
1/4 cup diced celery
1 tbsp diced garlic
1/2 cup sliced andouille sausage
1 cup diced yellow squash

1 cup diced zucchini
1/2 cup diced red bell pepper
3 cups heavy whipping cream
salt and cracked black pepper
   to taste
4 cups cooked rotini pasta
2 tbsps chopped parsley

In a heavy bottom saute pan, heat butter over medium high heat. Cut catfish fillets into one inch cubes and dust in unseasoned flour. Saute cubes until golden brown on all sides, approximately three to five minutes. Remove and keep warm. In the same saute pan, cook onions, celery, garlic, andouille, squash, zucchini and bell pepper three to five minutes or until vegetables are slightly undercooked. Add heavy whipping cream, bring to a low boil, reduce to simmer and cook three minutes. Add sauteed catfish and stir in gently to avoid breaking. Season to taste using salt and pepper. Reheat rotini pasta under hot tap water. Place equal amounts of pasta in each serving plate and top with catfish cream sauce. Garnish with chopped parsley.

Changes

_____

_____

_____

_____

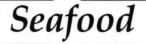

Baked Catfish Creole

1 Hour   6 Servings

FOR SAUCE:

3/4 cup melted butter
1 cup chopped onions
1 cup chopped celery
1/2 cup chopped bell pepper
1/4 cup diced garlic
2 whole bay leaves
2 8-ounce cans tomato sauce
1 cup fish stock (see recipe)

1/2 tsp sugar
pinch of dry thyme
pinch of dry basil
1 cup chopped green onions
1/2 cup chopped parsley
salt and cracked black pepper
    to taste

In a two quart heavy sauce pan, melt butter over medium high heat. Saute onions, celery, bell pepper, garlic and bay leaves until vegetables are wilted, approximately three to five minutes. Add tomato sauce and fish stock, bring to a low boil, reduce to simmer and cook thirty minutes, stirring occasionally. Add sugar, thyme, basil, green onions and parsley. Continue to cook ten additional minutes and season to taste using salt and pepper. Remove from heat and set aside.

FOR COOKING:

4 5-8 ounce catfish fillets
1 cup 90-110 count shrimp
    (peeled and deveined)

reserved Creole sauce
4 cups cooked white rice
1/4 cup chopped parsley

Preheat oven to 375 degrees F. Place catfish fillets in an ovenproof casserole dish large enough to hold the four fillets. Sprinkle the shrimp evenly over the top of the fillets. Spoon the Creole sauce generously until fish and shrimp are well covered. Place covered baking dish in oven and cook approximately thirty minutes or until fish is done. Heat rice under hot tap water and place an equal amount in the center of each serving plate. Serve catfish Creole on top of white rice and garnish with chopped parsley. This dish may also be served over pasta.

Changes

Catfish in Oyster Andouille Butter

1 Hour   6 Servings

6 5-8 ounce catfish fillets
3/4 cup vegetable oil
1 cup eggwash (1 egg, 1/2 cup
    water, 1/2 cup milk)
1/2 cup unseasoned flour
1/4 cup julienned andouille
    sausage
1 tsp garlic

1/2 cup sliced mushrooms
1/2 cup chopped green onions
24 fresh shucked oysters
1/2 cup dry white wine
1-1/2 cups heavy whipping cream
salt and white pepper to taste
4 chips cold butter

In a ten inch heavy bottom saute pan, heat oil over medium high heat. Blend eggwash to ensure that egg, milk and water are well mixed. Dip catfish fillets into eggwash and then into flour, coating evenly on all sides. Saute fish, three fillets at a time, until golden brown, approximately three to five minutes on each side. Once cooked, remove and keep warm. In the same saute pan, add andouille, garlic, mushrooms and green onions and saute until vegetables are wilted, approximately three to five minutes. Add oysters and saute until their edges are curly. Deglaze with white wine, add heavy whipping cream and cook until sauce is slightly thickened. Season to taste using salt and white pepper. Once sauce has thickened, swirl in butter chips, two at a time, until all is incorporated. The butter will finish the sauce to a nice sheen. Place two to three ounces of oyster butter in the center of a serving plate and top with catfish fillet. Garnish with four cooked oysters per serving.

Changes

_____

_____

_____

_____

Holiday Catfish Casserole

1-1/2 Hours   6 Servings

6 5-8 ounce catfish fillets   **1/4 cup chopped parsley**
1/4 cup paprika

Using a sharp knife, trim the thickest portion of the catfish fillet to the approximate thickness of the tail. Reserve all trimmed pieces. Spray bundt style pan with non-stick coating and sprinkle the pan with paprika and parsley. Line the mold with the catfish fillets, filling in all void spaces with trimmings of the fish. Allow enough fish to hang over the side of the pan to cover the stuffing. Set aside.

FOR STUFFING:

1/4 pound butter   **1 cup heavy whipping cream**
1/2 cup diced onions   **3 eggs**
1/2 cup diced celery   **5 cups cooked rice**
1/2 cup finely diced carrots   **salt and cracked black pepper to taste**
2 small summer squash, diced   **1/4 cup diced red bell pepper**
2 small zucchini, diced   **for garnish**
6 florets of broccoli, diced   **1/4 cup diced yellow bell pepper for**
1 cup sliced mushrooms   **garnish**
3/4 cup diced red bell pepper   **1/4 cup chopped parsley for garnish**
1/2 cup diced andouille sausage   **colored endive for garnish**

(Continued)

Changes
_____
_____
_____
_____

(Holiday Catfish Casserole continued)

Preheat oven to 375 degrees F. In a four quart sauce pot, melt butter over medium high heat. Saute onions, celery, carrots, squash, zucchini, broccoli and mushrooms until vegetables are wilted, approximately three to five minutes. Add bell pepper and andouille sausage and continue to cook two to three minutes. Add heavy whipping cream, bring to a light boil and remove from heat. Quickly blend in eggs, mixing well into the cream sauce. Add cooked rice and season to taste using salt and pepper. Allow mixture to cool slightly. Once cool, spoon rice mixture into center of fish mold. Fold fish pieces over the top of the rice and cover with aluminum foil. Place bundt pan in a baking pan filled with water one inch from the top. This will create a water bath for the bundt pan to cook in and will keep the fish from browning and overcooking. Place the pan in center of oven and bake one hour. When cooked, remove from water bath and turn mold over into serving platter. Garnish the mold using parsley sprigs and colored endive. Sprinkle with additional diced red or yellow bell pepper and parsley.

Changes

_____

_____

_____

_____

Catfish in Shrimp Chive Cream

1 Hour   6 Servings

6 5-8 ounce catfish fillets
24 21-25 count shrimp (peeled
   and deveined)
3/4 cup vegetable oil
1 cup eggwash (1 egg, 1/2 cup
   water, 1/2 cup milk, blended)
1-1/2 cups unseasoned flour
1/2 cup sliced mushrooms

1/2 cup chopped green onions
1/4 cup diced red bell pepper
1 tbsp diced garlic
1/4 cup dry white wine
2 cups heavy whipping cream
1/2 cup finely chopped chives
salt and cracked black pepper
   to taste

In a ten inch heavy bottom saute pan, heat oil over medium high heat. Dip fillets in eggwash and coat generously with unseasoned flour. Saute fillets, three at a time, until golden brown, approximately three to five minutes on each side. Once cooked, remove and keep warm. In the same saute pan cook mushrooms, green onions, bell pepper and garlic until vegetables are wilted, approximately three to five minutes. Add shrimp and saute until shrimp are pink and curled. Deglaze with white wine, add heavy whipping cream, bring to a low boil and cook until sauce is thickened. Add chopped chives and season to taste using salt and pepper. Place serving of chive cream sauce in the center of a serving plate, top with fish fillet and garnish with four jumbo shrimp.

Changes

_____

_____

_____

_____

Catfish Frangelico

1 Hour   6 Servings

6 5-8 ounce catfish fillets
3/4 cup vegetable oil
eggwash (1 egg, 1/2 cup water,
    1/2 cup milk, blended)
1-1/2 cups unseasoned flour
1 tbsp diced garlic
1/2 cup chopped green onions

3/4 cup chopped pecans
1-1/2 ounces Frangelico liqueur
2 cups heavy whipping cream
4 pats cold butter
salt and cracked black pepper
    to taste

In a ten inch heavy bottom saute pan, heat oil over medium high heat. Dip fillets in eggwash and coat generously with flour. Saute fillets in hot oil until golden brown, three to five minutes on each side. Once done, remove from saute pan and keep warm. In same saute pan, cook garlic, green onions and pecans until vegetables are wilted, approximately three minutes. Deglaze with Frangelico and add heavy whipping cream. Bring to a low boil and reduce until cream is thickened. Add cold butter, two pats at a time, swirling pan constantly until all is incorporated. Butter will finish sauce to a nice sheen. Season to taste using salt and pepper. Place sauce in center of serving plate and top with catfish fillet.

Changes

_____

_____

_____

_____

Catfish Provencal

1 Hour   6 Servings

6 5-8 ounce catfish fillets
3/4 cup olive oil
eggwash (1 egg, 1/2 cup water,
    1/2 cup milk, blended)
1 cup unseasoned flour
1/4 cup julienned andouille
    sausage
1 tbsp diced garlic
2 cups diced tomatoes

1 ounce rose wine
1 cup tomato juice
1/4 cup chopped green onions
1/4 cup chopped parsley
pinch of dry thyme
pinch of dry basil
salt and cracked black pepper
    to taste

In a ten inch heavy bottom saute pan, heat oil over medium high heat. Dip fillets in eggwash and coat generously with flour. Saute fillets in oil until golden brown, approximately three to five minutes on each side. Once cooked, remove and keep warm. In same saute pan, cook andouille, garlic and tomatoes until vegetables are wilted, approximately three to five minutes. Deglaze with rose wine. Add tomato juice, green onions, parsley, thyme and basil and continue to cook until sauce is slightly thickened. Season to taste using salt and pepper. Place equal amounts of Provencal sauce in center of each serving plate and top with catfish fillets.

Changes

_____

_____

_____

_____

Catfish Paella

1 Hour   6 Servings

4 5-8 ounce catfish fillets (cubed)
1/2 cup olive oil
1 cup chopped onions
1 cup chopped celery
1 cup diced red bell pepper
1 cup diced tomato
1 tbsp diced garlic

1/2 cup diced andouille sausage
1 cup frozen peas
4 1/2 cups fish stock (see recipe)
3 cups raw rice
salt and cracked black pepper
    to taste
1/2 cup sliced green onions

Preheat oven to 350 degrees F. In a paella pan or other ovenproof baking dish, heat olive oil over medium high heat. Saute onions, celery, bell pepper, tomato, garlic and andouille until vegetables are wilted, approximately three to five minutes. Add frozen peas and blend well into mixture. Add fish stock, bring to a rolling boil and reduce to simmer. Add cubed catfish, stirring once. Add rice and season to taste using salt and pepper. Blend in sliced green onions. Cover pan with aluminum foil and bake forty-five minutes to one hour. Remove from oven, stir and allow to set thirty minutes before serving.

Changes

233

Honey Spiced Catfish

1 Hour   6 Servings

6 5-8 ounce catfish fillets
4 cans Barq's root beer or Dr.
    Pepper
1/2 cup melted butter
1/4 cup honey
1 tbsp lemon juice
1 tbsp white wine

2 tbsps sherry
2 tbsps diced garlic
1 tbsp chopped parsley
1 tsp dry basil
1 tsp dry thyme
1-1/2 tbsps cracked black pepper
salt to taste

Preheat outdoor barbecue grill according to manufacturer's directions. Pre-soak pecan or hickory chips in Barq's root beer or Dr. Pepper. This technique will give the fish a unique and interesting flavor. In a large mixing bowl, combine all of the above ingredients. Blend well to ensure that spices are evenly mixed. Allow catfish to set in marinade one hour at room temperature. Brush the grill lightly with oil and sprinkle in wood chips. Grill fillets three to five minutes on each side or until fish is done to your liking. Do not overcook. The fish should be served hot as an entree, in a salad or blended into a mousse or terrine.

Changes

Grilled Catfish with Dijon Sauce

1 Hour   6 Servings

- 6 5-8 ounce catfish fillets
- 6 tbsps dijon mustard
- 2 tbsps olive oil
- 2 tbsps sherry
- 1 tbsp diced garlic
- 1/4 cup chopped parsley
- pinch of dry thyme
- pinch of dry basil
- 2 tbsps cracked black pepper
- salt to taste

Preheat outdoor barbecue grill according to manufacturer's instructions. In a large mixing bowl, combine all of the above ingredients, blending well to ensure that spices are evenly mixed. Allow fish to set in marinade at room temperature for one hour. Brush grill with light coating of oil and grill fillets three to five minutes on each side or until fish is done to your liking. Fillets may be served as an entree or hot over salad greens.

Changes

_____

_____

_____

_____

Low Calorie Catfish Linguine

1 Hour   6 Servings

4 5-8 ounce catfish fillets (cubed)
1/4 cup olive oil
1/2 cup diced onions
1/2 cup diced celery
1 tbsp diced garlic
1 cup broccoli florets
1/2 cup sliced mushrooms

1/2 cup diced red bell pepper
3 tbsps flour
3 cups skim milk
salt and cracked black pepper
    to taste
3 cups cooked linguine pasta

In a two quart heavy bottom sauce pan, heat olive oil over medium high heat. Add onions, celery, garlic, broccoli, mushrooms and bell pepper and saute until vegetables are wilted, approximately three to five minutes. Blend in flour, stirring constantly until light roux is achieved. (see roux technique) Add hot skim milk, blending well to form cream sauce. Bring to a low boil, reduce heat to simmer, add catfish cubes and cook five to ten additional minutes. Add additional skim milk if necessary should mixture become too thick. Season to taste using salt and pepper. Heat cooked pasta under hot tap water and place in center of plate. Spoon generous serving of catfish sauce on top of linguine pasta. This dish has approximately 400 calories per serving.

Changes

Baked Catfish Lombardy

1 Hour   6 Servings

6 5-8 ounce catfish fillets
6 tbsps olive oil
2 cups sliced mushrooms
1 cup sliced red onions
1 cup julienned red bell pepper
1 cup julienned yellow bell
   pepper
1/2 cup sherry wine

2 cups fish stock (see recipe)
2 tbsps lemon juice
1/4 cup chopped green onions
1/4 cup chopped parsley
2 tbsps corn starch (dissolved)
salt and cracked black pepper
   to taste

Preheat oven to 400 degrees F. Tear six pieces of heavy duty aluminum foil large enough to wrap a fillet of catfish. In a heavy bottom saute pan, heat olive oil over medium high heat. Add mushrooms, red onions and bell peppers and saute until vegetables are wilted, approximately three to five minutes. Add sherry, fish stock and lemon juice, bring to a low boil and reduce to simmer. Cook approximately ten minutes more. Add green onions and parsley, blend well into mixture and add dissolved corn starch. Mixture should thicken quickly and additional fish stock should be added if mixture becomes too thick. Season to taste using salt and pepper. Place fillet in the center of aluminum foil and top with portion of the sauce. Wrap fillet tightly in aluminum foil package and cook fifteen to twenty minutes or until fish is done to your liking. This recipe has approximately 250 calories per serving.

Changes

_____

_____

_____

_____

237

River Road Crawfish Stew

1 Hour   6 Servings

Comment:

This is the most popular of all crawfish dishes cooked in Bayou country. It is easy to prepare and although similar to crawfish bisque, this dish may be completed in half the time.

2 lbs cleaned crawfish tails
1 cup vegetable oil
1 cup flour
2 cups chopped onions
1 cup chopped celery
1 cup chopped bell pepper
2 tbsps diced garlic

1/4 cup tomato sauce
2 1/2 quarts crawfish stock or water
1 cup chopped green onions
1 cup chopped parsley
salt and cayenne pepper to taste
dash of Louisiana Gold
    Pepper Sauce

A rich crawfish stock will certainly make this dish a winner. (see stock techniques) Any shellfish stock or fish stock may be substituted, but the dish will be good even if plain water is used. In a two gallon stock pot, heat oil over medium high heat. Add flour and using a wire whip, stir constantly until dark brown roux is achieved. (see roux technique) When brown, add onions, celery, bell pepper and garlic and saute until vegetables are wilted, approximately three to five minutes. Add crawfish tails and cook until meat is pink and slightly curled. Stir in tomato sauce and slowly add crawfish stock stirring constantly until stew like consistency is achieved. Add more stock if necessary to retain consistency. Bring to a rolling boil, reduce to simmer and cook thirty minutes, stirring occasionally. Add green onions and parsley and season to taste using salt and pepper. When done, serve over white rice with a few dashes of Louisiana Gold Pepper Sauce.

Changes

Crawfish Etouffee

1 Hour   6 Servings

Comment:

The French word "etouffer" means to smother or braise. This technique is found in dishes using shrimp, crab, crawfish and in some cases, meat or game. Though more Creole in origin, etouffees are found throughout Cajun country.

2 lbs cleaned crawfish tails
1/4 pound butter
1 cup chopped onions
1/2 cup chopped celery
1/2 cup chopped bell pepper
1/2 cup chopped red bell pepper
1/2 cup diced tomatoes
2 tbsps diced garlic
2 bay leaves

1/2 cup tomato sauce
1 cup flour
2 quarts crawfish stock or water
1 ounce sherry
1 cup chopped green onions
1/2 cup chopped parsley
salt and cayenne pepper to taste
dash of Louisiana Gold
    Pepper Sauce

In a two gallon stock pot, melt butter over medium high heat. Add onions, celery, bell peppers, tomatoes, garlic and bay leaves and saute until vegetables are wilted, approximately three to five minutes. Add crawfish tails and tomato sauce and blend well into mixture. Using a wire whip, blend flour into the vegetable mixture to form a white roux. (see roux technique) Slowly add crawfish stock or water, a little at a time, until sauce consistency is achieved. Continue adding more stock as necessary to retain consistency. Bring to a rolling boil, reduce to simmer and cook thirty minutes, stirring occasionally. Add sherry, green onions and parsley and cook an additional five minutes. Season to taste using salt and pepper. Serve over white rice using a few dashes of Louisiana Gold.

Changes

_____

_____

_____

_____

Crawfish Bisque

2 Hours   6 Servings

Comment:

Crawfish bisque is a tradition in Louisiana. This dish is normally made in May or June, toward the end of crawfish season. Usually, an entire family gets together to make enough bisque at one time for everyone's freezer.

FOR STUFFING:

2 lbs cleaned crawfish tails
60 cleaned crawfish heads
2 cups diced onions
2 cups diced celery
1 cup diced bell pepper
2 tbsps diced garlic

1 cup diced parsley
4 slices day old bread
3 eggs, beaten
salt and pepper to taste
3 cups vegetable oil
2 cups unseasoned flour

Ask your seafood supplier to clean sixty crawfish heads for this dish. The heads may be frozen for an extended period of time. Prior to using, you may wish to soak the heads overnight in cold soda water. Grind crawfish, onions, celery, bell pepper, garlic, parsley and bread in a homestyle meat grinder. Once ground, add eggs and season to taste using salt and pepper. Stuff equal amounts into the sixty crawfish heads and set aside. In a saute pan, heat vegetable oil over medium high heat. Dust stuffed heads in flour and saute until golden brown. Remove and drain well.

(Continued)

Changes

_____

_____

_____

_____

(*Crawfish Bisque* continued)

FOR SAUCE:

1 pound cleaned crawfish tails
1-1/2 cups vegetable oil
1-1/2 cups flour
1 cup diced onions
1 cup diced celery
1 cup diced bell pepper
1 tbsp diced garlic
1/2 cup tomato sauce

3-1/2 quarts crawfish stock
  or water
1 cup chopped green onions
1 cup chopped parsley
salt and black pepper to taste
dash of Louisiana Gold
  Pepper Sauce

In a two gallon stock pot, heat oil over medium high heat. Add flour and using a wire whip, stir constantly until dark brown roux is achieved. (see roux technique) Add onions, celery, bell pepper and garlic and saute until vegetables are wilted, approximately three to five minutes. Add crawfish tails and tomato sauce, blending well into vegetable mixture. Slowly add crawfish stock, a little at a time, until all is incorporated. Bring to a low boil, reduce to simmer and cook fifteen minutes. Add stuffed crawfish heads and continue to cook thirty additional minutes, stirring occasionally as mixture will settle to the bottom and burn. Add green onions and parsley and season to taste using salt and pepper. Serve in a ten ounce soup bowl over white rice using a few dashes of Louisiana Gold.

Changes

Broiled Softshell Crawfish

30 Minutes   6 Servings

Comment:

The softshell crawfish is a new found delicacy from the bayous of Louisiana. The crawfish molt four times per year, producing this new cash crop. It was not until the mid 1980's that softshell crawfish appeared on menus in South Louisiana.

24 softshell crawfish
3/4 cup melted butter
2 cups flour
salt to taste

granulated garlic to taste
cracked black pepper to taste
dried thyme to taste

Preheat oven to 400 degrees F. Softshell crawfish must be cleaned before cooking. This process is quite simple since the crawfish molts in clear running water ensuring a clean product. A few days before molting, the crawfish stop eating, which certainly guarantees that no impurities are left in the body of the animal. To clean the crawfish, remove the two calcium stones located right above and behind the eyes. These stones are easily located by pressing the thumb and forefinger in this general vicinity and squeezing firmly until the stones, eyes and mouth tear away from the body. The crawfish should then be rinsed under cold running water. Place crawfish on a large baking pan with one inch lip. Pour melted butter evenly over the crawfish to ensure that each is well coated. Dredge crawfish in flour and place feet down and legs separated on the baking pan. Season to taste using all of the above spices. Place on center rack in oven and bake or broil ten to fifteen minutes. Serve as an appetizer or entree.

HINT: The most popular way of cooking softshell crawfish today is deep frying. Simply follow the procedures for cleaning the crawfish explained in the recipe, and deep fry as per the fried shrimp recipe.

Changes

_____

_____

_____

_____

Pan Sauteed Softshell Crawfish
with Three Peppers Sauce

30 Minutes   6 Servings

Comment:

*Softshell crawfish continue to increase in popularity here at Lafitte's Landing Restaurant. We are constantly creating new and interesting recipes for this rare delicacy. I designed this dish for a feature article introducing softshell crawfish to the nation in **Gourmet Magazine**.*

3 dozen softshell crawfish
3 large red bell peppers
3 large gold bell peppers
3 large green bell peppers
1/2 cup cooking oil
3 cups yellow corn flour
eggwash (2 eggs, 1 cup milk,
   1 cup water - blended)

1 tbsp chopped garlic
1/2 cup dry white wine
2 cups heavy whipping cream
1/2 tsp dried thyme
1/2 tsp dried basil
salt and cayenne pepper
   to taste

Clean softshell crawfish by removing stones from the rear of the eyes. Cut away eyes, mouth and feelers, rinse under cold water and set aside. On an outdoor barbecue grill over high heat, cook bell peppers until they are charred on all sides. When done, rinse peppers under cold water to remove all of the charred skin. Cut peppers in half and remove ribs and seeds. In a food processor, puree peppers separately and reserve in individual containers. In a ten inch saute pan, heat oil over medium high heat. Season corn flour to taste using salt and cayenne pepper. Dip crawfish, a few at a time, into the eggwash and then into the seasoned corn flour and pan saute until golden brown, approximately one to two minutes on each side. Once browned, remove and keep warm. In the same saute pan, add garlic and deglaze with white wine. Add heavy whipping cream, thyme and basil. Bring to a low boil and reduce by one half volume. Season to taste using salt and cayenne pepper. Pour an equal amount of the cream sauce into each of the containers of pureed pepper and blend well. Place six crawfish on a serving plate and top two crawfish with the yellow sauce, two with the green sauce and two with the red sauce.

Changes

243

The Crawfish Boil

It is a hot June day in Bayou country and the guests are beginning to arrive, filled with anticipation of the greatest social event of South Louisiana: the Crawfish Boil. Already under the giant oak, the men are gathered washing the crawfish in number three tubs. The children entertain themselves by selecting the largest crawfish from the tub, giving it a name, and lining it up at the imaginary starting gate for the race. The women, on the other hand, have convened in their own area near the house, away from the children, and are catching up on the latest news. In Bayou Country everybody seems to get along, especially at the crawfish boil. Here, a certain kinship develops as the evening passes on.

The crawfish are now washed and the men are busy quartering onions, halving lemons and discussing each one's idea of the correct amount of seasonings that must go into the pot, if the flavor is to be successful. The yard is now filled with a steady hum, punctuated by that distant sound of beer cans popping open and the outburst of laughter from a group of men in one corner of the yard.

Some of the boys are encouraged to add salt, cayenne pepper and garlic to the boiling pot of water. Two young men approach the pot with fresh ears of corn and the new red potatoes, just more evidence of progress toward the goal of getting those crawfish to the table! Just then, the host turns to the man in charge and yells "Let 'em boil!" As the crawfish are poured into the pot everyone watches, knowing they will soon be ready to eat. The migration begins toward the eating area, and as the crawfish are poured onto the tables lined with newspaper, it is amazing how the chatter ceases, and now it becomes almost impossible to engage anyone in conversation. Everybody is just eating crawfish, peeling them with automated fingers as they attack the task at hand. After a short period of silence, broken only by "compliments to the chef", the guests begin to relax once more and conversation resumes. Soon the big eaters are finished, only because there are no more crawfish on the table. All that can be heard now are people saying, "I can't believe I ate all of that" or "Ask me if I am going to sleep well tonight". Now the sun is down in Bayou Country and the lights are dim in Cajun cabins. The lively chatter of people is gone, replaced only by the distant chirping of crickets and swamp grenouilles.

Boiled Crawfish

2 Hours   12 Servings

Comment:

The crawfish boil is the premier social event in the spring time here in Louisiana. Friends and family gather for an afternoon under the shade of an oak tree to enjoy a delicacy unequaled in the Southland.

30 quarts cold water
12 medium onions, quartered
6 heads of garlic, split in half
   exposing pods
1 dozen lemons, quartered
1 quart cooking oil

4 pounds salt
1/2 pound cayenne pepper
4 3-ounce bags crab boil
24 medium red potatoes
12 ears of corn
50 lbs cleaned crawfish

Live crawfish may be purchased already washed from your seafood supplier. However, a second rinsing in cold water would not hurt. The purging of crawfish, that is, washing the crawfish in cold salted water, has been found to be useless other than to place the animal under unnecessary stress. So forget the purging — rinsing in cold water will suffice. In a sixty quart stockpot, bring water to a rolling boil. Add onions, garlic, lemons, cooking oil, salt, pepper and crab boil and continue to boil for thirty minutes. This boiling of the vegetables will ensure a good flavor in the boiling liquid. Add red potatoes and cook approximately ten to twelve minutes. Add corn and cook ten minutes before adding the crawfish. Once the water returns to a boil, cook crawfish seven to ten minutes, turn off heat and allow to set in boiling liquid twelve additional minutes. Crawfish should be served hot with potatoes and corn and pitchers of ice cold beer.

Changes

_____

_____

_____

_____

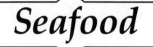

Seafood

Stuffed Hardshell Crab

1 Hour   6 Servings

Comment:

As you have noticed by now, Cajuns and Creoles stuff everything! Crabs are no different. The stuffed crab is presented in many ways on Louisiana menus, but mostly as an entree or as part of a seafood platter.

2 pounds white or claw crabmeat
12 crab shells, cleaned
3/4 cup melted butter
2 cups chopped onions
1 cup chopped celery
1 cup chopped bell pepper

1 cup chopped red bell pepper
1/4 cup diced garlic
salt and cracked black pepper to taste
2 cups seasoned Italian bread crumbs

Have your seafood supplier clean and package twelve hard shell crabs. These shells will freeze well, so you may consider buying them well in advance. In a heavy bottom saute pan, heat butter over medium high heat. Saute onions, celery, bell peppers, and garlic until vegetables are wilted, approximately three to five minutes. Add crabmeat and blend well into vegetable mixture. Continue to cook until juices are rendered from vegetables and crabmeat. Season to taste using salt and pepper. Remove from heat and sprinkle in bread crumbs, a little at a time, until proper consistency is achieved. Stuffing should not be too dry. Adjust seasonings if necessary. Place an equal amount of stuffing in each crab shell and continue until all stuffing is used. Additional bread crumbs may be sprinkled on top of stuffed crab. Allow to cool and wrap individually for the freezer or drizzle with a small amount of melted butter and bake at 350 degrees F, approximately fifteen to twenty minutes.

Changes

_____

_____

_____

_____

246

Broiled Softshell Crab

1 Hour   6 Servings

Comment:

The hard shell crab will molt its shell at different times during the year. During this period, this delicacy can be brought to the table. Whether broiled, deep fried or pan sauteed, softshell crab is a masterpiece in Cajun cooking.

12 softshell crabs	**2 cups flour**
eggwash (1 egg, 1/2 cup milk,	**1 pound melted butter**
1/2 cup water - beaten)	**salt and cayenne pepper to taste**

Preheat broiler to 500 degrees F or oven to 450 degrees F. Have your seafood supplier clean the softshell crabs in advance or clean them yourself in the following manner. Lift the pointed end of the top shell away from the main body. Scrape off the lungs or white spongy substance located at each end of the crab. Using a sharp paring knife or scissors, cut away the eyes and mouth portion located in the center-front of the crab. You may also wish to remove the "apron" or small loose shell which comes to a point in the middle of the undershell. Once completed, wash the crab thoroughly in cold water. Dredge crabs in eggwash and then in flour, shaking off all excess. On a large baking sheet with a one inch lip, place crabs shell side up. Drizzle each crab with melted butter. Crabs should be drenched. Season to taste using salt and pepper. Place crabs under broiler and allow to cook ten to twelve minutes. Turn crabs to opposite side and cook an additional ten to twelve minutes, basting occasionally. They may be served with lemon and parsley butter or with tartar sauce. This dish may also be eaten poboy style.

Changes

_____

_____

_____

_____

Blackened Louisiana Crabcakes

1 Hour   6 Servings

Comment:

Blackening, as a technique, has thrown the spotlight on Louisiana cooking. In the early 1980's just about every restaurant in America had a blackened dish on its menu. This recipe is used extensively as an appetizer at Lafitte's Landing.

FOR BLACKENED SEASONING:

1 tbsp sweet paprika
2 tsps salt
1/2 tsp cayenne pepper

1/2 tsp cracked black pepper
1 tbsp granulated garlic
1 tsp dried thyme

Blend all of the above spices and package into a container for future use.

FOR CRABCAKES:

3 pounds jumbo lump crabmeat
2 pounds white fish
1 cup finely diced onions
1/2 cup finely diced celery
1/2 cup finely diced bell pepper
1/2 cup finely diced red bell
    pepper
2 tbsps finely diced garlic
1 cup finely diced green onions

3 whole eggs
3/4 cup heavy whipping cream
1/4 cup lemon juice
1/2 cup mayonnaise
1 cup seasoned Italian
    bread crumbs
salt and cracked black pepper
    to taste
1/2 cup melted butter

(Continued)

Changes

_____
_____
_____
_____

(Blackened Louisiana Crabcakes continued)

In order to blacken, it is imperative that an outdoor propane burner and black iron skillet be used. The basic technique calls for the skillet to be "white hot". This may only be achieved on a very hot fire. In a food processor, blend fish into a fine paste. Remove from processor and place in a one gallon mixing bowl. Add onions, celery, bell peppers, garlic and green onions and blend well into fish mixture. Add eggs, whipping cream, lemon juice, and mayonnaise and combine well into mixture. Fold in lump crabmeat being careful not to break lumps, if possible. Sprinkle in bread crumbs, a little at a time, until proper consistency is achieved. The mixture should not be too dry. Season to taste using salt and pepper. Form mixture into four ounce cakes approximately three inches in diameter. Once all cakes are formed, they may be frozen or made ready for the skillet. To blacken, dredge each crab cake in melted butter and coat generously with blackened seasoning. Place in white hot skillet being cautious of flare-up. Crabcakes should saute two minutes on each side. The blackening will be caused when the butter crystalizes on the hot skillet. Continue until all are done and serve with tartar sauce or brown butter.

Changes

_____

_____

_____

_____

Cajun Garlic Crabs

1 Hour   6 Servings

Comment:

Garlic crabs have been around Cajun cottages for generations. When crabs became too plentiful, dishes such as this one began to emerge. I first tasted garlic crabs in a bar in Thibodeaux, Louisiana.

1 dozen hardshell crabs, cleaned   **1/4 cup cracked black pepper**
2 pounds melted butter   **1/4 cup pickling spice**
1/2 cup diced garlic   **salt to taste**
1/2 cup chopped parsley

Preheat oven to 475 degrees F. Have your seafood supplier remove the hardshell from live crabs and clean in the normal manner. Leave all legs and claws in place. Split the body into two pieces and set aside. In a two gallon baking dish, heat butter over medium high heat. Add all remaining ingredients and saute approximately two to three minutes. Add cleaned crabs and stir well to incorporate all seasonings. Once crabs are well seasoned with butter-garlic mixture, place in hot oven and cook, stirring occasionally, approximately ten to fifteen minutes. Serve crabs and a ladle of the garlic butter in a serving plate with hot French bread.

Changes

_____

_____

_____

_____

Shrimp Creole

1 Hour   6 Servings

Comment:

Without a doubt, this is the most famous dish in the city of New Orleans. As common as red beans and rice on Monday, the shrimp creole can be found on any table in Louisiana for Friday lunch.

3 pounds 21-25 count shrimp,
   peeled and deveined
3/4 cup vegetable oil
3/4 cup flour
1 cup chopped onions
1 cup chopped celery
1 cup chopped bell pepper
2 tbsps diced garlic
2 cups tomato sauce

1 cup diced tomatoes
1-1/2 quarts shellfish stock
   (see recipe)
1 cup chopped green onions
1/2 cup chopped parsley
salt and cracked black pepper
   to taste
dash of Louisiana Gold
   Pepper Sauce

The flavor of this dish will be greatly enhanced by the use of a rich shrimp stock. (see stock technique) This may be done by boiling the shrimp shells in shellfish stock to achieve a concentrated flavor. In a two gallon heavy bottom sauce pan, heat oil over medium high heat. Using a wire whisk, add flour, stirring constantly, until light brown roux is achieved. (see roux technique) Add onions, celery, bell pepper and garlic and saute until vegetables are wilted, approximately three to five minutes. Add tomato sauce and diced tomatoes and blend well into roux mixture. Slowly add shellfish stock, a little at a time, stirring constantly until sauce-like consistency is achieved. Allow to cook approximately fifteen minutes, stirring occasionally. Add stock should mixture become too thick. Add shrimp, green onions and parsley and continue to cook five additional minutes. Season to taste using salt and black pepper. Serve over hot white rice using a dash of Louisiana Gold.

Changes

_____

_____

_____

Barbecued Shrimp

1 Hour   6 Servings

Comment:

Barbecued shrimp originated at Manale's Restaurant in New Orleans. Long lines would form down Napoleon Avenue with customers waiting for the next table. Difficult for the novice to master, eating barbecued shrimp is an experience.

3 pounds 21-25 count head-on
    shrimp
1 cup melted butter
1/2 cup olive oil
4 tbsps diced garlic

4 tbsps cracked black pepper
4 tbsps Worcestershire sauce
2 tbsps dried basil
1 tbsp dried thyme
1 tbsp Louisiana Gold Pepper Sauce

It is important to realize that the head-on shrimp is best used when barbecueing. In Cajun country, it is a must to suck the heads of the butter-garlic flavored cooked shrimp. Preheat oven to 375 degrees F. In a heavy bottom saute pan, heat butter and olive oil over medium high heat. Combine all remaining ingredients and blend well into butter mixture. Cook one to two minutes. Place head-on shrimp in a large baking pan with a one inch lip. Pour melted butter mixture on top of shrimp, coating as evenly as possible. Place shrimp on center rack of oven and cook three to five minutes or until shrimp are pink and curly. Turn shrimp one time, baste well and allow to cook three to five additional minutes. Remove from oven and serve in soup bowls with the seasoned butter mixture. Hot French bread should accompany this dish.

Changes

_____

_____

_____

_____

Deep Fried Shrimp, Oysters or Catfish

1/2 Hour   6 Servings

Comment:

Deep frying is still quite common in the South. With the introduction of "lite" oils, the technique seems to live on forever. I feel it necessary to include my own frying technique since so many customers request it time and time again.

FOR BATTER:

1 egg	4 tbsps yellow mustard
1 cup milk	salt and cracked black pepper
1 cup water	to taste

In a one quart mixing bowl blend all ingredients well. Set aside.

FOR FRYING:

3 pounds 21-25 count shrimp, peeled and deveined	2 tbsps granulated garlic
oil for deep frying	2 tbsps cracked black pepper
4 cups yellow corn flour	1 tsp cayenne pepper
	2 tbsps salt

Using a homestyle deep frying unit, such as Fry Daddy, heat oil according to manufacturer's directions. A high quality vegetable oil or peanut oil should be considered. Corn flour is a double ground yellow corn meal. This ingredient may be found in the gourmet section of most food stores or as a pre-packaged fish fry such as Zatarain's. Combine corn flour, garlic, peppers and salt, blending well to ensure seasonings are evenly distributed. Dip shrimp in egg batter and then into seasoned corn flour. Deep fry, a few at a time, until they float to the top of the oil and are golden brown. Continue the process until all shrimp are done. Fried shrimp are best when served hot with cocktail sauce, tartar sauce or as a poboy.

Changes

_____

_____

_____

Bayou Shrimp Quiche

1-1/2 Hours   8 Servings

Comment:

Who would have thought of combining the quiche of France with the andouille and shrimp of Cajun country? Once again, we see the use of a combination of ingredients to create a unique dish in Louisiana cooking.

2 cups 170-190 shrimp, peeled
   and deveined
3/4 cup heavy duty mayonnaise
3 tbsps flour
4 eggs, beaten
1 3/4 cup heavy whipping cream
1/4 cup finely diced celery
1/4 cup finely diced red bell pepper

1 tbsp diced garlic
1/4 cup julienned andouille sausage
1 12-ounce package grated
   Swiss cheese
salt and cracked black pepper
   to taste
2 9-inch pie shells, unbaked

Preheat oven to 350 degrees F. Par boil shrimp in lightly seasoned water until pink and curly. Drain and set aside. In a large mixing bowl, combine mayonnaise, flour, eggs and whipping cream. Using a wire whisk, blend well until all is incorporated. Fold in onions, celery, bell pepper, garlic, andouille, and Swiss cheese until all ingredients are well distributed. Season to taste using salt and pepper. Divide shrimp equally into the bottom of the two unbaked pie shells. Pour the quiche mixture over the shrimp and cook on center rack of oven for approximately one hour and fifteen minutes. Quiche will be done when mixture is well set. Allow to sit ten minutes and cut each pie into four equal serving pieces. Quiche may be served hot or cold.

Changes

_____

_____

_____

_____

Jumbo Shrimp Viala

1 Hour   6 Servings

Comment:

This unique shrimp presentation was designed here at Lafitte's Landing Restaurant for use during the height of the white shrimp season. At this time of year, shrimp are plentiful and we only select ten to twelve count shrimp for this recipe.

3 dozen ten to twelve count
   head-on shrimp
1 pound jumbo lump crabmeat
1/2 cup melted butter
1/2 cup finely diced onions
1/4 cup finely diced celery
1/4 cup finely diced red bell
   pepper
2 tbsps finely diced garlic
1/2 cup sliced green onions
1 tsp dried thyme

1 tsp dried basil
1 tbsp Creole mustard
1 tbsp dry sherry
1/2 cup bechamel sauce (see recipe)
3/4 cup seasoned Italian
   bread crumbs
salt and cracked black pepper
   to taste
1/2 cup melted butter
1/2 cup dry sherry
1 cup water

Preheat oven to 350 degrees F. Place shrimp right side up on cutting board. Using a sharp paring knife, cut through the tail shell from the top of the tail to the bottom of the flipper, making sure not to separate head from tail. Using your thumbs, open the tail flat, remove the vein and gently pry the meat away from the shell, leaving it intact at the head. Set aside. In a large mixing bowl, combine all of the above ingredients except crabmeat, salt and pepper and the last three ingredients. Using a large mixing spoon, blend until all ingredients are well incorporated. Gently fold in crabmeat being careful not to break lumps. Season to taste using salt and pepper. Stuff tail of shrimp with generous portion of crabmeat stuffing. Once stuffed, the tail should lay flat on a baking pan. Place stuffed shrimp on a large baking sheet and drizzle with butter and sherry. Pour water into the bottom of the baking pan and place on center oven rack. Bake until stuffing is golden brown, approximately fifteen to twenty minutes.

Changes

Lafitte's Oyster Stuffing

1 Hour   1/2 Gallon

Comment:

This stuffing is used in many recipes in our restaurant. Though commonly used to stuff our baked quail, it is also used at Thanksgiving for our turkeys and capons.

2 pints select oysters in liquid
1/2 cup finely diced onions
1/4 cup finely diced celery
1/4 cup finely diced garlic
1/2 cup finely sliced green
    onions

1/2 cup finely chopped parsley
1/4 cup finely diced red bell pepper
salt and cracked black pepper
    to taste
3 cups seasoned Italian
    bread crumbs

Place oysters and oyster liquid in a food processor. Coarsely chop by using the pulse button once or twice. Remove to a large mixing bowl. Add onions, celery, garlic, green onions, parsley and bell pepper. Blend well to ensure that seasonings are evenly distributed. Season to taste using salt and black pepper. Sprinkle in bread crumbs, one cup at a time, until proper consistency is achieved. The stuffing should be moist but held together well by the bread crumbs. Correct seasonings if necessary. This stuffing may be made well in advance.

Changes

_____

_____

_____

_____

Deviled Oysters

1/2 Hour   6 Servings

Comment:

This recipe, though quite similar to the stuffing, is an excellent casserole side dish. It may also be considered for a brunch or light lunch item.

2 pints select oysters in liquid
1 cup melted butter
1 cup finely diced onions
1 cup finely diced celery
1/2 cup finely diced red bell
    pepper
1/2 cup sliced green onions
1 tbsp diced garlic
1 cup heavy whipping cream

1/2 cup diced egg
1/2 cup chopped parsley
1 tbsp Worcestershire sauce
1 tbsp Louisiana Gold
    Pepper Sauce
2 1/2 cups seasoned Italian
    bread crumbs
salt to taste

Preheat oven to 350 degrees F. In a two quart sauce pot, heat butter over medium high heat. Saute onions, celery, bell pepper, green onions and garlic until vegetables are wilted, approximately two to three minutes. Add heavy whipping cream, bring to a low boil and reduce to simmer. Add oysters and oyster liquid and cook until oysters are slightly curled. Remove from heat and add egg, parsley, Worcestershire and Louisiana Gold and blend well into mixture. Sprinkle in bread crumbs, one cup at a time, until proper consistency is achieved. Mixture should remain moist but should hold together well with bread crumbs. Season to taste using salt. Place in a well greased 9 x 13" baking dish or individual shells and bake approximately one half hour.

Changes

Oysters Castel

1 Hour   6 Servings

Comment:

This simple oyster dish will be a hit if used as an hors d'oeuvre item or as a side dish for a light lunch. Consider this casserole on the holiday table as an interesting seafood variation.

3 pints oysters in liquid	2 tbsps flour
2 cups chopped artichoke hearts	2 cups heavy whipping cream
1/4 pound butter	1 tbsp lemon juice
1/4 cup diced onions	1 ounce sherry
1/4 cup diced celery	salt and cracked black pepper
1/4 cup diced red bell pepper	to taste
1 tbsp diced garlic	pinch of nutmeg

In a ten inch heavy bottom saute pan, heat butter over medium high heat. Add artichokes, onions, celery, bell pepper and garlic and saute until vegetables are wilted, approximately three to five minutes. Add flour, blending well to form white roux. (see roux technique) Using a wire whip, add whipping cream, a little at a time, until white sauce consistency is achieved. Add oysters and oyster liquid, bring to a light boil and continue cooking fifteen to twenty minutes, stirring occasionally to keep mixture from sticking. Add lemon juice and sherry and blend well into sauce. Season to taste using salt, pepper and nutmeg. Continue to cook until oysters are curly and sauce is thick and creamy. Correct seasonings if necessary. Pour mixture into a hot chafing dish and serve with garlic croutons or on toast points as an entree.

Changes

_____

_____

_____

_____

Seafood Sauce Piquante

1-1/2 Hours   6 Servings

Comment:

The early Spanish certainly gave us the foundation for today's famous sauce piquante.
The most popular is a sauce piquante made with seafood or a combination of seafoods.

1 pound 21-25 count shrimp,
   peeled and deveined
1 pound jumbo lump crabmeat
1 pint select oysters in liquid
1 pound redfish, cubed
1/2 cup oil
1/2 cup flour
1 cup chopped onions
1 cup chopped celery
1 cup chopped bell pepper
2 tbsps diced garlic

1 8-ounce can tomato sauce
1 cup diced tomatoes
1 tbsp diced jalapenos
2 whole bay leaves
1/2 tsp thyme
1/2 tsp basil
1-1/2 quarts fish stock (see recipe)
1 cup chopped green onions
1 cup chopped parsley
salt and cracked black pepper
   to taste

In a one gallon heavy bottom sauce pot, heat oil over medium high heat. Using a wire whisk, add flour, stirring constantly until dark brown roux is achieved. (see roux technique) Add onions, celery, bell pepper and garlic and saute until vegetables are wilted, approximately three to five minutes. Add tomato sauce, diced tomatoes and jalapenos, blending well into roux mixture. Add bay leaves, thyme and basil. Slowly add fish stock, stirring constantly until all is incorporated. Bring to a low boil, reduce to simmer and cook thirty minutes. Add additional fish stock if necessary to retain volume. Add fish, shrimp, oysters and oyster liquid and continue to cook five to ten additional minutes. Add green onions and parsley. Season to taste using salt and pepper. When shrimp are pink and curled, carefully fold in lump crabmeat. Adjust seasonings if necessary. Serve over hot white rice or pasta.

Changes

_____

_____

_____

Pan Sauteed Trout
in Crabmeat Garlic Beurre Blanc

30 Minutes   6 Servings

Comment:

The compound butter sauces are part of our way of life here in South Louisiana. Two of my favorites are the beurre blanc and beurre cajun. This classic beurre blanc is flavored Louisiana style with lump crabmeat and andouille.

FOR SAUTEING:

6 5-6 ounce fillets speckled trout
1/2 cup oil
2 cups flour

salt and pepper to taste
eggwash (1 egg, 1/2 cup milk, 1/2 cup water - beaten)

In a heavy bottom saute pan, heat oil over medium high heat. Season flour to taste using salt and pepper. Dip trout fillets in eggwash and then in flour and saute in hot oil three to five minutes on each side until golden brown. Remove and keep warm.

(Continued)

Changes

_____

_____

_____

_____

Seafood

(Pan Sauteed Trout in Crabmeat Garlic Beurre Blanc continued)

FOR SAUCE:

1/4 cup melted butter
1/4 cup julienned andouille
2 tbsps diced garlic
1/4 cup sliced green onions
1/4 cup sliced mushrooms

1/4 cup dry white wine
1/2 cup heavy whipping cream
1 pound jumbo lump crabmeat
3/4 pound butter, chipped
salt and white pepper to taste

In a ten inch heavy bottom saute pan, heat butter over medium high heat. Add andouille, garlic, green onions and mushrooms and saute until vegetables are wilted, approximately three to five minutes. Deglaze with white wine and reduce to one half volume. Add heavy whipping cream, bring to a low boil and reduce volume to one half. Add lump crabmeat and blend well into cream mixture. Add chipped butter, a few pats at a time, swirling the pan constantly. Do not stir as hot spots may develop in pan and butter will separate. It is important that the pan is constantly swirled over the heat. Continue adding butter until all is incorporated. Remove from heat and season to taste using salt and pepper. Place generous serving of garlic beurre blanc in the center of a serving plate. Top with sauteed trout and a small portion of lump crabmeat.

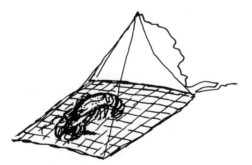

Changes

Broiled Fillet of Flounder
in Cajun Butter

1 Hour   6 Servings

Comment:

The Cajun butter or beurre cajun is my favorite of all compound butters. It is best when made with crawfish, but I have often substituted shrimp, oysters or crab. The natural fat in the crawfish seems to make the difference.

FOR BROILING:

6 5-6 ounce flounder fillets   salt and cayenne pepper to taste
1 cup white wine   paprika for color
1/2 cup water   1/4 cup chopped parsley
1/4 cup melted butter

Preheat oven to 375 degrees F. Place flounder fillets in a large baking pan with a one inch lip. Pour wine, water and butter over fish fillets. Season to taste using salt and pepper and sprinkle generously with paprika and parsley. Broil or bake ten to fifteen minutes or until fish is flaky to the touch. Do not overcook. Remove and keep warm.

(Continued)

Changes

_____

_____

_____

_____

(Broiled Fillet of Flounder in Cajun Butter continued)

FOR SAUCE:

1/4 cup melted butter
1 pound fresh crawfish tails
1 tbsp chopped garlic
1/4 cup chopped green onions
1/4 cup sliced mushrooms
1/2 cup diced tomatoes

1/2 cup dry white wine
1 tbsp lemon juice
1/2 cup heavy whipping cream
3/4 pound butter chipped
salt and cayenne pepper to taste

In a heavy bottom saute pan, heat butter over medium high heat. Add crawfish, garlic, green onions, mushrooms and tomato and saute until vegetables are wilted, approximately three to five minutes. Deglaze with white wine and lemon juice and reduce to one half volume. Add heavy whipping cream, bring to a low boil and reduce until thickened. Slowly add chipped butter, a few pats at a time, swirling pan constantly. Do not stir as hot spots may develop and butter will separate. It is imperative that the pan is constantly swirled. Continue until all butter is incorporated. Season to taste using salt and pepper. Place a generous serving of Cajun butter in the center of the serving plate and top with broiled or baked flounder. Top with a small amount of the crawfish tails.

Changes

_____

_____

_____

_____

Redfish Courtbouillon

1 Hour   6 Servings

Comment:

Courtbouillon in classical cooking refers to a poaching liquid flavored with onions, carrots etc. The Courtbouillon of Cajun and Creole country is a rich tomato sauce dish revered here for many centuries.

3 pounds redfish fillets
3/4 cup oil
3/4 cup flour
1 cup chopped onions
1 cup chopped celery
1 cup chopped bell pepper
2 tbsps diced garlic
2 cups sliced mushrooms
2 8-ounce cans tomato sauce

1-1/2 quarts fish stock (see recipe)
1 tsp dried thyme
1 tsp dried basil
2 bay leaves
3 lemon slices
1 cup chopped green onions
1 cup chopped parsley
salt and cracked black pepper
   to taste

Cut redfish fillets diagonally into two and a half inch strips. In a one gallon heavy bottom sauce pan, heat oil over medium high heat. Using a wire whisk, add flour, stirring constantly until dark brown roux is achieved. (see roux technique) Add onions, celery, bell pepper, garlic and mushrooms and saute until vegetables are wilted, approximately three to five minutes. Add tomato sauce, blending well into roux mixture. Slowly add fish stock, a little at a time, stirring constantly until well incorporated. Add thyme, basil, bay leaves and lemon slices. Bring to a low boil, reduce to simmer and cook thirty minutes. Add fish stock to retain volume. Add green onions and parsley and season to taste using salt and pepper. Cook an additional ten minutes and slowly add fish pieces. Stir occasionally until fish is done, approximately five to ten minutes. Correct seasonings if necessary. Serve over hot white rice or pasta.

Wild Game

Wild Game

I was born in St. James Parish, the cradle of Cajun cuisine. I grew up a few feet from the monument marking the first permanent settlement of the Acadians in Louisiana. This marker stands near Sainte-Jacques de Cabanocey Catholic Church, erected in 1757, which was the first chapel established in St. James Parish. St. Jacques de Cabanocey became the principle settlement of the Acadians along the Mississippi River.

Cabanocey is an Indian word meaning "clearing where mallard ducks roost". This was the new home of the Cajuns, a unique people imbued with extraordinary stamina, strength and courage. They created their feast from what was available on the swamp floor. The "Cabanocey" was their outdoor pantry and the birthplace of Cajun cuisine as we know it today.

During that initial era of Acadian history in South Louisiana, the only available resources for subsistence were wild game and seafood. Wild game played the most important role in the early development of Cajun cuisine.

The life of the Cajuns revolved around wild game. The cooking of wild game was instrumental in the development of "the trinity concept" of seasonings so crucial to the distinctiveness of our cuisine. The local Indians, to whom the Micmac Indians of Nova Scotia passed their tutorial caps, instructed the Cajuns on the unique wildlife available in Bayou country.

The duck hunts would always create a special excitement for the early Acadians. Back in Acadie, Canada, the arrival of the mallard ducks signified the beginning of Spring. To the Acadians, each year was a test of resourcefulness in surviving long and hard winters. As the ducks flew over, the settlers were filled with the anticipation of meals to come. These early Acadians soon came to realize that the flight of the mallards meant waterways free of ice, snow melting into clear streams and duck breasts preserved to ease hunger.

It is easy then, to see why the Acadians offered thanks to Saint Jacques upon their discovery of the Cabanocey in South Louisiana. The discovery of the winter home of the mallards proved a good omen to these weary exiles. Soon the Houmas, Choctaw and Chetimaches Indians had even more natural bounty to show the arriving Acadians in their new homeland.

Wild Game

What an extraordinary outdoor pantry the Cabanocey proved to be! Here were grosbecs, a premier small bird of the swamps, mallard ducks, geese, squirrel, rabbits, deer, quail, doves, woodcocks and wild turkey. Wild spices and seasonings were found everywhere. No Cajun cabin would be without a pot of rabbit fricassee or pot roasted venison smothered in wild Louisiana mushrooms simmering on the stove.

The Creoles of New Orleans utilized wild game brought into town by Indians, Cajun trappers, and hunters. Canvasback, mallard ducks and other wild game would be prepared in a salmis, a Creole stew made with wine and slowly cooked for hours. Recipes abound in Creole cuisine with such names as chevreuil a la chasseur (hunter style venison), salmis de canards, sauvages a la Creole, (stewed wild ducks) and lapin en matelote (a rabbit dish made with roux, tomatoes, spices and claret wine).

All of these principal players on this stage of South Louisiana's developing cuisine are still stars today. Duck hunters from all over the area bring the fruits of their labor here to Lafitte's Landing Restaurant for me to prepare in a traditional fashion or in new and evolving ways. Just the other day, a game dinner for a group of hunters included wild rabbit terrine, duck and andouille gumbo, charbroiled venison salad and boneless leg of rabbit stuffed with lump crabmeat on a sauce of grand veneur.

Don't hesitate to try any of the recipes in this section. If you must substitute a domestic game animal for the wild version, go ahead. If you cannot find the specific game called for in a recipe, substitute any local variety and all will be well. Go ahead, create! You certainly don't want to miss out on the most fundamental aspect of Cajun and Creole cuisine.

"Our Indian killed a deer and the other men some turkeys, but the Indian begged us not to cook the venison and turkey together because it would spoil his luck in future hunting and we should repent it with fasting and prayer."

William Byrd, First Thanksgiving

Wild Game

Principles of Wild Game Cookery

One major factor to keep in mind when preparing wild game is that the flesh tends to be dry. These are not domesticated animals that have been corn fed and have fat layers and marbling. Because of the constant movement of game animals, necessitated by their lifestyle, a lean sinewy meat is produced.

What first appears as the disadvantage of wild game is really its recommendation. This is, of course, what gives the meat its distinctive taste and unique flavor.

The trinity of seasonings in Cajun and Creole cooking evolved as a means of dealing with the tawny meat in a braising fashion. Moisture from the vegetables enhances the flavor of game and also keeps the flesh from drying out and toughening.

Placing pork fat in the roux and larding with bacon are additional means of providing succulent moist game dishes. Fruits and spices further tone down "wild" tastes and improve the flavor.

Many times though, judgement and experience make the difference as decisions are made as to what the game is and what it needs to be tasty, tender, and delicious! I've eaten fresh quail that needed no more than salt, pepper and a grill to become the finest food ever eaten.

With certain game varieties, the international cooking principles utilized in preparing tougher cuts of meat are what's needed. What makes Coq au Vin in French cuisine so tremendous? The fact that it requires an old rooster! Marinating and lengthy cooking of the meat in red wine produces a truly great dish that couldn't be duplicated with a young spring chicken. Certain wild game dishes stand as masterpieces in culinary repertoire because of the care that is taken in their preparation.

As you work through the wild game recipes, look for the following principles and remember them as your creativity grows. Since the "unknown" is such a factor in cooking wild game, improvisation is necessary and afterall, this is half the fun.

Wild Game

AROMATIC VEGETABLES — add moisture and flavor to wild game and are essential to a braise.

LARDING — with pork fat or bacon, bastes the meat and keeps it moist, protecting it from drying out during cooking.

WINES AND STOCKS — which are important in all cooking, are essential in wild game cookery. The wine aids in breaking down tough tissue and the stock adds gelatinous flavor and moisture.

SEASONINGS — round out the taste of game and tend to tone down some flavors while perking up others.

FRUITS — with their acidic bases, help to tenderize wild game as well as off-set some of the natural earthy flavors.

TRUSSING — closes the cavity and seals in stuffings or seasonings. The closed cavity aids in moisture retention.

BRAISING AND SIMMERING — two keys to successful wild game cooking. These slow cooking methods allow the flavor of the vegetables, fruits, wines, stocks, and seasonings to penetrate and moisturize the game. Over-cooking is a great danger when preparing wild game and these slow cooking techniques will help prevent this from happening.

HEATED PLATTERS FOR SERVICE — hot plates are essential because, due to its lack of natural fats and marbeling, game tends to cool quickly and takes on a slightly different taste.

CREATIVITY — as previously mentioned, is the first and last principle and the most important. When dealing with game, make each dish a signature of your heritage and style as you improvise in the style of the Cajuns and Creoles.

RM 89

Baked Mallard Ducks in Apple Essence

4 Hours   6 Servings

Comment:

The parish of St. James, located west of New Orleans, is the largest roosting area for mallard ducks in the southern United States. It is interesting to note that the Cajuns first settled at Cabanocey, a section of land on this mallard roost.

3 mallard ducks, cleaned

1 pint white vinegar

1 quart cold water

1/2 pound butter

4 medium onions, quartered

6 stalks celery, chopped

6 carrots, quartered

6 red apples, quartered

6 tsps garlic, diced

salt and cracked black pepper
   to taste

3 quarts chicken stock (see recipe)

Make sure mallard ducks have been well cleaned and any visible shot removed. Soak the ducks, breast down, in the vinegar and water mixture overnight. This process will help remove the extreme gamey taste. Preheat oven to 325 degrees F. In a heavy roasting pan or dutch oven place ducks, breast side up. Season the inside cavity generously with salt and black pepper. You should over-season this cavity since only a small amount of the seasoning will be transferred to the dish. Place one eighth pound of butter into the cavity of each duck. Follow with one quarter of onions, celery, carrots and apples. Place one teaspoon of garlic in the cavity. Season the outside of the ducks generously with salt and pepper and place all remaining fruits and vegetables including garlic tightly around the ducks. Pour in chicken stock, cover tightly with aluminum foil and bake approximately two and a half to three hours. Check occasionally for doneness. The ducks will be tender when the legs pull easily away from the body. When ducks are tender, remove aluminum foil and allow to brown thirty minutes to one hour.

Changes

_____

_____

_____

_____

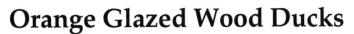

Orange Glazed Wood Ducks

3 Hours   6 Servings

Comment:

Since South Louisiana produces such a fine orange crop each year, it is simple to understand why the Cajuns and Creoles have taken advantage of this fruit flavor in their wild game cooking.

6 wood ducks
3/4 cup oil
2 cups flour
2 cups chopped onions
1 cup chopped celery
1 cup chopped bell pepper
1 cup diced carrots

2 tbsps diced garlic
3 oranges, peeled and sectioned
1/2 cup orange juice concentrate
1-1/2 quarts chicken stock (see recipe)
salt and cracked black pepper
    to taste
12 strips bacon

Preheat oven to 375 degrees F. Make sure ducks are well cleaned and all visible shot removed. Season ducks well inside and out using salt and pepper. In a large dutch oven, heat oil over medium high heat. Dust ducks evenly with flour and brown well on all sides. Remove and set aside. In the same oil, saute onions, celery, bell pepper, carrots and garlic until vegetables are wilted, approximately three to five minutes. Add oranges, orange juice and chicken stock and stir well to blend into vegetable mixture. Bring to a rolling boil and remove from heat. Season liquid to taste using salt and pepper. Place ducks, breasts side up, in hot mixture and top with two slices each of bacon. Cover tightly, bake for two hours and check occasionally for doneness. Ducks will be done when legs pull apart easily from the body. Remove cover and allow ducks to brown. You may serve with the natural drippings or strain all vegetables from the stock and thicken with a light brown roux. (see roux technique)

Changes

_____

_____

_____

_____

Smoked Breast of Mallard

1 Hour   6 Servings

Comment:

This is a very interesting variation for wild duck. We often use smoked duck breast in salads, pastas or sliced as a hot appetizer.

6 whole mallard duck breasts,
   deboned
1/2 cup dry red wine
3/4 cup Louisiana cane syrup
2 tbsps red wine vinegar
1/4 cup cracked black pepper
1 tbsp dried thyme

1 tbsp dried basil
1 tbsp dried tarragon
1 tbsp diced garlic
salt to taste
2 cans Barq's root beer
1 cup water

Preheat smoker according to manufacturer's directions. You may wish to soak pecan wood or hickory chips in Barq's root beer for a very unique flavor. In a large mixing bowl, combine duck breasts with all of the above ingredients except root beer and water. Allow to set at room temperature for one hour. Pour root beer and one cup of water into the water pan of the smoker. Place over the coals and position duck breasts on top rack of smoker. Cook for one hour and check for doneness. The breasts are best when served between medium rare and medium. Once done, breasts may be sliced and served hot or used as an ingredient in salads, pastas or other main dishes.

HINT: You may wish to try this same recipe with duck breasts grilled on your barbecue pit or charbroiler.

Changes

_____

_____

_____

_____

Roasted Goose

3 Hours   6 Servings

Comment:

South Louisiana is a haven for game birds. I suppose this is why our state motto is "Sportsman's Paradise". Canadian geese and speckled bellies are found by the thousands here in the marshlands of South Louisiana.

1 large wild goose or 2 small geese	2 cups sliced mushrooms
4 cups diced onions	2 cups red seedless grapes
2 cups diced celery	1-1/2 quarts chicken stock (see recipe)
2 cups diced carrots	salt and cracked black pepper to taste
4 tbsps diced garlic	

Preheat oven to 375 degrees F. Make sure goose is well cleaned inside and out. Season the inside cavity of the bird well with salt and pepper. Place a generous amount of onions, celery, carrots and garlic into the cavity. Season the outside of the goose with salt and pepper. Using a small paring knife, cut slits under the breasts of the goose and stuff generously with garlic. Place the goose into a heavy dutch oven and surround with remaining seasonings, mushrooms and grapes. Pour in chicken stock and cover tightly with lid or aluminum foil. Bake for two and a half hours and check for doneness. Bird will be done when legs pull away easily from the body. Once done, remove cover and allow goose to brown. The bird may be served with the natural drippings or the juices may be strained and thickened with a light roux. (see roux technique)

Changes

Wild Dove in Madeira Wine

1-1/2 Hours   6 Servings

Comment:

Though Louisiana is the dove capital of the South, many Louisiana hunters today are traveling south of the border to Mexico for their annual hunts. I get many requests for a dove recipe, so here is my favorite.

18 doves, cleaned	2 cups sliced mushrooms
1 cup butter	2 tbsps flour
2 cups flour	6 purple plums, quartered
1 cup diced onions	3 cups madeira wine
1 cup diced celery	1 quart chicken stock
1 cup diced bell pepper	salt and cracked black pepper
2 tbsps diced garlic	to taste

Wash birds well inside and out and remove any visible shot. In a large dutch oven, melt butter over medium high heat. Dust doves in flour and brown well on all sides in butter. Remove and set aside. Add onions, celery, bell pepper, garlic and mushrooms. Saute until vegetables are wilted, approximately three to five minutes. Sprinkle in two tablespoons of flour and blend well into vegetable mixture. Add purple plums, madeira wine and chicken stock and blend well until all is incorporated. Bring to a rolling boil, reduce to simmer and return birds to the hot sauce. Season lightly using salt and pepper. Cover and continue to cook one to one and a half hours. Add a small amount of chicken stock when necessary should mixture become too thick. When cooked, serve three doves per person with a generous amount of sauce.

Changes

_____

_____

_____

_____

Medallions of Venison and Oysters

1 Hour   6 Servings

Comment:

This is definitely a recipe that reflects the evolution of Cajun and Creole cooking. The marriage of wild game and seafood is quite common in Louisiana. However, to present it in a classical manner is truly nouvelle in style.

12 3-ounce medallions of venison tenderloin
24 select oysters
1/2 cup oil
1 cup flour
1/4 cup julienned andouille sausage
1/2 cup sliced mushrooms

1/2 cup sliced green onions
1 tbsp diced garlic
1/4 cup muscadet wine
2 cups game demi-glace (see recipe)
1/2 cup heavy whipping cream
1/4 cup chopped parsley
salt and cracked black pepper to taste

In a ten inch heavy bottom saute pan, heat oil over medium high heat. Dredge medallions in flour, shake off all excess and saute until golden brown, approximately three to five minutes on each side. Add andouille, mushrooms, green onions and garlic. Saute one to two minutes and add oysters. Continue to saute until oyster liquid is rendered and edges begin to curl. Deglaze in muscadet wine and add demi-glace and cream. Bring to a low boil and cook until sauce is slightly thickened. Garnish with parsley and season to taste using salt and cracked black pepper. Serve two medallions of venison in the center of dinner plate. Top with two oysters and generous serving of hunter sauce. This hunter sauce is made a little lighter with the addition of whipping cream. I have done this in order to compliment the delicate taste of the oysters.

Changes

_____

_____

_____

_____

Stuffed Tenderloin
of Venison with Hunter Sauce

1 Hour   6 Servings

Comment:

Venison seems to be more popular today than ever before in restaurants across the country. Customers tend to enjoy the heavier taste of wild game while benefitting from the lower cholesterol content of the meat.

FOR STUFFING:

1 5-pound tenderloin, trimmed
1 cup ground andouille sausage
1 cup ground crawfish tails
1/4 cup finely diced onions
1/4 cup finely sliced green
    onions

2 tbsps diced garlic
1/2 cup bechamel sauce (see recipe)
3/4 cup seasoned Italian
    bread crumbs
salt and cracked black pepper
    to taste

In a large mixing bowl, combine all of the above ingredients except tenderloin. Mix well to ensure that all spices are well blended into stuffing. Season to taste using salt and pepper. Using a sharp knife, cut a one inch pocket lengthwise through the center of the tenderloin. Use a pastry bag to force the stuffing into the tenderloin. Once stuffed, set aside.

(Continued)

Changes

_____

_____

_____

_____

Wild Game

(Stuffed Tenderloin of Venison with Hunter Sauce continued)

FOR COOKING:

1 stuffed tenderloin	1 tsp dried basil
1/4 cup melted butter	1 tsp dried tarragon
1/2 cup Louisiana cane syrup	1 cup dry red wine
1/2 cup dijon mustard	2 cups demi-glace (see recipe)
1 tbsp diced garlic	salt and cracked black pepper
1 tsp dried thyme	to taste

Preheat oven to 500 degrees F. Place stuffed tenderloin in the center of a large baking pan with a one inch lip. Season well with butter, syrup, mustard, garlic. thyme, basil, tarragon, salt and pepper. Rub all seasonings well into the meat. Place in oven and bake twenty-five to thirty minutes for medium rare. Check for doneness. A meat thermometer should read between 125 and 135 degrees for perfection. When done, remove tenderloin and keep warm. Deglaze pan with red wine, scraping all drippings into the wine. Add demi-glace, blend well and pour into a nine inch saute pan. Reduce over medium high heat until sauce is well thickened. Season to taste using salt and pepper. Use a sharp knife to slice three ounce medallions from the roasted tenderloin. Serve two medallions per person with a generous serving of hunter sauce.

Changes

_____

_____

_____

_____

Roasted Leg of Venison

3 Hours   6-8 Servings

Comment:

I have found this to be one of the great methods of preparing a leg of venison. Most methods will either overcook an already dry meat or tend to render it stringy and tasteless. Try this simple method and I feel you will agree it is worth the wait.

1 5-pound venison leg, deboned	dried thyme to taste
1/2 cup finely diced onion	dried basil to taste
1/2 cup finely diced celery	dried tarragon to taste
1/4 cup finely diced garlic	2 tbsps diced garlic
1/4 cup finely diced bacon	3/4 cup oil
1/4 cup salt	1 cup diced onions
1/4 cup cracked black pepper	1 cup diced celery
2 cups apple cider vinegar	2 cups diced carrots
salt and cracked black pepper to taste	

Rinse venison leg in cold water. In a small mixing bowl, combine onions, celery, garlic, bacon, salt and pepper. Using a paring knife, cut one inch slits at intervals around the leg and stuff with equal amounts of the seasoning-bacon mixture. Place the leg in a dutch oven, pour in the apple cider vinegar, cover and allow to set overnight in the refrigerator. The next day, preheat oven to 450 degrees F. Remove venison from refrigerator and season to taste with salt, pepper, thyme, basil, tarragon and garlic. Allow to set at room temperature for one hour. Remove the apple vinegar and pour oil into the bottom of the dutch oven. Cook over medium high heat until venison leg is well browned on all sides. Once brown, add onions, celery and carrots. Place dutch roaster in preheated oven and bake for one hour. At this time, the venison should be medium rare and perfect for slicing. You may wish to deglaze with red wine and add one or two cups of demi-glace (see recipe) should a sauce be desired.

Changes

_____

_____

Sauteed Rabbit Tenderloin in Brandy Cream

30 Minutes   6 Servings

Comment:

The tenderloin of domestic rabbit is perfect for this dish. The wild rabbit has a much smaller tenderloin, however, I have found it to be quite flavorful. Using either one, try this recipe. It is a delicacy!

12 rabbit tenderloins	1/2 tsp dried thyme
1/2 cup butter	1/2 tsp dried basil
1/2 cup flour	1/4 cup brandy
1 tbsp diced garlic	1 cup demi-glace (see recipe)
1/4 cup sliced green onions	1/2 cup heavy whipping cream
1/4 cup sliced mushrooms	salt and cracked black pepper to taste

In a ten inch heavy bottom saute pan, heat butter over medium high heat. Dredge rabbit tenderloins in flour and saute until golden brown on all sides. Add garlic, green onions, mushrooms, thyme and basil. Saute until vegetables are wilted, approximately one to two minutes. Remove saute pan from heat and add brandy. When pan is returned to the heat, brandy may ignite. This is fine. Reduce to one half volume and add demi-glace and whipping cream. Bring to a low boil and cook until sauce is slightly thickened. Season to taste using salt and black pepper. Serve two tenderloins in the center of a dinner plate and top with brandy cream sauce.

Changes

_____

_____

_____

_____

Cajun Stuffed Leg of Rabbit

2 Hours   6 Servings

Comment:

The stuffed leg of rabbit has been a gold medal winner in culinary competitions throughout Louisiana. In addition to being served on our menu, this dish has been the entree for many gourmet dinners served by us worldwide.

6 hind legs of rabbit, deboned
1 pound lump crabmeat
1/4 cup finely diced onions
1/4 cup finely diced celery
1/4 cup finely diced red bell
   pepper
2 tbsps diced garlic
2 tbsps sliced green onions
1/2 cup bechamel sauce
   (see recipe)
1/2 cup seasoned Italian
   bread crumbs

salt and cayenne pepper
   to taste
1/2 cup melted butter
1/2 cup Louisiana cane syrup
1 tbsp dried thyme
1 tbsp dried basil
1 tbsp dried tarragon
1 tbsp cracked black pepper
1/2 cup dry red wine
2 cups demi-glace
   (see recipe)

(Continued)

Changes

_____

_____

_____

_____

(*Cajun Stuffed Leg of Rabbit* continued)

Have your butcher debone six hind legs of rabbit to the knee joint. In a large mixing bowl, combine lump crabmeat, onions, celery, bell pepper, garlic, green onions and bechamel sauce. Blend well to ensure proper mixing of all ingredients. Slowly add bread crumbs until all are incorporated. Season to taste using salt and pepper. Inside the pocket formed when the leg was deboned, place crabmeat stuffing. Make sure to place an equal amount in all six legs. Once stuffed, place the legs on a large baking sheet and top with butter, cane syrup, thyme, basil, tarragon and cracked black pepper. Allow to set at room temperature for one hour. Preheat oven to 450 degrees F. Bake rabbit legs until golden brown and stuffing is cooked, approximately twenty-five to thirty minutes. Remove legs from baking pan and deglaze with red wine. Scrape all drippings into a nine inch saute pan and add demi-glace. Bring to a low boil, reduce to simmer and cook until sauce is slightly thickened. Slice rabbit leg into three equal pieces and place in center of serving plate. Spoon generous serving of sauce on the side of the rabbit.

RM89

Changes

_____

_____

_____

_____

Wild Game

Fricassee of Wild Rabbit

2 Hours   6 Servings

Comment:

The fricassee is probably the most popular method of cooking rabbit in South Louisiana. Slowly cooked in the black iron pot, this dish is considered simple, yet the best tasting rabbit dish in Bayou country.

2 young wild rabbits
3/4 cup oil
2 cups flour
2 cups chopped onions
1 cup chopped celery
1 cup chopped bell pepper
2 tbsps diced garlic

1 cup diced tomatoes
2 cups sliced oyster mushrooms
2 cups beef or chicken stock
   (see recipe)
salt and cracked black pepper
   to taste

Cut rabbit into eight serving size pieces. In a one gallon black iron pot, heat oil over medium high heat. Dredge rabbit in flour and brown well on all sides in hot oil. Once browned remove and set aside. In the same oil add onions, celery, bell pepper, garlic and tomatoes. Saute until vegetables are wilted, approximately three to five minutes. Return rabbit to pot and stir well into seasonings. Add mushrooms and beef stock. Season to taste using salt and pepper. Bring the stock to a light boil, reduce heat to simmer, cover pot and allow to braise for one and a half hours. Rabbit will be done when tender to the touch. Add stock, if necessary, should mixture become too dry. Correct seasonings if necessary. This dish should be served over hot white rice with a side dish of white beans. (see recipe)

Changes

_____

_____

_____

_____

Wild Game

Braised Quail on Toast

1 Hour   6 Servings

Comment:

As young boys, we always raised quail penned in the back yard, along with pigeons, ducks and a multitude of wild game. This recipe was created one Sunday morning using some of those corn-fattened quail.

12 quail breasts
3/4 cup bacon dripping
1 cup flour
1 cup finely diced onions
1 cup finely diced celery
1 cup finely diced green onions
2 tbsps finely diced garlic
2 cups sliced mushrooms

2 tbsps flour
2 cups rose wine
1 cup chicken stock (see recipe)
2 cups red seedless grapes
salt and cracked black pepper
   to taste
12 French bread croutons, toasted

In a heavy bottom dutch oven, heat bacon drippings over medium high heat. Season quail lightly with salt and pepper and dredge in flour. Brown well on all sides. When done, remove and set aside. Into the same oil add onions, celery, green onions, garlic and mushrooms. Saute until vegetables are wilted, approximately three to five minutes. Sprinkle in two tablespoons of flour, blending well into the vegetable mixture. Add rose wine, chicken stock and seedless grapes and stir until all are incorporated. Return quail to the sauce mixture, bring to a low boil and reduce to simmer. Cover and cook one hour. When quail are tender, serve two breasts on toasted croutons and top with a generous serving of sauce.

Changes

Oyster Stuffed Quail

1 Hour   6 Servings

Comment:

This is another one of the gold medal dishes of Lafitte's Landing Restaurant. This dish was served at the opening dinner of my Lafitte's Landing East in Moscow, May 15, 1988.

12 quail, deboned
2 pints select oysters
1/2 cup finely diced onions
1/2 cup finely diced celery
1 tbsp finely diced garlic
1/4 cup finely diced red bell
    pepper

1/4 cup bechamel sauce (see recipe)
1 cup seasoned Italian bread crumbs
1/2 cup melted butter
1/2 cup dry red wine
2 cups demi-glace (see recipe)
1/2 cup heavy whipping cream
salt and cracked black pepper
    to taste

Preheat oven to 450 degrees F. Have your butcher debone twelve quail, breasts only. The bones may remain in the legs and wings. Coarsely chop oysters and in a large mixing bowl, combine with onions, celery, garlic, bell pepper and bechamel sauce. Mix well to ensure proper blending of all ingredients. Slowly add bread crumbs, stirring constantly, until proper consistency is achieved. Stuffing should be moist but held together well with the bread crumbs. Season to taste using salt and pepper. Stuff each quail with an equal amount of the oyster stuffing. Once all quail have been stuffed, secure the legs with a toothpick. Place all quail in a large ten inch oven proof skillet or baking dish. Drizzle with melted butter and season to taste using salt and pepper. Place quail in oven and cook until golden brown, approximately thirty minutes. Remove quail from saute pan and deglaze with red wine. Add demi-glace and cream, bring to a low boil, reduce to simmer, and cook until sauce is slightly thickened. Place two quail in the center of a serving plate, remove toothpicks from the legs and top with generous serving of sauce.

Changes

_____

_____

Grilled Quail

1 Hour   6 Servings

Comment:

This is a simple yet elegant way to serve quail. I have seen grilled quail served as an appetizer, salad, entree and even grilled to order as an hors d'oeuvre item. Try it any way. It's spectacular.

12 quail, split at the backbone   **1 tbsp dried thyme**
1/2 cup dry red wine   **1 tbsp dried basil**
1/4 cup red wine vinegar   **1 tbsp dried tarragon**
3/4 cup Louisiana cane syrup   **2 tbsps cracked black pepper**
2 tbsps diced garlic   **salt to taste**

Preheat outdoor charbroiler or barbecue grill according to manufacturer's instructions. I suggest soaking a few chips of pecan wood for another unique flavor. Quail should be split across the backbone and completely flattened. Place quail on a large baking pan and coat with all remaining ingredients. Blend well to ensure that quail are well coated with the seasoning mixture. Allow to set at room temperature for one hour. Wet wood chips may be placed on the grill at this time. Position quail, bone side down, on the hot grill. Allow to cook three to five minutes, basting with the marinade ingredients. Turn quail meat side down, being careful not to burn them should fire become too hot. Cook two to three minutes and continue turning until birds are done to your liking. I prefer to serve the grilled quail hot with sweet mustard, however, they are also excellent served cold.

Changes

_____

_____

_____

_____

Alligator Chili

1-1/2 Hours   6 Servings

Comment:

Although alligator is served only as an appetizer in sausage form at Lafitte's Landing, I see it served in many ways around the state. The dish seems to have found renewed popularity over the past few years. Here is an old camp recipe.

3 pounds alligator meat, diced
1/2 cup oil
2 cups diced onions
1 cup diced celery
1 cup diced bell pepper
2 tbsps diced garlic
2 tbsps diced jalapenos

1 16-ounce can pinto beans
3 8-ounce cans tomato sauce
1 cup chicken stock
1 tbsp chili powder
1 tsp cumin
salt and cracked black pepper
    to taste

In a heavy dutch oven, heat oil over medium high heat. Add alligator and saute twenty minutes to render juices. Add onions, celery, bell pepper, garlic and jalapenos. Saute until vegetables are wilted, approximately three to five minutes. Add pinto beans, tomato sauce and chicken stock, bring to a low boil and reduce to simmer. Add chili powder and cumin, stir well into mixture and allow to cook one hour, stirring occasionally. Once alligator is tender, season to taste using salt and black pepper. This dish is always served at hunting camp dinners over spaghetti.

Changes

_____
_____
_____
_____

Desserts

Desserts

With such an emphasis on the seafood, game and vegetables of the area, South Louisianians regard dessert as a mellow ending to dinner, rather than the grand finale. This is not to say that people of the bayous don't like dessert; they love dessert. But true Louisiana desserts tend to be simple and understated.

With the Germans, came milk, eggs and butter. These three ingredients gave rise to the many custard-based dishes found on dessert menus in South Louisiana. Fresh berries growing wild in the Bayous supplied the ingredients for our blackberry and strawberry pies. Even vegetables such as carrots and squash found their way into the baking dishes and onto the dessert tables. New creations emerged from the Creole tables such as Bananas Foster and Pralines.

For a happy ending to any Cajun and Creole meal, rice pudding, bread pudding served with whiskey sauce, pecan or sweet potato pies, cakes and other fruit desserts were considered more than adequate. Once again, as with most recipes in South Louisiana, even our desserts, though simple in nature, stand alone in the world of international cooking.

"Once in a young lifetime one should be allowed to have as much sweetness and dessert as one can possibly want and hold."

Judith Onley

Bananas Foster in Cane Syrup

30 Minutes   6 Servings

Comment:

This famous New Orleans dessert was named after Dick Foster during the early 1950's. Mr. Foster was serving as a vice chairman of the committee in charge of cleaning up the French Quarter of New Orleans.

6 bananas, cut lengthwise in half	1/2 tsp nutmeg
4 tbsps butter	1/4 cup banana liqueur
1/2 cup Louisiana cane syrup	1/4 cup dark rum
1 tbsp brown sugar	6 scoops praline ice cream
1/2 tsp cinnamon	(see recipe)

The original dish calls for only brown sugar, however, since cane syrup is such a major player in Louisiana cuisine, I have elected to use this sweetener in the recipe. In a heavy bottom saute pan, heat butter over medium high heat. Add cane syrup and brown sugar and blend well. Add cinnamon and nutmeg and continue to cook until sauce is bubbly hot. Add bananas and cook into the syrup until they are tender to the touch. Remove from flame and add banana liqueur and dark rum. Return to the flame, being careful as liqueur will ignite. If using an electric range use a match to ignite the liqueurs. Swirl the pan slowly until the flame dies out. Place a single scoop of ice cream in a serving bowl, top with two slices of banana and a generous serving of the sauce.

Changes

_____

_____

_____

_____

Deep Dish Blackberry Pie

1-1/2 Hours   8-10 Servings

Comment:

Blackberries are so plentiful in the Bayous of South Louisiana that many interesting dishes are created using blackberries as a main ingredient. This simple blackberry cobbler was a mainstay in our home when I was a boy.

3 pints blackberries
2 9-inch pie shells
1/4 pound butter
2 cups sugar
1/2 cup water

3 tbsps corn starch
1/4 tsp salt
pinch of cinnamon
pinch of nutmeg

Preheat oven to 425 degrees F. Line an 8 x 12" oblong baking dish with one of the pie shells. Be sure that bottom and sides of baking dish are covered with the shell. In a heavy bottom saute pan, melt butter over medium high heat. Add sugar and dissolve into the butter. Remove from heat and cool slightly. Combine water and corn starch adding a little extra water, if necessary, for corn starch to dissolve. Add into butter-sugar mixture, stirring well. Blend in salt, cinnamon and nutmeg. Place berries in baking dish and top with butter-sugar mixture. Cover top with second pie crust, sealing edges well around the baking dish. Cut several two inch slits in the top of the pie crust using a sharp paring knife. Place on the bottom shelf of the oven and bake approximately one hour.

Changes

Desserts

Bread Pudding Souffle

1 Hour   6 Servings

Comment:

This is, simply stated, the evolution of bread pudding. The dish was created for the opening of my restaurant in Hong Kong in the mid 1980's. It has been a winner ever since.

1/4 cup melted butter	1/4 cup vanilla
1/4 cup sugar	1 tsp nutmeg
4 10-inch loaves French bread	1 tsp cinnamon
4 cups milk	1/2 cup raisins
8 eggs separated, reserve whites	1/2 cup pecans
1/2 cup sugar	1/4 cup sugar for meringue

Preheat oven to 400 degrees F. Butter and sugar six individual souffle molds. Cut French bread into one half inch croutons and place in an 11 x 14" baking pan with one inch lip. In a large mixing bowl, whip milk, egg yolks and sugar. Continue to whip while adding vanilla, nutmeg and cinnamon. You may wish to correct the sweetness of the custard should you prefer a sweeter taste. Sprinkle raisins and pecans over the croutons and slowly pour the custard mixture into the baking pan. Firmly press the croutons with your fingers until the custard is well absorbed. Bake until mixture is golden brown, about fifteen minutes. While bread pudding is baking, whip egg whites and sugar until stiff peaks form. When bread is golden brown, remove from oven and using a metal cooking spoon, break croutons into the custard mixture which has formed in the bottom of the baking pan. Fold in egg whites and blend into the bread-custard mixture. Pile mixture generously into the six souffle cups at least one inch above the rim. Return to hot oven and bake until golden brown, five to ten minutes. Serve with praline flavored sabayon (see instructions in previous recipe).

Changes

_____

_____

Bread Pudding

2 Hours   6-8 Servings

Comment:

This recipe was given to me by the master bread pudding chef, Sharon Jesowshek. I first tasted it in French Settlement, Louisiana, and could not rest until I had secured the recipe. It takes patience, but is a true masterpiece.

5 10-inch loaves French bread	1 tbsp cinnamon
1 quart milk	1 tbsp nutmeg
6 whole eggs	1 tbsp vegetable oil
1-1/2 cups sugar	1 cup raisins
1/4 cup vanilla	1 cup chopped pecans

Slice French bread into one half inch round croutons. In a large mixing bowl, combine milk, eggs and sugar. Using a wire whisk, blend these three ingredients well. Add vanilla, cinnamon and nutmeg. Continue to blend until all ingredients are well mixed. Oil a ten inch cheesecake pan. Press one layer of French bread croutons into the bottom of the pan, making sure there are no void spaces. Sprinkle a small amount of pecans and raisins over this layer. Ladle in one third of the custard mixture. Carefully press the custard into the croutons using the tips of your fingers. Continue this process until all croutons and custard are used up. You may find that one to two cups of the custard mixture will remain once the pan has been filled. This is normal and you must continue to add the custard, a little at a time, firmly pressing into the croutons until all has been used. This may take an hour or so. The bread pudding is always best if allowed to set in the refrigerator overnight before cooking. Preheat oven to 375 degrees F. Place the bread pudding pan into a larger pan filled with water. Cook in this water bath approximately one to one and a half hours. Allow to cool and serve with praline sabayon.

(Continued)

Changes

_____

_____

_____

_____

Desserts

(*Bread Pudding* continued)

FOR SABAYON:

3 egg yolks
1/4 cup sugar

3/4 cup dry white wine
1/2 cup praline liqueur

Place two inches of water in a one quart sauce pan over medium high heat. Bring to a low boil, reduce to simmer and hold. In a heavy mixing bowl, whisk egg yolks and sugar until creamy, approximately three to five minutes. Set aside. In a saute pan over medium high heat, combine white wine and praline liqueur. Bring to a slow boil and, whisking constantly, add into the egg mixture. Set the bowl on top of the sauce pan of water creating a double broiler, and continue to whip until mixture doubles in volume. Remove from heat and continue to whisk one to two minutes.

Changes

_____

_____

_____

_____

Praline Cheesecake

1-1/2 Hours   1 10 inch cake

Comment:

The flavor of pralines is as indigenous to Louisiana as gumbo is to bayou country. To adapt this wonderful pecan candy taste to a classical cheesecake recipe makes good sense to a Louisiana cook.

FOR CRUST:

1-1/2 cups graham cracker
   crumbs

1/4 cup sugar
4 tbsps melted butter

Combine cracker crumbs and sugar. Drizzle melted butter into the mixture to moisten. Using your fingertips, press the graham cracker mixture into the bottom of a ten inch round springform pan. Place the pan in the refrigerator for fifteen minutes or until crust is firm to the touch.

FOR CHEESECAKE:

1-1/2 pounds cream cheese
1/4 cup heavy whipping cream
4 medium eggs
1 cup sugar

1/2 tsp praline extract
1 ounce praline liqueur
1 tsp vanilla
1/2 cup chopped pecans

(Continued)

Changes

(Praline Cheesecake continued)

Preheat oven to 300 degrees F. In a large mixing bowl, combine softened cream cheese and heavy whipping cream. Blend well to remove all lumps from the cream cheese. This can be done in a blender or with a hand held mixer. Add one egg at a time, whipping completely before the next one is added. Continue until all are incorporated. Add sugar, a little at a time, while continuing to whip. Add the three flavorings, blending well after each is added, then fold in chopped pecans. Remove crust from the refrigerator and pour batter into the baking pan. Rotate pan until batter mixture flattens out. Place in preheated oven and bake approximately one hour or until firm to the touch. The cake may be topped with a sour cream topping made by combining one pound of sour cream, four tablespoons of sugar and one half teaspoon of vanilla. Blend all together well until creamy. Add to the top of the slightly cooled cheesecake and place in 400 degree oven for five minutes.

Changes

_____

_____

_____

_____

Carrot Cake

1-1/2 Hours   1 9-inch cake

Comment:

The orange glaze used in place of frosting on this cake is just another example of putting the Louisiana orange to work. It is quite common to see fruit glazes used in place of icings or frostings.

FOR CAKE:

3 cups grated carrots
2 cups sugar
2 cups flour
2 tsps baking powder
2 tsps baking soda
2 tsps cinnamon

1 tsp salt
1 cup chopped pecans
1-1/4 cups salad oil
4 eggs
3 tbsps butter

Preheat oven to 325 degrees F. In a large mixing bowl, combine all dry ingredients. In a separate bowl, whip together oil and eggs, blending well to ensure that all is incorporated. Add to the dry mixture and slowly blend until all ingredients are well mixed. Grease three 9 inch baking pans with butter. Pour batter into pans and bake on center shelf of oven for approximately one hour and fifteen minutes. Cool and set aside.

FOR GLAZE:

1 cup sugar
1/4 cup corn starch
1 cup fresh orange juice
1 tsp lemon juice

2 tbsps grated orange peel
2 tbsps butter
1/2 tsp salt

In a heavy bottom sauce pan, combine sugar and corn starch. Add orange and lemon juice and stir over medium heat until mixture is well blended and bubbly. Add all remaining ingredients and cook over low heat until mixture is thick and glossy. Remove from heat and cool slightly. Once cool, pour orange glaze over carrot cake and spread.

Changes

_____

_____

Plantation Dump Cake

1 Hour   12 Servings

Comment:

This simple concoction was developed by the black cooks on the plantations. It was quite tasty and usually made with whatever ingredients were available.

1 21-ounce can cherry or other fruit pie filling

1 18-ounce package yellow cake mix

2 8-ounce cans crushed pineapple, drained

1/2 pound butter, chipped

1 3-1/2 ounce can coconut flakes

1 cup chopped pecans

Preheat oven to 325 degrees F. Spoon pie filling evenly into a 9 x 13" baking dish. Sprinkle cake mix over the filling. Evenly distribute crushed pineapple over the cake mix. Slice butter into one quarter inch pats and layer evenly over pineapple. Sprinkle with coconut and chopped pecans. Bake for one hour and check for doneness. Remove from oven, leave in baking dish and serve with a generous portion of whipped cream or a scoop of praline ice cream. You may wish to add or substitute whatever ingredients are on hand.

Changes

Floating Island

1 Hour   6-8 Servings

Comment:

One of the original desserts of early Louisiana, the floating island arrived with the French in the late 1600's. I remember thinking at one time in my life there was no better dessert on the face of the earth than "Isle Flotante".

6 cups heavy whipping cream	**pinch of nutmeg**
8 eggs separated	**2 tsps corn starch**
1-1/2 cups sugar	**3 tbsps vanilla**
pinch of cinnamon	**1/2 cup sugar**

In a two quart sauce pot, heat cream over medium high heat. In a large mixing bowl, combine egg yolks, sugar, cinnamon, nutmeg, corn starch and vanilla. When cream has come to a low boil, ladle one cup of the hot cream into the egg mixture, stirring constantly while pouring. Once the cream has been incorporated, pour the egg mixture slowly into the pot of hot cream. Remember, you must stir constantly, otherwise eggs will scramble. Reduce heat to simmer and, stirring constantly, cook until slightly thick custard is achieved. Pour into a serving bowl and allow to cool. In a large mixing bowl, beat egg whites until stiff peaks form. Add one half cup of sugar and continue beating for an additional one to two minutes. Poach spoonfuls of these floating isles in hot water over low heat, approximately two minutes on each side. When done, remove from hot water and place on top of the custard in the bowl. Serve two floating isles in a soup bowl of custard.

Changes

_____

_____

_____

_____

Fruitcake

3 Hours   1 tube cake

Comment:

I haven't located the origin of fruitcake in Louisiana, but I suspect that it has roots in English plum pudding. No matter where it originated, the fruitcake is found throughout Louisiana at Christmas time.

4 ounces candied red cherries
4 ounces candied green cherries
8 ounces candied pineapple
8 ounces packaged pitted dates
1 cup raisins
1/2 cup white raisins
2 cups chopped pecans
2 cups chopped walnuts

3 cups self rising flour
4 large eggs
1-1/2 cups sugar
1 cup melted butter
2 tsps cinnamon
1/2 tsp nutmeg
1 cup pineapple juice
1/2 cup brandy

Preheat oven to 275 degrees F. Grease one ten inch tube pan and set aside. On a cutting board, chop all fruit and nuts and combine into a large mixing bowl. Add one cup of flour and, using your hands, combine flour, nuts and fruit until well coated. In a separate bowl, combine eggs, sugar and butter. Whip thoroughly and slowly add remaining two cups of flour, cinnamon, nutmeg and pineapple juice. Use a metal spoon to whip these ingredients until well blended. Pour in brandy and mix well. Pour this batter over the fruit mixture and continue to whip until well blended. Pour into the buttered tube pan and bake approximately two and a half hours until done. Once the cake has cooled, cover with aluminum foil and store in the refrigerator. From time to time, ladle one or two tablespoons of brandy or cognac over the cake for a spiked flavoring. I suggest making four or five of these cakes at a time and giving them as Christmas gifts.

Changes

_____

_____

_____

German Chocolate Cake

1 Hour   1 9-inch cake

Comment:

This recipe came from the German Coast of Louisiana at the turn of the century. The Germans created many traditional recipes here in Louisiana and this one was handed down for us to enjoy today.

FOR CAKE:

2 cups sugar
1 cup Crisco
4 egg yolks
1/2 cup boiling water
4 ounces German sweet
    chocolate

2-1/2 cups flour
1 tsp baking soda
1-1/4 cup buttermilk
1 tbsp vanilla
pinch of salt
4 egg whites, beaten to peaks

Preheat oven to 350 degrees F. In a large mixing bowl, cream sugar and Crisco until fluffy. Add egg yolks, one at a time, until all have been incorporated. Bring one half cup water to a low boil and add chocolate, stirring until melted. Add chocolate to sugar-Crisco mixture blending well to incorporate. In a separate mixing bowl, combine flour and baking soda. Sprinkle alternate amounts of flour and buttermilk into the sugar-Crisco mixture. Continue until all is well blended. Add vanilla and salt. Fold in stiffly beaten egg whites and blend well into the mixture. Pour into three greased nine inch cake pans and bake approximately thirty to forty-five minutes or until done. Allow pans to cool completely before removing cakes.

(Continued)

Changes

_____

_____

_____

_____

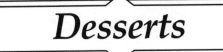

(*German Chocolate Cake* continued)

FOR ICING:

1-1/2 cups sugar
1-1/2 cups evaporated milk
3/4 cup butter
4 egg yolks, beaten

2 cups coconut flakes
1 cup chopped pecans
2 tsps vanilla

Over a double boiler, combine sugar, milk, butter and egg yolks. Using a wire whip, cook over low heat until well thickened. Remove from heat and add coconut, pecans and vanilla. Remove cake from baking pans and spread icing between layers. Stack and ice cake with the remaining mixture.

Changes

_____

_____

_____

_____

Cajun Fig and Pecan Pie

1 Hour   1 9-inch pie

Comment:

Figs were the most plentiful fruit available to the early Cajuns and Creoles. During the late summer, figs were canned in every household in bayou country. To combine fig preserves with pecan pie is a natural.

1/2 cup sugar	1 cup chopped pecans
1 tbsp corn starch	1/2 cup chopped fig preserves
1 cup Karo syrup	pinch of cinnamon
1/4 cup Louisiana cane syrup	pinch of nutmeg
1 tbsp vanilla	1 9-inch uncooked pie shell
3 eggs, beaten	

Preheat oven to 425 degrees F. In large mixing bowl, combine sugar and corn starch. Add syrups, vanilla and beaten eggs and, using a wire whisk, blend thoroughly. Add chopped pecans and fig preserves and blend well into the mixture. Season with a pinch of cinnamon and nutmeg. Pour into pie shell and bake on center rack of oven for 10 minutes. Then reduce temperature to 375 degrees F and bake for 35 minutes. Remove and allow to cool.

Changes

_____

_____

_____

_____

Honey Pecan Pies

1 Hour   1 9-inch pie

Comment:

There are as many variations for pecan pie in Louisiana as there are pastry shops. This recipe was given to me many years ago by a wonderful black chef. I often wonder how wealthy she could have become, had she sold this dessert.

1/4 pound butter	**1 tsp vanilla**
1 cup sugar	**1 cup chopped pecans**
3 eggs, beaten	**pinch of cinnamon**
1/2 cup Karo syrup	**pinch of nutmeg**
1/2 cup honey	**1 9-inch uncooked pie shell**
1/2 tsp lemon juice	

Preheat oven to 425 degrees F. In a heavy bottom saute pan, brown butter over medium high heat. Do not burn. Remove and allow to cool slightly. In a large mixing bowl, combine sugar, eggs, syrup and honey. Using a wire whisk, blend all ingredients well. Add the brown butter, lemon juice, vanilla and pecans. Season with cinnamon and nutmeg. Continue to whip until all ingredients are well blended. Pour into pie shell and bake on center rack of oven for 10 minutes. Then reduce temperature to 375 degrees F and bake for 35 minutes. Remove and allow to cool.

Changes

_____

_____

_____

_____

Oreilles De Cochon

1 Hour   8-10 Servings

Comment:

This old Cajun recipe gets its name from the shape the dough takes in the cooking process. The "pig's ear" is shaped by twisting the flattened dough with a fork as it hits the hot oil. This dessert is found mainly in the bayous.

1/4 pound butter	1 quart peanut oil
1/2 tsp salt	1/2 cup brown sugar
1 tsp baking powder	1/2 cup Louisiana cane syrup
3 eggs	1 cup chopped pecans
2 1/2 cups flour	

In a large mixing bowl, combine butter, salt, baking powder and eggs. Using a metal spoon, cream all ingredients together. Slowly sprinkle in flour, one cup at a time, blending well into a ball. Remove from bowl, place on a well floured surface and knead dough five to ten minutes. Using a dough cutter, divide into twelve equal pieces and roll each piece out into a one eighth inch thick circle. In a ten to twelve inch saute pan, heat oil over medium high heat. If a candy thermometer is available, try to maintain a 375 degree F temperature. Cook the pig's ears, one at a time, in the hot oil until they begin to float. Using a long handled fork, twist the pastry at the top center to give it the curled shape of a pig's ear. Continue to fry on each side until golden brown. Remove and drain on paper towels. To make the sugar topping, combine sugar, syrup and pecans in a heavy bottom sauce pan. Bring to a light boil and continue cooking until mixture forms a soft ball when dropped in cold water. Once cooked, drizzle the pecan sugar on top of the pig's ears until all are well coated.

Changes

Pralines
A Creole Tradition

The story of pralines is a perfect example of how the innovative Creoles adapted to their new surroundings. How else could French confections find their way into the grand ballrooms of New Orleans. The entire history of pralines centers around man's life-long interest; women and the pursuit of women. During the reign of Louis XII, the Marechal duc de Choiseul Praslin had gained quite a reputation, not only on the battlefields of Europe but in the boudoirs of France as well. The Marechal had a fancy for candy and always kept a supply to give to the ladies when he called upon them. One day, legend has it, he ran out of his sugar coated bon bons and summoned his chef, Jean Dulac, into the kitchen to create a new supply. The chef did not have the ingredients necessary to produce his normal fare but created a new dish that received rave reviews. His friends congratulated the Marechal for his ingenuity in creating this new candy and pressed him for the recipe and its name. These friends christened the candy "prasline". The new name, however, evolved into praline, as we know it today.

Another legend states that the candy came to New Orleans with the Ursuline nuns who were so familiar with the classical cuisine of France. They substituted native South Louisiana pecans in place of almonds and hazelnuts, which were required in the original recipe, but the name remained the same.

Regardless of their origin, pralines today are loved throughout the South and are prepared with many variations.

Praline Crepes

1 Hour   10 Crepes

Comment:

This evolution of the Louisiana praline came about during the opening of our Lafitte's Landing in Fukuoka, Japan, in 1986. We have since used the recipe for many high level affairs.

FOR PASTRY CREAM:

2 cups heavy whipping cream	1/2 tsp salt
1/2 cup sugar	2 ounces praline liqueur or Frangelico
6 egg yolks	1-1/2 tbsps vanilla
1/2 cup flour	1 tbsp softened butter

In a heavy bottom sauce pan, bring cream to a low boil and reduce heat to simmer. In a large mixing bowl, combine sugar, eggs, flour and salt, blending well. Using a wire whisk, continue to blend until creamy and smooth. While whisking, pour one cup of hot cream into the egg mixture. When well blended, return all of egg mixture to the hot sauce pan of cream, stirring constantly while pouring. Add praline liqueur and vanilla. Remove from heat and allow to cool. Once cool, fold in one tablespoon of softened butter. Cover with clear wrap and refrigerate.

(Continued)

Changes

_____

_____

_____

_____

Desserts

(*Praline Crepes* continued)

FOR CREPE:

2 eggs	3/4 cup milk
1/2 cup flour	pinch of salt
1/2 tsp sugar	1 ounce melted butter
1/2 tsp vanilla	1/4 cup sugar
1 tbsp praline liqueur	3/4 cup chopped pecans
1 tbsp melted butter	

In a large mixing bowl, beat eggs and flour until creamy. Add sugar, vanilla, praline liqueur, butter and milk. Continue to whip until all ingredients are well blended. Batter should have the consistency of heavy whipping cream. Season with a pinch of salt. Heat an eight inch crepe pan over medium high heat. Add one half ounce of melted butter, swirling to coat the pan. Pour excess butter from crepe pan back into the original container. Butter should just film coat the pan. Place approximately two ounces of the crepe batter into the hot pan, tilting in a circular motion until the batter spreads evenly over the pan. Cook crepe until outer edges begin to brown and loosen. Flip crepe to other side and cook approximately one minute. Using a thin spatula, lift crepe from pan and sprinkle with sugar. Continue until all crepes are done. Place one tablespoon of pastry cream in the center of crepe and top with chopped pecans. The crepe may be heated in the oven or served cold. It may also be served on a sauce of cream anglaise.

Changes

_____

_____

_____

_____

Desserts

Cajun Pralines

1 Hour   25 Pieces

2 cups light brown sugar   **1 tbsp vanilla**
1 cup white sugar   **1-1/2 cups chopped pecans**
1 cup water   **1/2 cup pecan halves**
1 cup heavy whipping cream

In a heavy bottom sauce pan over medium high heat, combine sugars, water and cream. Cook, stirring constantly, until sugar forms a soft ball when dropped in a cup of cold water, approximately 238 degrees F. Remove from heat and, using a heavy wire whisk, whip until creamy, approximately ten to fifteen minutes. Quickly add vanilla and nuts and drop by spoonfuls onto a buttered sheet pan. Allow to cool at room temperature.

Changes

_____

_____

_____

_____

Praline Ice Cream

2 Hours   6 Servings

Comment:

The Cajuns and Creoles preferred the flavor of pralines to any other and even adapted the taste to produce ice cream. As a child, we would sit and churn the ice cream freezer for hours to produce this delicacy.

4 egg yolks
1/2 cup brown sugar
1/2 cup sour cream
1 pint heavy whipping cream
1 pint milk

1 tbsp vanilla
1/2 cup praline liqueur or Frangelico
1 cup chopped pecans
pinch of salt

In a large mixing bowl, combine egg yolks and sugar. Using a wire whisk, blend until ingredients are creamy. Add sour cream, heavy cream and milk and continue to whip until well blended. Add vanilla, praline liqueur, chopped pecans and salt. Whip two to three minutes more to ensure proper blending of flavors. Pour mixture into an ice cream freezer container and, following manufacturer's directions, freeze until ice cream is set. Place container in the freezer for two to three hours to allow the ice cream to harden.

Changes

_____
_____
_____
_____

Creole Rice Pudding

1-1/2 Hours 6 Servings

Comment:

The rice pudding, I feel, was a gift from the Germans. These early settlers had a good supply of milk and eggs and were known for their custard type desserts. Here is an interesting twist to an old method.

2 eggs	**pinch of nutmeg**
3/4 cup sugar	**pinch of salt**
2 cups heavy whipping cream	**1-1/2 cups cooked rice**
2 tbsps vanilla	**1 cup raisins**
pinch of cinnamon	**1/2 cup chopped pecans**

Preheat oven to 350 degrees F. In a large mixing bowl, combine eggs, sugar and whipping cream and, using a wire whisk, blend until mixture is creamy. Add vanilla, cinnamon, nutmeg and salt and continue to whip until flavor has developed. Fold in cooked rice, raisins and pecans. Place the mixture in a buttered two quart casserole dish. Place dish in a larger pan filled with water to create a water bath. Bake on the center oven rack for approximately one hour or until pudding is set.

Changes

_____

_____

_____

_____

Desserts

Sweet Potato Pie

1 Hour   1 9-inch pie

Comment:

Sweet potatoes and Louisiana yams were growing wild here in the Bayous in 1755 when the Cajuns arrived. Many interesting sweet potato desserts were developed in South Louisiana, but this simple pie was always a winter favorite.

2 cups mashed sweet potatoes	**1/2 cup heavy whipping cream**
1/4 pound melted butter	**1 tsp lemon juice**
1 cup sugar	**1 tsp vanilla**
1/2 cup brown sugar	**pinch of cinnamon**
4 tbsps flour	**pinch of nutmeg**
3 eggs	**1 9-inch unbaked pie shell**

Preheat oven to 325 degrees F. Boil or bake sweet potatoes until tender and set aside to cool. In a large mixing bowl, combine butter, sweet potatoes, sugars and flour. Using a metal spoon, mash all ingredients until well blended. Add eggs, heavy whipping cream, lemon juice and vanilla and continue to whip until the batter is smooth and creamy. Season with cinnamon and nutmeg and pour into unbaked pie shell. Place on center oven rack and bake approximately forty-five minutes. Remove and allow to cool.

Changes

_____

_____

_____

_____

Tart a la Bouie

2 Hours   1 9-inch pie

Comment:

This is another of the custard desserts given to the Cajuns and Creoles by the Germans. Although the French lay claim to this simple custard pie, I feel the Germans first brought the dish to Louisiana.

4 cups heavy whipping cream   **1/4 cup melted butter**
3 eggs   **pinch of cinnamon**
1-1/4 cups sugar   **pinch of nutmeg**
2 tbsps corn starch   **2 9-inch pie shells, uncooked**
2 tbsps vanilla

Preheat oven to 350 degrees F. In a heavy bottom sauce pan, heat cream until scalding. In a large mixing bowl, combine eggs, sugar and corn starch and using a wire whisk, blend all ingredients until creamy. Add vanilla, butter, cinnamon and nutmeg and continue to whip until all ingredients are well blended. Once cream has come to a low boil, ladle one cup into the egg mixture, stirring constantly while pouring. Once well blended, pour egg mixture into the hot cream and stir continuously. Remove from heat and allow to cool slightly. Pour slightly cooled mixture into one of the pie shells. Using a sharp paring knife, cut the other pie shell into one half inch strips. Lattice the strips across the top of the pie in a decorative fashion. Place pie on center oven rack and bake for forty-five minutes or until crust is golden brown.

Changes

_____
_____
_____
_____

Lagniappe

Lagniappe means "something extra" in South Louisiana. It is a Cajun custom to always throw in a little lagniappe, whether at the bakery with an extra cookie added to the dozen, in the gumbo pot with a few extra shrimp or at the end of my cookbook. This section of lagniappe includes specialty recipes such as New Orleans drinks for that special party, biscuit recipes handed down from generation to generation, and the history of coffee in Cajun country.

Take a minute to browse through this "lagniappe" and I think you will quickly understand the importance of that little something extra in South Louisiana.

"What? Sunday morning in an English home and no more sausages, no extra gifts on the table? God bless my soul, what's the world coming to, eh...?"

Dorothy Sayers

Sazerac

10 Minutes   1 Drink

Comment:

The Sazerac cocktail was named by John Schiller in 1859 after the famous Sazerac de Forg Cognac served in his coffee house in New Orleans. The business was sold to Tom Handy in 1870 and the recipe was changed to the one we know today.

**2 3-1/2 ounce old fashioned
   glasses**
1/2 cup crushed ice
1 tsp sugar
1 dash Peychaud bitters

1 dash Angostura bitters
1-1/2 ounces rye whiskey
1 dash Herbsaint liqueur
1 lemon twist

Pack a three and a half ounce old fashioned glass with crushed ice. In a second glass, mix sugar with Peychaud and Angostura bitters and blend well. Add rye whiskey and continue to blend until sugar is well dissolved. Place a few cubes of ice into the glass and stir until liquid is chilled. Discard ice from the first glass, add a dash of Herbsaint and swirl around coating the inside of the chilled glass. Pour out all excess Herbsaint. Pour the mixed drink into the chilled glass, twist lemon peel into the cocktail and serve.

Changes

_____

_____

_____

_____

Brandy Milk Punch

10 Minutes   1 Drink

Comment:

Brandy milk punch is the most popular brunch drink served in South Louisiana. It is also believed that a little warm milk punch will cure the ills of a bad hangover.

1 9-ounce old fashioned glass   **1-1/2 ounces brandy**
2 tsps powdered sugar   **1/2 cup crushed ice**
1 tbsp light creme de cocoa   **dash of nutmeg**
3/4 cup heavy whipping cream

Place sugar, creme de cocoa, cream and brandy in a cocktail shaker with crushed ice. Shake briefly and strain into an old fashioned glass. Garnish with nutmeg.

Changes

_____
_____
_____
_____

Ramos Gin Fizz

10 Minutes   1 Drink

Comment:

This famous drink was named after Henry Ramos of the Imperial Cabinet Saloon in New Orleans. Although the drink existed before his time, he brought it back to its highest level of popularity.

1 9-ounce cocktail glass   **4 drops of orange flower water**
1 egg white   **1-1/2 ounces gin**
1 ounce heavy whipping cream   **2 ounces soda water**
1-1/2 tbsps powdered sugar   **1/2 cup crushed ice**
juice of one lemon

Pour all of the above ingredients into a cocktail shaker and shake vigorously for at least three to four minutes. The drink should be fairly thick at this point. You may wish to add a drop or two of vanilla extract and one more quick shake. Strain into cocktail glass and serve immediately.

Changes

_____

_____

_____

_____

White Oak Mint Julep

10 Minutes   1 Drink

Comment:

This southern cooler was extremely popular during the Plantation Era. The mint fragrance gives the drink an extremely refreshing aroma which makes it perfect for those hot southern afternoons.

1 9-ounce old fashioned glass   **1 ounce Southern Comfort**
6 mint leaves   **1 ounce simple syrup**
2 tsps powdered sugar   **1 cup crushed ice**
1 ounce bourbon   **1 sprig fresh mint**

Place mint leaves in the bottom of old fashioned glass along with powdered sugar. Using a muddler, crush mint leaves into powdered sugar. Add bourbon, Southern Comfort, simple syrup and crushed ice. Using an iced tea spoon, blend all ingredients well into the mint-sugar mixture. Garnish with fresh mint sprig and serve with a straw. This cocktail should be stirred long enough for frost to form on the outside of the glass. It has been said that the early planters would only drink mint juleps from silver tumblers.

Changes

_____

_____

_____

_____

Absinthe Frappee

10 Minutes   1 Drink

Comment:

This is another one of the creations to come out of Cayetano Ferrer's Absinthe House in the 1870's. Since Absinthe was eventually outlawed in New Orleans because of the wormwood it contained, the recipe was changed and the drink remained popular.

1 9-ounce highball glass   **1 ounce Anisette**
1 cup crushed ice   **soda water**
1 ounce Herbsaint or Pernod

Fill highball glass with crushed ice and add Herbsaint and Anisette. Using an iced tea spoon, mix in soda water, a little at a time, until glass is full. Continue to stir mixture until frost forms on the outside of the glass. You may wish to add a teaspoon of simple syrup or powdered sugar to the drink for additional sweetness. All Absinthe substitutes are flavored with anise and since this flavor is quite pronounced, the drink should only be served to those who enjoy this particular taste.

Changes

_____

_____

_____

_____

Hurricane

10 Minutes   1 Drink

Comment:

Everyone who visits the city of New Orleans eventually finds his way to Pat O'Brien's for one of his famous Hurricanes. The drink, with its fruit punch taste, has packed a wallop on many unsuspecting partiers.

1 10-ounce highball glass
1 ounce lemon juice
4 ounces dark rum

4 ounces red passion
    fruit cocktail mix or
    hawaiian punch
crushed ice
orange slice and cherry garnish

Into a cocktail shaker, pour lemon juice, rum and cocktail mix. Shake vigorously for one to two minutes. Pack crushed ice into cocktail glass and pour drink mixture over the crushed ice. Garnish with orange slice and cherry. To my knowledge, this is the original recipe and not quite the same as the one served at Pat O'Brien's today.

Changes

_____

_____

_____

_____

Lagniappe

Planters Punch

10 Minutes   1 Drink

Comment:

This drink was undoubtedly named in jest of the southern plantation owners and their afternoon delight. This potent rum punch was consumed daily, as was the julep, on the front verandas of the antebellum mansions.

12 ounce stemmed wine glass
1-1/2 ounces light rum
1/2 ounce grapefruit juice
1/2 ounce orange juice

1/2 ounce grenadine
1/2 ounce dark rum
slice orange and cherry

Into a cocktail shaker, pour light rum, grapefruit juice, orange juice and grenadine. Shake vigorously for one minute. Fill wine glass with ice cubes and pour drink mixture over the ice. Float dark rum on top of drink and garnish with a slice of orange and cherry. I feel that this drink was more popular in plantation country than the mint julep simply because the large plantations had grapefruit and orange orchards to supply the main ingredients.

Changes

_____

_____

_____

_____

Angel Biscuits

30 Minutes   4 Dozen biscuits

Comment:

Angel biscuits get their name from the lightness of the batter. This recipe was given to me by Mrs. Emily Bruno of The Emily House in St. Joseph, Louisiana. The recipe is double in size because the dough refrigerates well and may be made ahead.

5 cups flour	**1 cup Crisco**
1/4 cup sugar	**1 package of yeast (dissolved**
5 tsps baking powder	**in four tbsps warm water)**
1 tbsp baking soda	**2 cups buttermilk**
1-1/2 tsps salt	**4 tbsps melted butter**

Preheat oven to 400 degrees F. Sift together flour, sugar, baking powder, soda and salt. Mix well to ensure proper blending. Using a pastry blender, cut shortening into the flour mixture. Add dissolved yeast and buttermilk and continue to mix until biscuit dough forms. Roll the dough, one inch thick, onto a floured board. Cut biscuits with a two inch biscuit cutter. Continue rolling the dough until all has been used. Drizzle biscuits with melted butter, place on a sheet pan and bake for fifteen to eighteen minutes. Since it refrigerates well, you may wish to make the dough a few days in advance. I might also suggest slightly under-baking the biscuits and freezing them for later use. They may be reconstituted in a 500 degree oven for five to six minutes.

Changes

Crackling Biscuits

30 Minutes   8-10 Biscuits

Comment:

The Cajuns, always looking for variation in recipes, certainly created a winner here. Adding the hog crackling to the biscuit mixture created a unique breakfast item. You may wish to substitute salted pork skins.

4 cups all purpose flour	2/3 cup unsalted butter
2 tbsps baking powder	1-1/2 cups buttermilk
1 tsp baking soda	3/4 cup chopped hog crackling
1-1/2 tbsps sugar	1/4 cup melted butter
1 tsp salt	

Preheat oven to 400 degrees F. In a large mixing bowl, combine flour, baking powder, baking soda, sugar and salt. Mix well to ensure proper blending. Using a pastry blender, cut butter into flour mixture. Once butter has been well blended into flour, add buttermilk and chopped crackling. Continue to mix until biscuit dough is well formed. Place dough on a floured board and knead lightly. Roll dough out until approximately one inch thick. Cut biscuits with a three inch biscuit cutter until all are formed. Place biscuits on a buttered baking sheet and drizzle with melted butter. Bake until golden brown, approximately twenty-five minutes.

Changes

_____

_____

_____

_____

Purple Plum Pie

1-1/2 Hours   1 9-inch pie

Comment:

Gaston and Olga Hirsch arrived in the United States shortly after World War II. Having family in the Donaldsonville area, they decided to settle in this small Louisiana town, forty-five miles West of New Orleans. Soon after their arrival, they opened a clothing store on Mississippi Street in Donaldsonville. "Gaston's" prospered and became a landmark in the city until it was sold upon his retirement in 1984.

Both Gaston and Olga had been trained in the restaurant/hotel business. Gaston's family owned "La Marne," a grand hotel in the town of Saverne, France. The hotel was well-known for its magnificent cuisine, even prior to World War II. The hotel was founded in 1872 and is still in business today. Olga's family owned "La Forestiere," a family restaurant in the town of Veymerange, Lorraine. Her specialties were pates, terrines and tarts. Numerous culinary awards were proof of the quality of the products produced in La Forestiere.

Many hours have been spent in my twenty years knowing these two people, discussing fine food and restaurant service. Olga not only taught me the fine art of pate making but on many occasions, gave me pointers on pies and tarts. This recipe is one of her specialties and I hope you will enjoy it as much as I have enjoyed their friendship over the years.

FOR PIE CRUST:

1-1/3 cups flour	**1 tbsp sugar**
1/4 pound chipped cold butter	**1/4 cup iced water**

(Continued)

Changes

_____

_____

_____

_____

(*Purple Plum Pie* continued)

In the bowl of a food processor equipped with a metal blade, place all of the above ingredients except iced water. Using pulse button, blend mixture until a coarse meal texture is achieved, approximately one minute. Slowly add iced water, a little at a time, until dough forms into a ball. Remove and place on floured surface. Roll dough to a one eighth inch thickness. Firmly press into a nine inch pie or tart pan. Set aside.

FOR FILLING:

18 ripe purple plums	1/4 cup vanilla
1/4 cup heavy whipping cream	pinch of cinnamon
2 whole eggs	pinch of nutmeg
1/2 cup granulated sugar	1/4 cup powdered sugar

Preheat oven to 375 degrees F. Using a sharp paring knife, cut plums into one fourth inch slices and discard seeds. Arrange plum slices neatly around the dough until all have been used. Place the pie on the bottom oven rack and bake approximately twenty minutes to render juices from the fruit. While pie is baking, combine all remaining ingredients, except powdered sugar, in a mixing bowl. Using a wire whisk, whip until well blended. Remove the pie from oven and pour egg mixture evenly over the baked plums. Return to oven and allow pie to cook approximately twenty minutes longer or until custard is set. Remove from oven and dust generously with powdered sugar. This pie may be duplicated using red or green apples.

Changes

_____

_____

_____

_____

Beignets

A night on the town in New Orleans is not complete without a stop at Cafe du Monde for cafe au lait and beignets. These forerunners of the doughnut, when sprinkled heavily with confectioner's sugar and coupled with that cup of hot coffee, give more pleasure than even a Ramos Gin Fizz. These delightful, rectangular shapes of puffed dough were also brought to New Orleans by the Ursuline nuns who came to Louisiana in 1727. They were so well versed in French baking that today many basic sweets in Creole cooking can be traced to these industrious nuns.

There are many variations of beignets and fritters in classical cooking today and some are even made with vegetables and fruit. Although the beignets of New Orleans are well known to the tourist, the Cajuns have their own delightful counterpart. Beignets de aubergines, or eggplant beignets, are prepared during the season when eggplants are prolific. They are also made with summer squash or pumpkin.

The beignet recipe brought by the Ursuline nuns was similar to what we know as Beignets Viennois. This beignet is filled with cream or fruit during preparation and sprinkled with sugar after frying. Whether preparing the Creole puffed beignet or the Cajun eggplant beignet, I know you will enjoy this creation, a classic in Cajun and Creole cooking.

Lagniappe

Beignets

30 Minutes   35 Beignets

1 package dry yeast (dissolved   **1/4 cup sugar**
in 4 tbsps water)   **1-1/4 cups milk**
oil for deep frying   **3 eggs, beaten**
3-1/2 cups flour   **1/4 cup melted butter**
1 tsp salt   **1 cup powdered sugar**

Dissolve yeast in four tablespoons of warm water or according to package directions. Set aside. Using a homestyle deep fryer, such as the Fry Daddy, heat oil according to manufacturer's instructions. In a large mixing bowl, combine flour, salt and sugar and mix well to ensure proper blending. Fold in dissolved yeast, milk, eggs and butter. Continue to blend until smooth beignet dough is formed. Place dough in a metal bowl, cover with a towel and allow to rise for one hour. Remove to a well floured surface and roll out to one quarter inch thickness. Cut into rectangular shapes, two by three inches, and return to lightly floured pan. Cover with a towel and allow dough to rise. Deep fry, turning once, until golden brown. Drain and dust generously with powdered sugar. Enjoy beignets with a cup of Louisiana cafe au lait. (see recipe)

Changes

_____

_____

_____

_____

Lagniappe

Cajun Eggplant Beignets

30 Minutes   30 Beignets

Comment:

Here again, we see the Cajun variation of the classical beignet. Having such an abundance of fresh vegetables, it seems natural that eggplant and squash have found their way into the beignet batter.

3 medium sized eggplants, peeled and diced	1 pinch of nutmeg
oil for deep frying	1 cup milk
2 cups flour	2 eggs, beaten
2 tbsps sugar	1 tsp vanilla
1 tbsp baking powder	1/4 cup raisins
1 pinch of cinnamon	1/4 cup chopped pecans
	1 cup powdered sugar

In a one gallon stock pot, cover diced eggplant with cold water. Bring to a rolling boil and cook approximately thirty minutes or until eggplant is very tender. Drain and cool. This should yield approximately one level cup of eggplant. In a homestyle frying unit, such as a Fry Daddy, preheat oil according to manufacturer's instructions. In a large mixing bowl, combine flour, sugar, baking powder, cinnamon and nutmeg and mix until all ingredients are well blended. Add eggplant, milk, eggs and vanilla. Using a metal spoon, blend until beignet dough is formed. Add raisins and chopped pecans. Spoon batter into hot oil, one beignet at a time, and cook until golden brown on all sides. It is advisable to cook one beignet as a sampler, adjusting seasonings and cooking time if necessary. Continue cooking until all beignets are done. Remove, drain and dust generously with powdered sugar.

Changes

_____

_____

_____

_____

Rice

Rice is second in importance only to the roux in Cajun and Creole cooking. In South Louisiana, we begin the day with rice for breakfast. Riz jaune or yellow rice, two eggs cracked over fried rice and seasoned with boudin blanc, is considered a mainstay in many homes. Throughout the day, rice continues to find its place on the table. You will find rice everywhere, served with gumbo, etouffee, sauce piquante, crawfish bisque, and of course, our famous red beans. Even in dessert, we incorporate rice. One of the finest desserts in Cajun country is rice pudding, cooked rice blended into vanilla custard and served warm.

Rice was a natural for the hard-working Cajun who needed something to stick to his ribs. Upon their arrival in South Louisiana, the Cajuns found rice being cultivated by the Indians and quickly assimilated it into their cuisine.

It is said that the definition of a true Cajun is one who can look over a rice field and calculate how many gallons of seafood gumbo it will take to cover it. From time to time, we in bayou country may eat potatoes, pasta or grits, but nothing will ever take the place of rice in Cajun cuisine.

White Rice

30 Minutes   3 Cups

1 cup long grain rice   **1 tsp salt**
1-1/2 cups water   **1 tbsp butter**

Wash rice a minimum of two times in clear cold water. This process will remove all excess dust and starch from the outside of the grains. Drain well. In a heavy bottom sauce pot, combine all of the above ingredients. Place sauce pot on medium high heat and bring to a rolling boil. Reduce temperature to simmer, cover sauce pot and cook for thirty minutes. During the thirty minute cooking time, it is imperative that you do not remove the cover or attempt to stir the rice. One cup of raw rice will yield approximately two and a half to three cups of cooked rice. I suggest one half cup of cooked rice per serving.

RIZ AU LAIT   RM89

Changes

_____

_____

_____

_____

Hushpuppies

Hushpuppies are one of those unique items found everywhere in Cajun country. I have traveled the world over but have never seen hushpuppies or fritters served as often as in South Louisiana. Once again, legend has it that the hushpuppy was developed in the early 1700's by the Ursuline nuns. The nuns converted corn meal, given to them by the Indians, into a delicious fritter called "Croquettes de Maise."

The name hushpuppy came about when an old Creole cook was frying a batch of catfish and croquettes. His hungry hunting dogs began to howl in anticipation of a chance to savour some of the catfish. The innovative Creole instead tossed a few of the croquettes de maise to the dogs and yelled, "hush, puppies!" The name has since been associated with this corn meal delicacy.

Hushpuppies

30 Minutes   15-20 Hushpuppies

oil for deep frying
1-1/4 cup yellow corn meal
1/2 cup flour
3 tsps baking powder
1 tsp sugar
1 pinch of salt

1 tsp cracked black pepper
1 small onion, finely diced
1 egg, beaten
1/2 cup milk
1/2 cup whole kernel corn
1/4 cup sliced green onions

In a homestyle deep fryer, such as a Fry Daddy, heat oil according to manufacturer's directions. In a large mixing bowl, combine corn meal, flour, baking powder, sugar, salt and pepper. Mix until all ingredients are well blended. Add diced onion, egg, milk, corn and sliced green onions. Continue to mix until all ingredients are well blended. The batter should be smooth and free of any lumps. Using a soup spoon or a small ice cream scoop, dip one hushpuppy and deep fry as a sampler. The hushpuppy will be done when it floats and is golden brown. Correct seasonings and cooking time if necessary. Continue to fry until all are done.

Changes

_____

_____

_____

_____

Lagniappe

Coffee in Cajun
and Creole Cuisine

No coffee can compare to the coffee of South Louisiana. Soon after you have visited with us, you will come to understand that the coffee the rest of America drinks is a nice, warm beverage but certainly could not pass for coffee here.

The coffee of the Cajuns is different from the New Orleans chicory coffee of the Creoles. What Cajun boy or girl has not heard the story of "Grandmere", sitting next to her old wood stove on a foggy morning, dripping that first cup of coffee through her apron. It was imperative for the water used in dripping to be taken from the rain barrel and not the well. Everyone knew that the soft water, collected in a rain barrel, was preferable to the hard well water when dripping a good pot of coffee. Each child would be enchanted to hear how she would carefully drizzle the hot water one spoonful at a time over the dark roasted, fresh, ground coffee. The aroma that permeated the Cajun cabin was as memorable to the children as to the grown-ups who were privileged enough to savor this dark, rich brew. It left an indelible mark in their minds and brought back fond childhood memories for years after.

Still today, a dark roast coffee is used, always slowly dripped with Grandmere in mind. When combined with hot milk, this cafe au lait makes a morning beverage unparalleled outside of Cajun Country which is enjoyed by adults and children alike.

The chicory coffee of the Creoles is not only enjoyed in New Orleans but its fame is recognized throughout the world. Cafe au lait with hot beignets, heavily sprinkled with confectioner's sugar, is a must for visitors to the Vieux Carre'.

No sumptuous Creole feast would be complete without its traditional Cafe Noir, that swarthy blend of dark roasted coffee and chicory, still recognized for its therapeutic values. Many old Cajuns and Creoles have testified to its worth in reaching that ripe old age, as well as adding a lot of pleasure to those years.

In New Orleans, Cafe Brulot is often served. Brulot in French means spicy or burned with sugar. The recipe for this famous blending of dark roasted Creole coffee with cognac or brandy and vermouth, spiced with cinnamon and orange peel, is attributed to none other than Dominique Youx, top lieutenant to the pirate, Jean Lafitte. Some say Dominique hailed from Santo Domingo and brought with him this famous recipe. The pirates, under Dominique's leadership, frequently acquired beautiful porcelain tableware. Included in their "finds" were stemmed porcelain demi-tasse cups that later became the receptacles for his famous drink.

Dominique was known to be quite a romancer and has become more famous here in South Louisiana for the phrase that he coined than his delicious Brulot. The custom of giving young girls a handful of bon bons or pralines to win their fancy was well known in the city of New Orleans. From the following saying, it is quite obvious that Dominique was a lot more successful in his amorous adventures armed with his Cafe Brulot, spiked with cognac and vermouth, than others with their handful of candy.

Dominique's infamous saying goes like this:

> *"LES BONBONS ACCUEILLIS*
> *PRODUISENT LEUR EFFET,*
> *MAIS LA LIQUEUR TRAVAILLE*
> *PLUS VITE A CET EFFET"*

Loosely translated it says:

CANDY IS DANDY BUT LIQUOR IS QUICKER

As you can see, from a small bayou cottage to the Old Absinthe House of Bourbon Street, coffee is more than just a beverage in South Louisiana. Yes, to us, ma chere, it is a way of life.

"Kind sir, if this is coffee, please bring me some tea. If this is tea sir, please bring me some coffee."

Abraham Lincoln

Coffee

1 Hour   4-6 Cups

CAJUN COFFEE:

8 level tbsps ground dark roast
coffee

4-1/2 cups cold water

In the top of a French drip coffee pot, place eight tablespoons of dark roast coffee. In a one quart sauce pot, bring water to a rolling boil. Drip boiling water through coffee, two to three tablespoons at a time, until all water has been used. This recipe makes a very strong black coffee that is enjoyed in the bayous. Once the coffee is dripped, the Cajuns place the coffee pot in a small frying pan filled with water. This frying pan is placed on low heat to keep the coffee hot all day. The longer it sets, the stronger it gets. A demi-tasse of coffee with one heaping spoon of sugar was the normal serving.

CAFE AU LAIT:

4 cups heavy whipping cream
2 cups brewed Cajun Coffee
(see recipe)

6 tbsps sugar

Scald cream in a small sauce pot over medium high heat. Do not boil. Add the hot Cajun Coffee, blend well into the cream and sweeten with sugar. Remember, cafe au lait is normally a little sweeter than regular coffee. This recipe is served to the children at breakfast time with a heaping platter of beignets.

(Continued)

Changes

_____

_____

_____

_____

Lagniappe

(*Coffee* continued)

CREOLE CAFE NOIR:

5 level tbsps dark roast coffee and chicory   **5 cups cold water**

In the top of a French drip coffee pot, place ground coffee and chicory. In a one quart sauce pot, bring water to a rolling boil. Drip the hot water, a few tablespoons at a time, through the coffee until all is used. Once dripped, the coffee pot may be placed in a small frying pan filled with water on low heat to keep warm. However, the coffee may be placed in a glass jar in the refrigerator and heated whenever needed. This coffee is normally served black and only in demi-tasse cups.

CAFE BRULOT:

1 lemon   **1-1/2 ounces triple sec**
1 orange   **1 ounce brandy**
6 whole cloves   **1-1/2 cups cafe noir**
2 small cinnamon sticks

Every household in early New Orleans had its brulot bowl on the buffet. A brulot bowl is any silver or copper bowl that can be heated with sterno or candle flames from the bottom. Over your brulot bowl, peel lemon in one continuous motion so that the peel is a long spiral. Any juice from the lemon should fall directly into the bowl. Peel orange in the same fashion. Once peeled, insert cloves into the orange and lemon peels at one inch intervals. Into the brulot bowl, place cinnamon stick, triple sec and brandy. Place a sterno or candle under the bowl and bring the liquid to a slight simmer, stirring constantly. Once the liquor is simmering, carefully ignite using a kitchen match. A ribbon of golden blue flame may be achieved by ladling the liquors into the air above the bowl. While the liquor is flaming, hold the lemon and orange peels in the heat to "cook out" the flavor. Slowly add hot coffee, pouring around the edges of the bowl so that the sizzling sound may be heard. Continue stirring until flame dies out. Squeeze a small amount of orange and lemon juice into the bowl to naturally sweeten the coffee. Ladle hot brulot into hot demi-tasse cups.

Changes

336

Pecan Rice Dressing

1 Hour   8-10 Servings

Comment:

The pecan rice dressing is found on most holiday tables in South Louisiana. It incorporates all of the best of bayou country: the seafoods, meats and nuts. It has been a tradition in our family for over 150 years.

6 chicken livers
1 pound ground beef
1 pound ground pork
1/4 pound butter
1 cup diced onions
1 cup diced celery
1 cup diced bell pepper
1/4 cup diced red bell pepper

2 tbsps diced garlic
1 pint select oysters and liquid
6 cups cooked white rice
1/2 cup sliced green onions
1/2 cup chopped parsley
1/2 cup chopped pecans
salt and cracked black pepper
   to taste

In a small saute pan, poach chicken livers in lightly salted water until done. Remove and set aside to cool. Once cool, chop and reserve. Retain poaching liquid. In a large heavy bottom saute pan, melt butter over medium high heat. Add ground beef and pork and saute until golden brown and grains of meat are totally separated, approximately thirty minutes. Add chopped chicken livers, onions, celery, bell peppers and garlic. Continue to saute an additional thirty minutes or until vegetables are totally cooked. You may need to add the poaching liquid from the livers to keep the mixture moist during cooking. Add oysters and oyster liquid and continue to cook until oysters have almost cooked away. Chop oysters into the meat mixture as they cook. Add cooked rice, stir well into the mixture and garnish using green onions, parsley and pecans. Season to taste using salt and black pepper. Serve as a rice casserole or stuff a turkey or duck with this mixture.

Changes

337

Creole Dirty Rice

1 Hour   6-8 Servings

Comment:

This dish is much better known in New Orleans than in the bayous. The name dirty rice was given to the dish because of its dark color, once the liver and giblets are added. It is truly a unique Creole dish and definitely worth trying.

1/2 pound chicken giblets
1/2 pound chicken livers
1/2 cup melted butter
1 cup diced onions
1 cup diced celery
1 cup diced bell pepper
2 tbsps diced garlic

1 cup chicken stock (see recipe)
6 cups cooked rice
1/2 cup sliced green onions
1/2 cup chopped parsley
salt and cracked black pepper
    to taste

In a small sauce pot, poach chicken giblets in lightly salted water until tender, approximately forty-five minutes. Once cooked, remove and cool. Using a sharp paring knife, chop the giblets into tiny pieces, removing all tough membrane. Set aside and reserve poaching liquid. In a large heavy bottom saute pan, heat butter over medium high heat. Saute chicken livers until golden brown on all sides, approximately fifteen to twenty minutes. Remove chicken livers from saute pan and place on a chopping board to cool. Into the same saute pan, add onions, celery, bell pepper and garlic. Saute until vegetables are wilted, approximately three to five minutes. Once vegetables are done, coarsely chop chicken livers and return with giblets to the saute pan. Add chicken stock and a small amount of the poaching liquid, bring to a low boil and cook until volume of liquid is reduced to approximately one fourth cup. Add cooked white rice, blending well into the meat mixture, and garnish using green onions and parsley. Season to taste using salt and cracked black pepper.

Changes

_____

_____

_____

_____

Fried Grits Patties

1 Hour   8 Patties

Comment:

This is a good example of the evolution of Cajun cooking. Grits are beginning to disappear from breakfast tables, however, this interesting variation will guarantee the survival of this unique Cajun fare.

1-1/2 cups hominy grits
5 cups water
3 tbsps butter
salt to taste
1/2 cup finely diced andouille
4 tbsps shredded cheddar cheese
1 tbsp cracked black pepper

1/4 cup oil
eggwash (1 egg, 3/4 cup milk - beaten)
1 cup flour
1 cup seasoned Italian bread crumbs

In a one quart sauce pot, bring water to a rolling boil. Add butter and season to taste with salt. Fold in grits and reduce heat to simmer. Stirring occasionally, cook until grits are tender. Once cooked, remove from heat and stir in andouille, cheddar cheese and cracked black pepper. Pour hot grits onto a sheet pan with one inch lip. Smooth to about three fourth inch thickness and allow to cool overnight in the refrigerator. The next morning, place cold grits on a cutting surface. Cut grits circles with a three inch cookie cutter. Heat oil in a ten to twelve inch saute pan over medium high heat. Dip grits patties into eggwash, then into flour, again into eggwash, and then into bread crumbs. Pan fry until golden brown. The patties may be served as a side dish or under poached eggs.

Changes

_____

_____

_____

_____

Choucroute Garnie

1-1/2 Hours   8 Servings

Comment:

Since St. James Parish hosted the largest settlement of Germans in Louisiana, it is easy to understand the reason for this recipe. Olga and Gaston Hirsch have prepared this recipe on many occasions for me, and I dedicate this to them.

2 jars sauerkraut
2 ham steaks, bone-in
3 smoked ham hocks
3 links heavy smoked sausage
3 links Polish sausage
6 1-inch cubes slab bacon
1 cup diced onions

1 tbsp diced garlic
2 small bay leaves
8 peeled white potatoes
1-1/2 tbsps flour
2 cans beer
1 ounce dry white wine
cracked black pepper to taste

Wash sauerkraut once or twice under cold running water. This will remove some of the sour taste as well as the salt. Place equal layers of sauerkraut and meat into a heavy bottom stock pot. Add onions, garlic, bay leaves and potatoes and distribute evenly over the sauerkraut. Sprinkle in flour and add beer and wine. Allow to simmer over medium heat for one to one and a half hours before serving. Season to taste with cracked black pepper. Continue to cook until most of the excess liquid has evaporated. To serve, arrange sauerkraut in a mound in the center of a serving platter and surround with meats and sausages.

Changes

Cream Anglaise

1 Hour   3 cups

Comment:

Cream Anglaise or whiskey sauce is the best accompaniment for bread pudding and custard. I've even seen Cream Anglaise served with ice cream. Try adding different liqueurs for a unique flavor.

2 cups heavy whipping cream	**1 tbsp vanilla**
1 cup sugar	**4 egg yolks, beaten**
pinch of cinnamon	**1 tbsp corn starch**
pinch of nutmeg	**1/4 cup bourbon**

In a heavy bottom sauce pan, scald whipping cream over medium high heat. In a separate mixing bowl, combine sugar, cinnamon, nutmeg, vanilla, eggs and corn starch. Using a wire whip, blend until well mixed and creamy. Add bourbon and fold once or twice until blended. Into the mixing bowl, ladle one cup of hot cream, stirring constantly while pouring. Return egg mixture to the pot of hot cream, whisking constantly with a wire whip. Cook one to two minutes and remove from heat. Should mixture become too thick, add a little cold whipping cream.

Changes

_____

_____

_____

_____

Caramel Custard

1-1/2 Hours   6 Servings

Comment:

This classic recipe was brought to New Orleans by the early French settlers. This rich smooth custard with caramel sauce is perfect for light lunches or elegant ballroom dinners.

FOR CARAMEL:

1 cup sugar   2 tbsps cold water

In a small heavy bottom saute pan over medium high heat, combine sugar and water. Constantly stir sugar over heat until it melts and turns a smooth rich brown color. Remove from heat and continue to stir to keep the sugar from burning. You may add an additional tablespoon of hot water should mixture be too thick. Spoon one to two tablespoons of caramel into each of six four-ounce custard cups.

FOR CUSTARD:

2-1/2 cups milk   pinch of cinnamon
3 eggs   pinch of nutmeg
3 egg yolks   1 tbsp vanilla
1/2 cup sugar

Preheat oven to 350 degrees F. Scald milk in a heavy bottom sauce pot. Do not boil. In a large mixing bowl, combine eggs, sugar, cinnamon, nutmeg and vanilla. Using a wire whip, whisk until well blended. Ladle one cup of scalded milk into the mixing bowl, stirring constantly while pouring. Gradually whip egg mixture back into the hot sauce pan until well blended. Remove from heat and ladle custard into cups to approximately one half inch from the top. Place cups in a large baking pan filled with enough water to reach 3/4 the height of the custard cups. Bake on the center oven rack for approximately one hour. The custard is best when chilled overnight.

Changes

_____

_____

Pain Perdu (Lost Bread)

30 Minutes   6 Servings

Comment:

The struggling Cajuns certainly would never have discarded anything from the kitchen. Stale bread, for example, was made into bread crumbs, stuffings, desserts or Pain Perdu. This breakfast item has become a dessert favorite.

2 10-inch loaves day-old French bread	**1 tsp nutmeg**
3 eggs	**1-1/2 cups heavy whipping cream**
1/4 cup sugar	**3/4 cup melted butter**
2 tbsps vanilla	**1 cup powdered sugar**
1 tsp cinnamon	**1 cup Louisiana cane syrup**

In a large mixing bowl, cream eggs and sugar until well blended. Add vanilla, cinnamon and nutmeg and mix until well blended. Slowly whisk in whipping cream until well incorporated in the egg mixture. Cut the French bread into three fourth inch thick croutons, discarding ends. Soak croutons in the cream-egg mixture. In a heavy bottom iron skillet, heat butter over medium high heat. Once hot, remove bread from cream-egg mixture and saute on each side in butter until golden brown. Remove sauteed lost bread to a serving platter and dust with powdered sugar and drizzle with cane syrup. You may wish to allow your party guests to saute their own lost bread and top with a variety of fruit compotes.

Changes

_____

_____

_____

_____

343

Louisiana Fig Ice Cream

1-1/2 Hours   2-3 Quarts

Comment:

During the late summer, when figs are plentiful, it is not uncommon to find fig preserves topping a bowl of vanilla ice cream. I am sure that this combination inspired the following ice cream recipe.

3 cups fresh figs   3 eggs
1 cup milk   2 cups milk
1-1/2 cups sugar   3 cups heavy whipping cream
2 tbsps lemon juice   pinch of cinnamon
1 ounce light creme de cocoa   pinch of nutmeg

In the bowl of a food processor, combine figs, one cup of milk, one cup sugar, lemon juice and creme de cocoa. Blend until pureed. In a large mixing bowl, combine fig mixture, eggs, remaining sugar, two cups milk and whipping cream. Using a wire whip, whisk until all ingredients are smooth and well blended. Add cinnamon and nutmeg. Place mixture in a four quart ice cream freezer and freeze according to manufacturer's directions. Once frozen, place container in your home freezer for two to three hours for best results.

Changes

_____

_____

_____

_____

Creole Cream Cheese Ice Cream

1 Hour   3 Quarts

Comment:

Creole cream cheese has always been a favorite of the Cajuns in Bayou country. I remember sitting on the front porch spooning sugar into a one pint container of cream cheese and enjoying the treat. Herein lies the origin of this dish.

4 12-ounce cartons Creole cream
    cheese
4 cups heavy whipping cream
2-1/2 cups sugar

3 egg yolks
pinch of cinnamon
pinch of nutmeg
4 tbsps vanilla

In a large mixing bowl, mash Creole cream cheese with the bottom of a serving spoon. Force the cream cheese through a fine colander to mash all large pieces. Add heavy whipping cream, sugar and egg yolks. Using a wire whip, whisk until well blended. Season mixture with cinnamon, nutmeg and vanilla. Continue whipping until smooth and creamy. Pour mixture into your homestyle ice cream freezer and freeze according to manufacturer's instructions. Once frozen, place the container in your home freezer for a few hours to ensure the best results. A cream cheese sauce may be made by mashing one twelve ounce package of cream cheese with one cup of cream anglaise. (see recipe)

Changes

_____

_____

_____

_____

Index

Meats

Beef

Lamb

Pork

Poultry

Wild Game

LOUISIANA SPECIALTY PRODUCTS

When cooking the cuisine of South Louisiana, numerous specialty products such as; black iron pots (a 200 year old tradition), crawfish tails and andouille sausage are utilized. Most of these unique items are grown or manufactured here in our State.

At my Lafitte's Landing Restaurant, we are able to make these unique items available to you anywhere in the country. If you are interested in purchasing or obtaining information on any of the products featured in this cookbook or on my PBS series, "A Taste of Louisiana with Chef John Folse & Company," please write or phone me at:

Chef John Folse & Company
P.O. Box 1128
Donaldsonville, Louisiana 70346

(504) 473-1232 Phone
(504) 473-1161 Fax

We look forward to assisting you with any special product needs or additional information on the cuisine and culture of the Cajuns and Creoles!